# The Desire to be God

# Studies in Phenomenological Theology

Steven Laycock
*General Editor*

Vol. 1

PETER LANG
New York • San Francisco • Bern
Frankfurt am Main • Berlin • Wien • Paris

James M. McLachlan

# The Desire to be God

## Freedom and the Other in Sartre and Berdyaev

PETER LANG
New York • San Francisco • Bern
Frankfurt am Main • Berlin • Wien • Paris

B
819

.M39

1992

**Library of Congress Cataloging-in-Publication Data**

McLachlan, James M.
    The desire to be God : freedom and the other
in Sartre and Berdyaev / James M. McLachlan.
        p. cm. — (Studies in phenomenological
theology ; v.1)
        Includes bibliographical references.
        1. Existentialism.    2. Liberty.    3. Sartre,
Jean Paul, 1905-1980.    4. Berdiaev, Nikolai,
1874-1948.    I. Title.    II. Series.
B819.M39    1992    142'.78—dc20    91-31770
ISBN 0-8204-1711-4                                CIP
ISSN 1056-4969


**Die Deutsche Bibliothek-CIP-Einheitsaufnahme**

McLachlan, James M.:
The desire to be God : freedom and the other in
Sartre and Berdyaev / James M. McLachlan.—
New York; Berlin; Bern; Frankfurt/M.; Paris; Wien:
Lang, 1992
    (Studies in phenomenological theology ; Vol. 1)
    ISBN 0-8204-1711-4
NE: GT

Cover Design by Geraldine Spellissy.


The paper in this book meets the guidelines for permanence and
durability of the Committee on Production Guidelines for
Book Longevity of the Council on Library Resources.

Printed in the United States of America.

*To my friends:*

*Carrie, Jimmy, Jonny, and Elizabeth*

# ACKNOWLEDGEMENTS

I am grateful to the following for permission to reprint quotes from the thinkers who appear in the text.

*Literary and Philosophical Essays*, Jean-Paul Sartre, translated by Annette Michelson, reprinted by permission of S. G. Phillips.

*Whitehead's Philosophy: Selected Essays, 1935-1970*, by Charles Hartshorne, reprinted by permission of the University of Nebraska Press. Copyright c 1972 by the University of Nebraska Press.

The Library of the Living Philosophers, Vol. XVI, *The Philosophy of Jean-Paul Sartre*, edited by Paul Arthur Schilpp, reprinted by permission of the publisher (La Salle, IL: Open Court Publishing, 1981), pp. 9-10.

*Sartre's Ontology,* by Klaus Hartmann, 1966, reprinted by permission of Northwestern University Press.

I am indebted to the Graduate School of Western Carolina University and Dean Anthony Hickey for a research grant in 1991 that facilitated the publication of this book.

I am also indebted to several interpreters of both Sartre and Berdyaev. Appropriate recognition of these debts are found in the footnotes and bibliography.

I want to thank my colleagues in Philosophy and Religion at Western Carolina University, Michael Jones and Eric Szendrei, who have heard most of my ideas many times already but will still argue with me. I am very indebted to several of my teachers. First to Paul Spade at Indiana University who introduced me to Sartre in 1980. I owe a very large debt to Professor James Hart at Indiana University who, after several discussions with me while a first year graduate student, recommended I read Berdyaev. I am also indebted to Professor Hart for the direction he gave my studies, for reading the text and for his criticisms as the outside examiner when this book was a dissertation at the University of Toronto. I also thank Professor Steven Laycock of the University of Toledo, editor of the series on Phenomenological Theology, whose close reading of the manuscript and many suggestions helped me to improve both the expression and the argument. To my teachers at Toronto, especially Professors Richard Marshall and Thomas Langan, I owe much for their friendship as well as for what they taught me. Most importantly, I owe an immense debt to Professor Donald D. Evans of the Department of Philosophy and the Centre for Religious Studies at the University of Toronto who directed the writing of the dissertation. I thank him for his infinite care in reading and suggesting possibilities for the development of the ideas, and for his friendship and personal example as a teacher and thinker.

I also need to thank the staff at Peter Lang and especially Ms. Kathy Iwasaki for her help in getting me through the process of publication.

I want to thank my children, Jimmy, Jonathan, and Elizabeth and my extended family for their great patience. Especially my mother Winifred Morse McLachlan who read a large section of the manuscript and my father James W. McLachlan whose example led me to study philosophy. Finally, I want to thank my friend Carrie Ann McLachlan who read a good deal of the manuscript and who has argued with me for years about truth. Life with her always reveals to me the necessity of going beyond what has already been thought and the assurance that, enclosing our efforts, there is a better world coming.

# CONTENTS

# The Desire to be God

# INTRODUCTION

Among twentieth century philosophers who have written about human freedom none have taken such radical positions in its defence as Jean-Paul Sartre and Nicholas Berdyaev. They were contemporaries in the Paris of the 1930s and 1940s. They held similar views in some significant area's of their thought. Both place the description of freedom at the center of their philosophies. They both took the individual point of view to be one of the essential pillars of existentialism. Both held an almost monadic conception of the person. Both rejected the idea of a human nature and rejected the possibility of philosophizing outside of a situation. For both human beings are those beings whose essence is constantly in question and must continually be created; and both claimed that there is no permanent meaning that exists independently and permanently by which human freedom was determined. Yet, as if to prove once again the fundamental vagueness that has been associated with the title of existentialist, Sartre and Berdyaev differed radically on the most fundamental issues of their interpretations of the meaning and essence of human freedom. The most obvious difference is Sartre's insistence on atheism as essential to the existence of freedom and Berdyaev's commitment to theism, (even if Berdyaev's theism is quite untraditional). In *Being and Nothingness* Sartre describes as the fundamental human project, the desire to be God and insists that all human attempts at the creation of permanent meanings and relations are doomed to fail. Berdyaev, though he accepts the primacy of change and becoming still insists on the possibility of meaning. In relation to the fundamental human project Sartre insists that community between human beings is ultimately impossible, while Berdyaev insists that community, or *Sobornost*, is the meaning of human existence and depends on the relation between the human and the divine.[1] These different interpretations of the possibilities of religion,

---

[1]It can be argued that Sartre himself is not nearly so pessimistic about the human condition as he has sometimes been portrayed. Francis Jeanson argues that even the early Sartre from a Marxist position argues that human freedom is attainable although human relationships are by their nature conflictual. Jeanson argues that the conflicts are the expression of freedoms that can be directed toward community.

anthropology, and ethics grow out of their attitudes toward ontology--radically different accounts of Being and Nothingness.

At the heart of this dispute is question of ontology. It is central in the divergent positions adopted by Sartre in *Being and Nothingness* and Berdyaev in all his philosophical works. Sartre develops what seems a dualistic conception of Being. It consists of a wholly positive material foundation of phenomena called Being-in-itself and a wholly negative projection on this positive Being that differentiates being and, though dependent on the ground of Being-in-itself, creates the objects as objects. This negating, differentiating form of being is being-for-itself, the foundation of freedom and consciousness. Sartre makes freedom, being-for-itself, dependent on the in-itself in his effort to avoid what he considers the pitfalls of idealism. It is just this point: making freedom dependent on Being where Berdyaev questions Sartre's ontology in particular and the whole project of ontology in general. Berdyaev thinks making freedom dependent on being eliminates the reality of freedom. Berdyaev creates what could be termed an anti-ontology and thinks that this is the central question in all efforts to talk about human freedom. For Berdyaev, freedom cannot be dependent on anything and still be freedom.

These different orientations I will characterize as Cartesian existentialism in Sartre's case, and personalist existentialism in Berdyaev's. Both versions of existentialism are centered in the subject, but Berdyaev attempts to get beyond the subject-object dichotomy by the introduction of a personalist metaphysics.[2] Sartre

---

*Sobornost* has been called by one of Berdyaev's translators "the despair of all translators from Russian." The same translator says "altogetherness," the dynamic life of the community, would come near to its meaning. Berdyaev himself writes that sobornost is a concrete universalism in which the individual overcomes the alienation of the external objectified world to include his environment.

There is only one acceptable, non servile meaning of the word *sobornost*, and that is the interpretation of it as the interior concrete universalism of personality, and not the alienation of conscience in any kind of exterior collective body whatever. The free man is simply the man who does not allow the alienation, the ejection into the external of his conscience and his judgment.

Nikolai Berdyaev, *Slavery and Freedom*, trans. R. M. French (New York: Charles Scribner's Sons, 1944), p. 68-69.

[2]Hartshorne considers Berdyaev a process thinker as well as an existentialist and has compared his conception of tragedy in God with Whitehead's. Charles Hartshorne, *Philosophers Speak of God*, (Chicago: University of Chicago Press, 1953), pp. 233-243. And Charles Hartshorne, "Berdyaev and Whitehead: Is there

remains in the subject-object dichotomy by adopting the subjective standpoint of the cogito as the starting point of his philosophy. He also introduces an objective metaphysics by way of an objective ontology. This results in very different conclusions as to the possibility of real relation to others and the possibility of human community or even real communication. These divergent anthropologies can be focused on the Sartrean characterization of the desire to be God as the basis of human effort.

Sartre and Berdyaev see human meaning as something that is continually created by human action. For both there is no overarching meaning that exists apart from human beings. But the way that this meaning is created and the possibility that this is any more than a private and completely transitory meaning is a point on which the two would disagree. Sartre thinks that the desire to be God characterizes the impossible human desire "to be." By this he means that "I" have the contradictory desire to create a permanent meaning that applies to all of Being and to which I am subject, and yet which is more than my creation. This meaning is also necessarily a private meaning because it can never be shared with others or completely accepted by them. In fact, others pose a threat to my created meaning; because they do not share it, they threaten to destroy the illusion that my created meaning applies to the whole of Being.

Berdyaev's idea of the desire to be God and the relationship with others is similar to Sartre's in some respects, yet remains fundamentally different. Though Berdyaev's basic anthropology is as subject-oriented and monadic as Sartre's, Berdyaev holds that the desire for unity and meaning reflects two possible attitudes. The first is very close to Sartre's position: an individual effort to create a private yet universal meaning that is frustrated by the encounter with others. The second is Berdyaev's conception of an ideal of unity which is possible, though perhaps never realized in time: that meaning is created within the relation of the community of human subjects and God. Herein lies a fundamental difference between Sartre's version of existential freedom and Berdyaev's. For Sartre, in *Being and Nothingness*, community is impossible because each individual creates values which reflect the fundamental desire to be God. Berdyaev grants this is one way the human being approaches the world but not the only one. The desire to create values can also reflect the creation of meaning that is the unity of community and its preservation as the ground for future meanings. But the question arises whether Sartre's ontology might allow for community in another fashion. That free authentic action on the part of individuals could include the possibility of free and authentic relations between persons.

The religious tone of Berdyaev's thought and the atheistic outlook of Sartre's receive their theoretical backing from the way they confront these two interrelated

---

Tragedy in God," in *Whitehead's Philosophy* (Lincoln: University of Nebraska Press, 1972), pp. 183-199.

problems--the desire to be God, and the relation to the other. But the different approach each takes toward these questions does not stem from their atheism or theism. Although the issues are connected, the fundamental disagreement is based on the very different ontological paths each takes in his efforts to explain freedom. It can and has been argued by some of Sartre's best commentators that *Being and Nothingness* is not the last word that Sartre had to say about community. And indeed in that work Sartre was concerned with the desire to be God and the denial of freedom in bad faith and not the possibilities of freedom. I think a case can be made for this. Sartre indicates as much himself in several passages that point out that the desire to be God is in bad faith and a denial of freedom, that community can only come about through the completely free activity of individuals who have passed beyond any maxims or ideas of nature that would either coerce them toward or away from community. But at this point I think that Berdyaev's objection to Sartre's ontology must be examined. Berdyaev maintained the possibility of both community and the meaningfulness of human freedom are undercut by Sartre's interpretation of nothingness.

Both Berdyaev and Sartre equate freedom with nothingness, and both regard freedom as the central meaning of consciousness and humanness. But for Sartre, nothingness alone is not an adequate definition of the subject. The subject is nothingness over against Being. It cannot be nothingness alone because nothingness is not and could not be a negation of Being. The subject therefore must be a nothingness sustained by Being. The subject represents its own type of being; being and nothingness held together is the flow of consciousness. The subject, consciousness, is constantly changing. Consciousness is a stream that is never present to itself or is never what it is. Nothingness, or freedom, is dependent on a wholly positive Being-in-itself. Berdyaev attempts to present an alternative to the ontological explanation of freedom produced by Sartre in *Being and Nothingness*, resulting in a most original and comprehensive metaphysics. At the heart of Berdyaev's "originality" is his appropriation of Jacob Boehme's image of the "Ungrund." Through this image Berdyaev is able to take what could be termed an anti-ontological position in which freedom is regarded as prior to Being.

Though in many ways Berdyaev seems close to Sartre's position in regard to freedom, he, and the tradition he represents, offers an alternative possibility to the conflictual theory of human relationships held by Sartre in *Being and Nothingness*. Berdyaev's position is eschatological. Like Sartre, he accepts a fundamental disharmony in the human condition. But unlike Sartre he argues that this is not an ontological structure of being human, but a stage in the development of humanity toward community, or *Sobornost*. Berdyaev felt that Sartre's existentialism fell into important difficulties in the attempt to derive freedom from Being: in making the for-itself dependent on the in-itself, Sartrean existentialism misunderstood the question of nothingness and human freedom.

[For Sartre] The freedom of man is not his nature, his essence, it is rather an act, it is existence and to that supremacy belongs. The freedom of man has its roots not in being but in non-being, it is not determined by anything at all. This is a true thought and I myself have often developed it, but here it is associated with a false metaphysics.

Sartre . . . considers the historical process as devoid of meaning. He seeks no support in it and wishes to rely simply upon the freedom of man. Man is made into a god. But the *néant* in Sartre is of a different kind from the *néant* in Heidegger and again in Hegel. In Boehme's teaching the *Ungrund* precedes being and it is fecunding. It is the same in Hegel's thought, where the negative gives birth to becoming. But Sartre compares the *néant* to the worm which is the cause of the apple's becoming rotten. This means that non-being in his view comes after being and is a corruption of it. On that account it is incapable of giving birth to anything positive.. . . Freedom is an ideal principle in Sartre, and that sets a limit to the gloom of his philosophy. But this freedom is empty and futile, it leads to no result and has no aim in view. The fundamental mistake is in his unwillingness to admit that a denial presupposes an assertion of something positive.[3]

The argument Berdyaev has with Sartre, evidenced in this passage, is that Sartre sees freedom and nothingness as a defect in Being, something that destroys the absolute positivity of Being like a worm in an apple. Non-being comes after Being and is a corruption of it. Berdyaev thinks that Sartre has abandoned the tradition of thinkers, including Boehme, Hegel and Heidegger, who have discussed

---

[3]Nicholas Berdyaev, *Truth and Revelation*, trans. R. M. French (London: Geofrey Bles, 1953), pp. 97-98. Taking *Being and Nothingness* as a whole, one cannot fail to notice the vast number of negative terms. This is what offended many of Sartre's critics in the early years of Sartre's philosophical career. Man, as consciousness, is referred to as a worm at the heart of the apple of Being: his freedom is the negation of the totality, the destruction of totality. The negative terms in the book seem to reflect common themes such as infection, degradation, and disintegration. They make it seem that the for-itself has infected the world with sickness that is the spoiling of the totality of pure Being. This theme is also a component of Sartre's literary pieces. It should be asked whether or not these images are of philosophical importance or if they are merely the intrusion of Sartre's temperament into his philosophy. Simone de Beauvoir wrote, "I knew how readily Sartre's imagination tended toward disaster." Simone de Beauvoir, *Prime of Life*, tr, Peter Green (New York: World Publishing Company, 1962) p. 170.

the relationship of nothingness and freedom. Sartre's position is Cartesian and he has abandoned the possibility of the negative element at the beginning of his ontology. He completely rejects the Hegelian notion of the ingredience of negation in Being.

Berdyaev's fundamental insight is that freedom is primarily, ultimately real. As such, its essence lies outside any kind of external determination. It cannot be derived from a more fundamental kind of reality. Freedom cannot be subordinated to Being qua Being, because the concept includes the possession of an objective and determinable character, whereas freedom eludes all determination. If there is any freedom, any real freedom, it must be metaphysically ultimate, and if it is metaphysically ultimate, it cannot be taken as a mode of Being. Berdyaev would accept the objection from traditional metaphysics that it is impossible to conceive anything more ultimate than Being since anything must be in order to have attributes. However, while it would appear to the traditional metaphysician that freedom is an attribute of a Being, for Berdyaev freedom is not an attribute of Being. Freedom is no-thing.

Berdyaev appeals to Jacob Boehme's image of the *Ungrund*. Strictly speaking the *Ungrund* is not anything; our idea of it is a myth, a symbol, whereby a fundamental truth about existence is expressed that is incapable of being expressed in an objective conceptual arrangement.[4] This incapacity is not due to the limitation of the knower but is in the nature of knowledge itself, the world itself. All novelty and uniqueness is unexplainable unless freedom is prior to Being. What Berdyaev does in his metaphysics is to reverse the priority that Aristotle assigned to actuality and potentiality and return to the Heraclitean metaphor of the world as fire.

Freedom is the key to Berdyaev's entire philosophy. Freedom cannot be derived from Being because the concept of Being includes the possession of objective and determinate character. Freedom, if it is to be taken seriously, is the absence of external determination. Any derivation of freedom from something more ultimate gives it determinedness and destroys its reality. Freedom must be metaphysically ultimate, it is then not a mode of Being, of *"ov"* but of *"me ov me on."* It is what Berdyaev, coining his own term, called meonic, non-or, not being.[5] In Berdyaev's freedom precedes Being and Nothingness and is the ground of both.

---

[4]Nicholas Berdyaev, *Freedom and the Spirit*, trans. Oliver Fielding Clarke (1935 reprint ed. New York: Books for Libraries Press, 1972), p. 73.

[5]In Boehme's myth, the *Ungrund* is the pre-existential abyss out of which all things come into being. The *Ungrund* is not being. It is the no-thing, pure potentiality, freedom that is as yet undetermined. This is closer to eastern conceptions than any conception of non-being in the western philosophical tradition. The Upanishadic term netti netti (not this not this) is close to the idea that Berdyaev is attempting to convey.

This study will examine two major areas in the philosophies of radical freedom put forward by Berdyaev and Sartre. First, and perhaps most important, is an exposition of each thinker's idea of freedom. Both thinker's ideas of freedom are contingent on their different attitudes toward the question of ontology.[6] Second, built into the fundamental attitudes to ontology and freedom that embody the groundwork of their respective philosophies are conceptions that each develops about the possibility of meaning (that which Sartre calls the desire to be God) and how it relates to the possibility of communion with the Other. Both, because of their interpretations of the meaning of freedom, develop subjectively-oriented philosophies. But Berdyaev, based on his different interpretation of freedom and being, has a much more optimistic appraisal about the possibilities of the creation of community with the Other than does Sartre. In relation to this, Berdyaev also sees the desire to be God, taken to mean (as Sartre characterizes it) the possibility of the creation of unity, as not necessarily an inauthentic quest. The desire, as the desire for unity, has the possibility for continual satisfaction (and frustration) in the creative advance.

This comparison will raise several questions about the philosophical projects of each thinker and about the limitations of the kind of monadic, subjective, existentialism in which each thinker is engaged. First, in the creation of his ontology, has Sartre left the phenomenological method and strayed into a metaphysical explanation of the totality of Being that he says he wants to avoid? Second, if this is the case, is it necessary to accept the interpretation of the possibilities of the for-itself and the for-others that Sartre puts forward? Along with this, if Sartre's description of the human condition is accepted, does Sartrean existentialism imply the absurdity of existence or the creation of meaning from ambiguity? Thirdly, there remains Berdyaev's question about Sartre's existentialism: does it really describe freedom?

To examine these questions it will be necessary to get an overview of the philosophy of freedom that Sartre presents in *Being and Nothingness* and the questions it raises. Chapter One will examine the Sartrean conception of freedom and the ontological position upon which it is based. Chapter Two will examine Sartre's version of the desire to be God as the basic pattern of human efforts to create meaning. Chapter Three will present the implications of Sartre's ontology and the desire to be God for his theory of the Other. Chapter Four presents a critical evaluation of Sartrean existentialism. At this point there will also be a

---

[6]As I have suggested in this introduction, Berdyaev's and Sartre's respective positions arise from different perspectives on the history of thought. For though both are in large part indebted to idealism, they take basically different stances in relation to idealism and its possibilities. I have characterized Sartre's existentialism as Cartesian and Berdyaev's as process existentialism. The senses in which these two characterizations hold true I will establish later in this discussion.

particular focus on Berdyaev's critique of Sartre's ontology from a philosophical tradition that favors some conception of the ingredience of negation in Being. Chapter Five centers on Berdyaev's anti-ontology as a possible alternative to Sartre's interpretation of human freedom. Chapter Six considers how Berdyaev's conception of the desire to be God differs from Sartre's. Chapter Seven discusses Berdyaev's idea of *Sobornost* and the relation of the self to others. Finally, the conclusion involves an evaluation of the possibilities of Berdyaev's idea of freedom.

PART ONE


FREEDOM AND THE DESIRE TO BE GOD


IN


SARTRE'S *BEING AND NOTHINGNESS*

# I. THE FOUNDATION OF SARTRE'S IDEA OF FREEDOM: THE ONTOLOGY OF *BEING AND NOTHINGNESS*

## Introduction

Sartre describes the basic form of the human condition in a famous passage from *Being and Nothingness*. In it he asserts that human reality is an effort to create the in-itself-for-itself, to become God, a contradiction that asserts that consciousness, which is the negation of positive being, is the foundation of its own positive being.

> Each human reality is at the same time a direct project to metamorphose its own For-itself into an In-itself-For-itself and a project of the appropriation of the world as a totality of being-in-itself, in the form of a fundamental quality. Every human reality is a passion in that it projects losing itself so as to found being and by the same stroke to constitute the In-itself which escapes contingency by being its own foundation, the *ens causa sui*, which religions call God. Thus the passion of man is the reverse of that of Christ, for man loses himself as man in order that God may be born. But the idea of God is contradictory and we lose ourselves in vain. Man is a useless passion.[1]

This passage concludes the section on "Existential Psychoanalysis" of *Being and Nothingness* in which Sartre summarizes the type of philosophical anthropology that is the basis of his existentialism. The two main characters who appear in the passage: being-in-itself and being-for-itself represent the major components of the ontology of *Being and Nothingness*. Being-in-itself is brute positive being. It is not conscious and it does not change but is the basis of all that is. Being-for-

---

[1]Jean-Paul Sartre, *Being and Nothingness*, trans. Hazel Barnes (New York: Washington Square Press, l956), p. 754. Jean-Paul Sartre, *L'être et le néant* (Paris: Gallimard, 1943), p. 708. (Here after *Being and Nothingness* will be abbreviated *BN* and *L'être et le néant*, *EN*.

itself is the negation of the in-itself. It is consciousness and freedom characterized by change and negation of what it was. A third character is implied in the passage but is conspicuous in its absence: Being-in-and-for-itself or God. God is an impossibility and God's absence haunts the for-itself. God would be that being that is both what it is, changeless and yet free and capable of consciousness and change, such a being is a contradiction.

The desire to be God is the basis and pattern of human desire. By this Sartre means the ultimate human desire is "to be," to be the foundation of one's own being in the same sense that the theological tradition of the West has seen God's perfection in being the foundation of his own being. This control over Being grants a permanent meaning to existence that is prior to existence and independent of the destructiveness of freedom. Sartre, in the tradition of Feuerbach and left-Hegelianism, sees God as the projection of this human desire. The desire is to be unchangeable, to have a determined essence that is given to it by the very fact of its being and yet at the same time to be free and capable of the changes that freedom implies, free to create and to change. So for Sartre, the problems of the Western tradition in theology are, in reality, problems of philosophical anthropology. The Western theological tradition has wrestled incessantly with problems in its attempts to describe that Being which is the foundation of its Being i.e. an all-powerful, all-knowing creator for whom all things are present, and yet He is able to create creatures who are in some sense free. This all perfect, all powerful deity is described as being conscious and in action, yet immutable. The tradition describes a "relation" "between" a deity that is not related to creatures but to which creatures are related. Sartre sees these problems and the others engendered by the theological tradition as mere reflections of the human condition in which we are caught between freedom and being, movement and resistance. They are efforts to come to terms, by the use of a "magical" projection, with the fundamental problems that human consciousness faces in existence. The human condition is a being-in-the-world in which there is no clear or complete prior meaning provided by a God or being-in-itself. Being-in-the-world entails a being-for-others who are in the same condition. But just as there is no meaning prior to existence provided by God, neither is it possible, as implied by Nietzsche's madman, to carry out the fundamental human project and in one way or another imagine ourselves to be gods. The human desire for completion that haunts all our actions is impossible to fulfill.

For Sartre essentially two factors deprive me, as a consciousness, of the comfort of living in the illusion that I can become the foundation of my own being. My facticity, or finitude, is one constant reminder that I did not create my situation ex nihilo. But the second factor is the most glaring reminder of this, my being-for-others. The Other is, for Sartre, the constant reminder that the world of my consciousness is not the permanent structure that I would like it to be, but rather, a fragile creation that I constantly make and remake in relation to my existing in a situation that is not completely of my choosing. The Other, as other, possesses the ability to destroy this creation simply by the contrariness of his alien freedom; his presence forces me constantly to rebuild my world anew. It is essentially for this reason that in "No Exit" Garcin utters the famous line "Hell is--other people."[2] In *Being and Nothingness*, Human relationships are primarily ones of conflict. There is no third consciousness who acts as arbitrator; no ultimate ground, no God to appeal to in the arbitration of disputes between myself and the Other. By the same token there is no ground that ultimately, as a type of metaphysical guarantee, binds the Other and myself together.

Francis Jeanson, one of Sartre's best sympathetic commentators and for years an associate at *Les Temps Modernes*, has argued that Sartrean existentialism and the ontological gulf that it creates between the self and the Other is ultimately a statement, not of the absurdity of the human condition, (which is the way that it was popularized), but of the ambiguity of the human condition. Jeanson's interpretation attempts to move Sartrean existentialism away from the popular interpretation of heroic man attempting to create meaning in an absurd and meaningless universe to a conception that man creates meaning from what he terms an ambiguous situation. Ambiguity, in Jeanson's interpretation, relates to the Sartrean definition of throwness into a situation. The situation affords us several possible but as yet undetermined meanings. Human beings create meaning out of the infinite possibilities that exist in the limited range afforded by the situation. Human beings, taking these possibilities, create a synthesis of meaning out of them. Human freedom is the root of this ambiguity that characterizes human existence. And ambiguity constantly requires the creation of meaning, the creation of a new synthesis, although no synthesis can ever be seen as final or all encompassing.

Sartrean existentialism maintains that consciousness is never at one with itself. But this is not to maintain that the universe is absurd, as Kafka does, but only that its meaning is always ambiguous in the sense of being unfinished. Sartre's existentialism walks the narrow ridge between the rigid consciousness that would erase itself in the spirit of seriousness, one that stubbornly adheres to magical absolute values, and the other that in rebellion maintains there is no significance to anything. Both views, Sartre argues, attempt to take the God's eye view of the situation. To go in either direction is a manifestation of bad faith because each requires a view of the universe that is absolute and unambiguous.[3]

---

[2]Jean-Paul Sartre, *No Exit and Three Other Plays* (New York: Random House, 1946), p. 47.

[3]Jeanson attacks the "theological" attitude in political thought in both its manifestations as conservative and radical ideology. Each reflects the spirit of seriousness which endeavors to impose an artificial state of affairs upon reality that prohibits further change. What is needed is a moral attitude that creates new meaning out of each new situation. The moral attitude is associated with the creation of the possibility of freedom whereas the political attitude seeks to create

Therefore authenticity, which Sartre maintains is the only escape from bad faith, is not and cannot be taken as a state that is accessible to man. Authenticity is not a condition in which it is possible to exist in forever, it is a continual creative activity. To live authentically is to always be aware that a person is responsible for her existence. Except in death, no one ever comes to a state of final relation where she is completely at one with herself, there is no absolute state in the sense of a final liberation: I am never free of my being-in-the-world, of my situation; which includes my relationship to the Other. I only exist authentically or creatively by engaging myself in the world with others and each authentic choice I make only orients me toward other choices and other problems.

In this interpretation Sartrean existentialism resembles aspects of the process philosophies of Whitehead and Hartshorne, and Berdyaev's existentialism. According to these positions God, in relation with the world, constantly creates a new synthesis encompassing the creative diversity of the universe, but this synthesis is constantly surpassed toward the future and requires constant adjustment.[4] But this comparison breaks down almost immediately because Sartre would see even the process philosopher's God as a type of metaphysical guarantee of permanence. In process metaphysics, God guarantees that the past is not lost, and guarantees at least that it is possible that the conflicts between individuals may be resolved in the creation of communion. For Sartre this kind of a relation with the Other is an ontological impossibility; the Sartrean ontology prohibits such a synthesis and communion between consciousnesses as is found in Whitehead's cosmic organism or Berdyaev's relation of the divine and the human in *Sobornost*. Sartre sees the for-itself as the negative derivation of the in-itself. It has no reason for its

---

a new situation in the name of certain principles. This is artificial. Both the conservative and the revolutionary make this error. They seek to establish some ideal norm in differing situations. The conservative believes in the absolute value of fact, the revolutionary in the absolute value of the ideal. They both disregard the ambiguity of the human situation. Francis Jeanson, *Sartre and the Problem of Morality*, trans. Robert V. Stone (Bloomington: Indiana University Press, 1980), p. 219-220.

[4]Some of this resemblance to process thought might be, as has been noted by Sartre's critics as well as admirers, attributed to the influence of Bergson. Despite Sartre's animosity to Bergsonian philosophy, it was an all pervasive influence in early twentieth-century French thought. Jacques Salvan, *The Scandalous Ghost* (Detroit: Wayne State University Press, 1967), pp. 17-54. Leszek Kolakowski, *Bergson* (Oxford: Oxford University Press, 1985). "Conversation with Jean-Paul Sartre" in *The Philosophy of Jean-Paul Sartre, The Library of the living Philosophers*, vol. XIV, ed. Paul Arthur Schillp (La Salle: Open Court, 1985), pp. 6ff. Luc-Jean Lefèvre, *L'existentialiste est-il un philosophe?* (Paris: Alsatia, 1946), pp. 21-22.

existence there is no reason the in-itself has secreted it but it is completely dependent on the in itself for its being just as creatures are dependent on God for their being in traditional Christian theology. As is the case in traditional theological interpretation of time the human world, the world of the for-itself, is the source of all temporality and becoming; temporality can only be a feature of human reality. Worldly time originates with the for-itself. Sartre's ontological structure prohibits possibility of raising the notion of the for-itself to a universal concept of Being.[5]

For Sartre it is individual finite man, consciousness for-itself, that resembles Whitehead's attempt to project the consequent nature of God. It is man who creates, or tries to make his world toward the future. But unlike Whitehead's God there is no possibility of the projects of these disparate centers coming together in the task of the creation of a common meaning. By the nature of Sartre's ontology the totality that haunts consciousness can never be realized. Concrete relations with the Other are conflictual in nature, common meaning in the sense of communion is prohibited by the Sartrean ontology found in *Being and Nothingness*. For this reason Jeanson's interpretation of Sartrean existentialism as the philosophy of the ambiguity of all human meanings, though helpful in many respects, appears to be misleading. It may be that absurdity is a better characterization of the Sartrean universe than ambiguity. In Sartre's existentialism there is a metaphysical guarantee that no human meanings can ever be fulfilled because all human values and meanings aim at a unity and permanence that can never be. And Sartre also maintains it is the nature of the human condition that consciousnesses have intentions toward totality that cannot be escaped. Totality haunts being-for-itself; but these intentions are doomed to frustration in that even our finite aspirations are impossible.[6] An eschatological conception that unites the disparate elements of reality into a totality is a part of many religious metaphysical systems from Plotinus to Teilhard. In them there is a progression from an imperfect being-in-itself toward

---

[5] According to Hartshorne both Whitehead and Berdyaev attempted, in their cosmologies, to introduce succession or process as a universal feature of the universe, leaving no opposition of a temporal subject and an atemporal object, and by using the notion of the "actual entity" which in its finitude resembles the structure of the for-itself. Hartshorne, "Berdyaev and Whitehead: Is there Tragedy in God?," pp. 183-199.

[6] A comparison between Being-in-itself and the primordial nature of God and between Being-for-itself and the consequent nature of God would not be unfruitful. But the major difference is that these poles are and can be harmonized in God in Whitehead's philosophy, but the harmonization of the poles in man for Sartre is impossible and God is not a possibility by definition. Whitehead's consequent nature of God resembles more closely the in-itself-for-itself which is a magical entity because it is the blending of ideality and experience.

a being that is only for-itself and, beyond that, to one that is in-and-for-itself. Sartre expresses the progression in this way.

> The for-itself is the being which is to itself its own lack of being. The being which the for-itself lacks is the in-itself. The for-itself arises as the nihilation of the in-itself and this nihilation is defined as the project toward the in-itself. Between the nihilated in-itself and the projected in-itself the for-itself is nothingness. Thus the end and the goal of the nihilation which I am is the in-itself. Thus human reality is the desire of being-in-itself. But the in-itself that it desires cannot be pure contingent, absurd in-itself, comparable at every point to that which encounters and which it nihilates.. . . The being which for the object of the desire of the for-itself is then an in-itself which would be to itself its own foundation; that is, which would be to its facticity in the same relation as the for-itself is to its motivations. In addition the for-itself, being the negation of the in-itself, could not desire the pure and simple return to the in-itself. Here as with Hegel, the negation of the negation cannot bring us back to our point of departure. Quite the contrary, what the for-itself demands of the in-itself is precisely the totality detotalized--"In-itself nihilated in for-itself." In other words the for-itself projects **being as for-itself**, a being which is what it is.[7]

The nihilated in-itself is the first phase of the process of the growth of consciousness. The nihilating for-itself is the second phase but it lives in isolation from the in-itself. The projected third phase is the unification of the for-itself and the in-itself in a new in-itself-for-itself, a plenum which is also conscious of itself. It involves the fullness and substantiality of a body with the emptiness and agility of Spirit. As in the Hegelian dialectic, one does not return through the negation of the negation to previous structures of the for-itself. Rather, the for-itself aims at the being that it projects, **being as for-itself**. The for-itself would become the foundation of its own being, it would encompass Being itself.

This projected structure has been a part of the religious tradition of various groups. Gnostic and Neo-Platonic sects spoke of a fall from an original plenitude and the eventual return. There is a Plotinian character to much of what Sartre writes in *Being and Nothingness*. In fact, the projected totality of the in-itself-for-itself is reiterated again and again. For example, in the passage from "Existential Psychoanalysis" quoted above, the for-itself is seen as an emanation from the in-itself that aims at a return to positivity and totality.

---

[7]*EN* p. 653. *BN* p. 693.

Each human reality is at the same time a direct project to metamor-
phose its own For-itself into an In-itself-For-itself and a project of the
appropriation of the world as a totality of being-in-itself, in the form
of a fundamental quality. Every human reality is a passion in that it
projects losing itself so as to found being and by the same stroke to
constitute the In-itself which escapes contingency by being its own
foundation, the ens causa sui, which religions call God.[8]

The basic project of the for-itself is the appropriation and reinterpretation of the
world totality of being-in-itself. The in-itself which is not conscious must become
both in-and-for-itself. But this is precisely what Sartre denies: the possibility that
the project of the for-itself, the projected totality of existence toward which the for-
itself is oriented, can ever be fulfilled. In this Sartre, in a strange way somewhat
resembles some forms of traditional Western theology which he repudiates. The
for-itself, like human creatures, is completely dependent on a transcendent being
that it cannot affect. Its efforts to create a basis for its own existence are all
doomed to failure. But where an irrational grace is available to the believer no
such option is available to Sartrean man.

In order to understand the idea of the desire to be God and its relation to
freedom in Sartrean existentialism it is necessary to examine some of the major
themes of the key work of Sartrean existentialism: *Being and Nothingness: An
Essay in Phenomenolgoical Ontology*. As the title indicates *Being and Nothingness* is an example of phenomenology. But in what respects and to what extent it
is phenomenological questions that now must be examined.

## Sartre's Relation to Phenomenology

In Sartre's early phenomenological works, *The Psychology of the Imagination*
and *The Transcendence of the Ego*, he outlines the road toward the position he
takes on consciousness in *Being and Nothingness*. In *The Transcendence of the
Ego* Sartre explains that consciousness is either positional or non-positional and
reflective or pre-reflective. Sartre maintains that consciousness is always
intentional. It always focuses on something, be that an object or an idea. In
pre-reflective consciousness, the object is not consciousness itself, but consciousness is absorbed in its object. In reflective consciousness the self becomes the
object of consciousness. But even here we can say that it is not consciousness
itself but the past states of consciousness that we project into an object for our
reflection. A very good example of this is in Sartre's famous description of an

---

[8]*EN*, p. 653. *BN*, p. 693.

incident of being caught spying through a keyhole. When I am looking through a keyhole I am completely absorbed in what I see, I am not aware of myself but of the room that is my object, but if I hear footsteps and become aware of the presence of another in the hallway I immediately become aware of myself. I, or my actions, become the object of my consciousness, I reflect on my actions. A less dramatic example of this is the case reflecting on the action of writing. When a person is writing he is absorbed in his project but then I can withdraw into refection and think my act of writing. Pre-reflective and reflective modes of consciousness are mutually exclusive; one is only involved in one mode or the other at any given moment.

Every act of consciousness is consciousness of something and is positional in relation to the object of consciousness. Non-positional consciousness is not an act of consciousness but is self-consciousness itself, it exists alongside of positional consciousness, it is a point of view. We always adopt a vantage point of perception. There is a sense in which we are always aware of this point of view throughout the story or vision of what we are taking in. I am always vaguely aware of my place at the keyhole. Every act of consciousness is always non-positionally aware of itself. Thus, no act of consciousness is, or rather becomes, the property of the unconscious. All acts of consciousness, then, are both positional and non-positional and either pre-reflective or reflective.

Sartre's theory of the work of the imagination in consciousness is given in *The Psychology of the Imagination*. Sartre relates the differences in perception, imagination, and conception in relation to the work of consciousness in relation to its world. The following table indicates the difference in the three forms of conscious activity. For example, in perceiving, imagining, or conceiving a cube, consciousness is involved in the following ways. In the first case, perception, one regards a cube from one side, but others are promised. There is a risk involved because the promised sides may not be there. In the second, imagination, the sides are promised but there is no risk of my being mistaken. Finally, in conception, I have the idea of the cube immediately present, there is neither the promise of further sides nor the risk of my being mistaken.

|             | Promise | Risk |
| ----------- | ------- | ---- |
| Perception  | Yes     | Yes  |
| Imagination | Yes     | No   |
| Conception  | No      | No   |

The phenomenon of a perceived cube presents a reference to something further, not to a reality hidden behind the phenomenon. The reference is to further phenomena, an infinity of further phenomena. Sartre argues that looking at the world phenomenologically does not mean that we have lost the world but only that we have lost a bad theory, one that asks us to look for a reality beyond the appearances and forces on us a series of dualisms. Husserl's phenomenology has replaced the dualisms of science, of interior-exterior, the Kantian dualism of being and appearance, phenomenon-noumenon, the psychological dualism of potency and act, and the metaphysical dualism of appearance versus essence, with the phenomenological dualism of finite and infinite appearances.[9] One phenomenon refers to an infinity of phenomena. The essence of the thing then becomes the principle of the series of appearances, like the ties or ganglia of nerves. The distinction between illusion and reality is made to disappear through the testing of promises. In the imagination the cube still appears from a point of reference just as in perception but there is no risk of testing for it is always a cube. Frequently one confuses imagination with a false perception and the tradition, since Hume, has been wrong on this point. Imagination is not at all like perception. Hallucinations are false perceptions, not imagination. Likewise, with conception, the cube is given all at once in conception--we learn nothing from it.

But even in the phenomenological theory there is also a re-establishment of the problem of dualism because the infinity of appearances always seems to outstrip the creation of an essence for those appearances. Husserl's theory has not done away with all dualisms, but only reduced them to the dualism of finite and infinite. Sartre wants to move to a position that maintains that individuals are primary and to dispense with the primacy of knowledge. We cannot arrive at the individuals through conception but only through experience. It is only through certain privileged moods that one encounters the individual or the other as a brute existent. In thought, objectivity requires the possibility of an infinite series of aspects or perspectives. All the dualisms reappear in the Husserlian dualism of the finite and infinite series. Sartre concludes that there is nothing behind the appearances. They are supported by no being but their own. But if appearances or phenomena are no longer opposed to Being, then what is the being of the phenomena? It is here that Sartre arrives at his formulation of the in-itself and the for-itself to characterize Being and beings. The in-itself or the being of the phenomenon is the substratum which allows the phenomenon to appear and the for-itself is that which gives to the being the characteristic of a phenomenon. Sartre must prove the existence of the in-itself otherwise than phenomenologically and this he attempts throughout the adoption and modification of the Cartesian version of the Ontological argument. This shift away from phenomenology is extremely important for the rest of *Being and Nothingness* because all of the major ideological statements of the work arise from this ontological move by which Sartre sets up the objective and subjective poles of his ontology. This dichotomy also is the basis of Sartre's attempt to contain both realist and idealist elements in his thought.

---

[9]*EN*, pp. 12-13. *BN*, pp. lv-lvi.

## The Move from Phenomenology to the Ontology of Intentionality

As the subtitle of *Being and Nothingness* indicates, Sartre desires the work to be *An Essay in Phenomenological Ontology*. But it is not clear whether or not Sartre has abandoned phenomenology in creating the ontological principles of the in-itself and for-itself. Sartre wants to be a phenomenologist, starting from consciousness as the cogito. But he also wishes to bring a subjective orientation to ontology, like that of Heidegger in *Being and Time*. But unlike Heidegger, Sartre makes the Cartesian cogito the basis of the analysis.

Early in the introduction to *Being and Nothingness* Sartre shifts from the phenomenological to the ontological level. His ontological proof for grounding his notion of the being of the phenomenon is not a phenomenological description but an ontological one that is similar to Anselm's proof of the existence of God. Sartre wants to show the presence of the in-itself as neither determinate nor indeterminate being. The phenomenon has to be, for its material content, dependent on a transcendent being of the phenomenon (being in-itself). Consciousness is congenitally orientated toward a being which it is not.[10] The in-itself is the basis of all phenomena perceived by consciousness and there is little else that can be said about it.

Through the creation of the dichotomy of the in-itself and the for-itself, Sartre attempts to create a philosophy with an objectively ontological perspective (being-in-itself) on the one hand and a subject-oriented perspective (being-for-itself), in terms of phenomenology and transcendental ontology, on the other. In this Sartre seems to more closely resemble Hegelian than Husserlian phenomenology. But Sartre indicated that the contradiction between the in-itself and the for-itself is what is dialectical about his early thought and that this dialectical character was something he only saw later. In the interview for the volume on his thought in The Library of the Living Philosophers, Sartre maintained that it was not until after 1945 that he became truly interested in Hegel and dialectical thinking. When pressed on the issue he indicated that there is a dialectic between the in-itself and the for-itself, but only in the sense that ". . . there is a dialectic in every author's work; we find everywhere contradictions that oppose each other and are transformed into something else, et cetera."[11]

The conflict between the subjective and objective orientation of Sartre's thought is reflected in the two types of being; the in-itself and the for-itself.

---

[10]*BN*, pp. 108-110, *EN*, p. 132-133.

[11]This denial may seem strange in that in-itself, for-itself, and in-and-for-itself are all Hegelian terms. Sartre admitted that he knew Hegel much earlier than 1945 from seminars and lectures but that he didn't begin serious study of Hegel until after that date. "An Interview with Jean-Paul Sartre," in Paul Arthur Schillp ed., *The Philosophy of Jean-Paul Sartre* (La Salle, Illinois: Open Court, 1981) pp. 9-10.

Being-in-itself is uncreated, it does not depend causally on anything else. There is not supposed to be a metaphysical first cause. Being-in-itself is without essence. It is not dependent on anything, it is "de trop", simply there, overflowing, superfluous, absurd. There is no reason for its existence, it simply is. Being-in-itself is a violation of the principle of sufficient reason. The in-itself is solid or "massif," "filled with itself," "opaque to itself." It has no "inner" and "outer" and no reference to what it is not. The in-itself is identical because it is only what it is and has no relation to another. It is completely positive. There is nothing negative about it. There are no distinctions within it.

As with the in-itself, Sartre abandons phenomenological method in positing the existence of the for-itself. He approaches the demonstration of the for-itself through a regressive analysis that aims to start with concrete examples and move back to the origin of negation. Sartre endeavors to offer what amounts to a me-ontological proof, one that will show the presence of nothingness in the world of phenomena. The objective negative is the original starting point from which he works back toward the original negation in consciousness. Not nothingness but consciousness is the opposite of being-in-itself because consciousness is a combination of being and nothingness. Nothingness is encountered in the object world but it cannot be being-in-itself because being-in-itself is pure positivity. Neither can it proceed from nothingness for nothingness is not, therefore it must proceed from a being which is concerned with its own nothingness, a being that "must be its own nothingness."[12] This being is the very opposite of being-in-itself. It is not simply nothingness but both being and nothingness. How this nothingness emerges from the Being upon which it depends is not clear, but the regressive analysis is intended to show that without it there is no other possible explanation for negation and negativities. It is through its own nothingness that the for-itself negates being and thus creates objects. Its negative action has no effect on being-in-itself which is absolutely transcendent; the being which the for-itself negates is itself. The for-itself is absolutely dependent on being-in-itself for its being; it creates the objective negative because it is its own negation of being, the material character of phenomena.[13] Following Husserl, the essence of an object for Sartre is the principle of a series of perceptions, thus the existence of objects presupposes consciousness. Consciousness (the for-itself) provides the objects with their essences, with their objective character. The in-itself, like Parmenidean Being, is completely positive and non-objective. This movement to a conception

---

[12]*EN*, p. 59, *BN*, p. 27.

[13]This discussion is like Augustine's discussion in *The Confessions* of the origin of evil in freedom as the lack of being. Indeed, in Sartre's article on "Cartesian Freedom" he argues that in the Christian world-view human freedom can only be seen as a negative. St. Augustine, *Confessions*, Book VII, trans. R. S. Pine-Coffin (Harmondsworth, England: Penguin Books, 1961), pp. 136-149.

of intentions with negative noetic character that establish an ontological relationship between the for-itself and being-in-itself is the basis of the link between Sartre's ontological and phenomenological analyses.[14]

The notions of the in-itself as a trans-phenomenal being that underlies all phenomena and the for-itself as consciousness which is the negation of being are important to Sartre's entire endeavor. But the separation of the in-itself and the for-itself seems to exist as much by assertion as by phenomenological description of the ontological basis of reality.

> As we have seen, consciousness is a real subjectivity and impression is a subjective plenitude. But this subjectivity can not go out of itself to posit a transcendent object in such a way as to endow it with a plenitude of impressions. If then we wish at any price to make the being of the phenomenon depend on consciousness, the object must be distinguished from consciousness not by its presence but by its absence, not by its plenitude, but by its nothingness.[15]

This returns us to Sartre's assertion that in any series of appearances most of what is does not appear. Sartre attacks the position of the idealists, among whom he lists Husserl. Sartre thinks that if consciousness is intentional it therefore must have an object. This passage seems to mean an object with real existence, thus the trans-phenomenal being-in-itself. But this is a another way of restating Husserl's phenomenological maxim that all consciousness is intentional. Thus, Sartre offers a proof for the trans-phenomenal phenomenon of being that makes possible the objective being of the phenomenon.[16] It is only through the subjective reality of

---

[14]Klaus Hartmann, *Sartre's Ontology* (Evanston: Northwestern University Press: 1973), pp. 50-51.

[15]*EN*, p. 28, *BN*, p. lxxii.

[16]The being of the phenomenon is the foundation of all Being but the objcetive being is founded on the nothingness of the for-itself.

> . . . It is an impossibility on principle for the terms of an infinite series to exist at all at the same time before consciousness, along with the real absence of all these terms except the one which is the foundation of objectivity. If present these impressions--even infinite in number-- would dissolve into the subjective, it is their absence which gives them objective being. Thus the being of the object is pure non-being. It is defined as a lack.

*EN*, p. 28. *BN* p. lxxii.

the for-itself that sees the object as an infinite series of appearances that objects can exist in the world as objects. Trans-phenomenal being is in a wholly positive and merely brute way, there are no distinctions or negations within it. What Sartre has attempted to do is to illustrate, non-phenomenologically, that for phenomenological analysis to work, intentionality requires a trans-phenomenal being that exists by-and-in-itself. "Consciousness is supported by a being which is not itself." The being of the objects that subjectivity beholds intends a being that is beyond subjectivity, the in-itself: ". . . consciousness is a being such that in its being, its being is in question insofar as this being implies a being other than itself."[17] So Sartre presents a type of logical proof for that which could not be proven because its existence is a brute fact.

The project of establishing the existence of the in-itself is pivotal to all of *Being and Nothingness*. Sartre's conception of freedom depends on establishing the separation of the in-itself (Being) and the for-itself (negation). The entire notion of freedom that Sartre develops is based on the ontological situation which sees human freedom as the negation of the in-itself, a wholly negative activity. Without this grounding, the descriptions and explanations that follow hang in mid-air, as brilliant "as if" characterizations of human existence.

Even though he temporarily abandoned phenomenology in founding his ontology, Sartre's shift to the ontological level took its start from phenomenology, specifically his interpretation of the idea of intentionality, i.e., the giveness of phenomena for a subject. Phenomena and subject establish a "being." The division results in the division between subjective being and the being of phenomena. The ontological proof purports to show that intentionality implies the in-itself or the being of the phenomenon. Sartre's ontology is based on this disjunction between a totally positive, objective being and a subjective negation of this being by a being which is also its own negation. These two forms of being illustrate the tension in Sartre's philosophy between its realist and idealist elements. Because of this disjunction between the objective and subjective sides of his ontology, Sartre must provide an explanation of the relation between its two members. He needs to show how beings of the subjective type are related to the being of phenomena.[18]

In attempting to describe the relation between the in-itself and the for-itself, Sartre tries to back up the regressive analysis (by which he arrived at the existence of the self-contradictory for-itself as the origin of negation) with phenomenological descriptions. The relation of the for-itself to the in-itself is a negation. The for-itself is the negation of the in-itself. Being-in-itself cannot account for negation, nothingness, or non-being because Being is completely positive. Yet our

---

[17]*EN*,29.  *BN*, p. lxxiv.

[18]Hartmann, p. 33.

pre-judgmental activities seem to indicate the presence (or absence) of these negations. For example, the questioning attitude often does not involve judgments but it reveals non-being. Non-being is not conceptually on a par with Being. Non-being exists only on the surface of Being, it is dependent on Being. Sartre criticizes Heidegger's description of nothingness as the void out of which the world emerges. Sartre thinks the encounter with non-being is much more mundane. One encounters non-being in everyday sorts of things, in the very nature of things. Things can only be because they are distinguished from that which they are not. Consciousness makes these distinctions by negation. Through negation consciousness ideally creates the objects whose material being depends on being-in-itself. Consciousness is taking a point of view on being-in-itself, the withdrawal of the subject by setting an object at a distance. This is the creation of individual entities; the idea of separation and individuality is shot through with negation. Consciousness is the being by which nothingness comes into being. As being-in-itself is the material basis of things, being-for-itself provides their ideational separation.

Because being-in-itself is wholly positive, there must be a being that nihilates, that makes nothingness appear. Being-for-itself, says Sartre, arises from both being and nothingness. This is why consciousness has to be contradictory; it is that being that nihilates. Sartre thinks that we cannot argue with the conclusion that contradiction is at the heart of being-for-itself because the regressive analysis has shown that it is the only way of explaining what the phenomenological method has shown, namely the reality of non-being. In Sartre's thought, the for-itself is the being which is its own nothingness.[19]

_____

[19]Nothingness is not alone an adequate definition of the subject. The subject is nothingness over against Being but it cannot be nothingness alone because nothingness is not and could not be a negation of Being. The subject, therefore, must be a nothingness sustained by Being. The subject represents its own type of being which is being and nothingness, unity, or presence to itself. Drawing on phenomenology, Sartre claims that consciousness is intentional, consciousness of something. Ontologically this is supposed to be a reference to Being and this reference is termed a negation. But why must consciousness of something be termed a negation? We will observe in the desire to be God that Sartre maintains the negation of a negation, of the for-itself by itself. But Sartre does not make clear how the for-itself as its own negation is also consciousness of something. Being surrounds me, I am simply the negation by which my presence-to-myself excludes all being from itself, thus separated from it and therefore connected with it. In spite of his criticism of Hegel, Sartre is forced to say something somewhat like him because the for-itself can only emerge through the relation of Being and nothingness. For a more complete discussion of the for-itself see Hartmann, p. 100.

Differentiation is only possible through negation and negation is only possible through consciousness. Difference is projected onto being-in-itself by consciousness, being-for-itself. Consciousness, for Sartre, is more than the intellect, it is the complete mental and emotional framework of the being. Consciousness is a negation of the in-itself, it is a negation of the past. He describes it in almost Bergsonian terms: consciousness flows out from the in-itself and is in state of constant change, it is constantly not what it is. In an early article Sartre described this empty character of consciousness.

> . . . consciousness purified itself, it is bright as great wind, there is nothing in it except a movement to flee itself, a sliding beyond itself; if by the impossible you would enter "in" a consciousness, you would be seized by a whirlwind and be cast out, next to the tree, in the dust; for consciousness has no "within," it is nothing but the outside of itself and it is this absolute fight, this refusal to be substance which constitutes it as consciousness.[20]

The in-itself is a necessary but not a sufficient reason for the existence of the for-itself. In particular, the for-itself is not its own foundation, but it is the basis of its own nothingness. The phenomenon is, for its material content, dependent on being-in-itself. As such, objects in the world are connected to each other by an external relation, an inessential otherness, they could appear in other configurations. The only necessary relation is between consciousness and the being of the phenomenon. Consciousness is "congenitally orientated" toward a being which it is not.

Being-for-itself is a brute given because its being-there has no sufficient reason. To say, with Sartre, that consciousness exists is not to make an abstract statement. Consciousness only exists in its own very particular and concrete ways, in individuals. There is no generalized form of existence.[21] Following from this there is no sufficient reason for the fact that I exist in the particular way that I do. There is no foundation for my being. The for-itself in general has its foundation, though not a sufficient foundation, in the in-itself. But my particular being has no particular reason to be the way it is; my existence is superfluous. Despite my

---

[20]Jean-Paul Sartre, "Une idée fondamentale de la phénoménologie de Edmund Husserl: L'Intentionalité," in *Situations I* (Paris: Gallimard, 1947), p. 33. The passage is translated and quoted in Thomas M. King, S. J., *Sartre and the Sacred* (Chicago: University of Chicago Press, 1974), p. 23.

[21]But, as will be shown, this point of view seems problematic because Sartre also maintains that all particular forms of consciousness are symbolic of the basic project of all consciousness: the desire to be god.

desires to the contrary, I am not a necessary existent. I exist as a gratuitous negation of the in-itself. There is no foundation for "my" being per se.

The individual existent is, in the sense that it exists, its facticity; its existence is a fact, a definite and fixed one. In its existence the individual consciousness has connections with the in-itself because it exists materially as a brute fact. Consciousness is necessarily related to the in-itself but it is a one-way reference; the in-itself is not affected by the for-itself.

This form of Sartre's relation of the for-itself to the in-itself has Neo-Platonic overtones. It is similar to the Plotinian emanations from Being. The emanations refer to the Transcendent Being and to the One, but the One is more than its emanations and is in no way lessened by their emanation. The relation of the in-itself and for-itself and the relation of the for-itself and the in-itself are also similar to traditional theological conceptions of God and creatures, wherein the creature is related to the creator but not the creator to the creature. This similarity is important because of Sartre's claim that he is not involved in a theological-/metaphysical exercise but in a phenomenological investigation that requires neither God nor first principle. But the proof of the existence of the in-itself and the use of the regressive analysis to establish the existence of the for-itself are metaphysical efforts to explain reality--no different in character from similar efforts in Aristotle, Whitehead, Bergson, or Berdyaev. So, one of the questions that follows from Sartre's description of the for-itself is how does being-for-itself ever come to be? If being-in-itself is pure positivity why is there an original upsurge of consciousness at all? In this respect Sartre's being-in-itself is quite like Parmenides' being. There is something unreal about negation, and hence consciousness, in both Parmenides and Sartre. Being can only be described in positive terms. In being-in-itself there is no change, reality is stable. Being-in-itself does not come to be. There is no becoming, no time, and no differentiation. Sartre, like Parmenides, never deals with the question of why negation comes to be, or in Sartre's terms, why there are beings rather than just being-in-itself. For although Sartre eschews metaphysics in his rhetoric, he lets metaphysics in the back door with his ontological proof. The way we get to the in-itself is not through phenomenological analysis but by way of logical proof. He wants to return to the phenomenological method to arrive at the description of consciousness, but even here the proof of the existence of the for-itself is provided by a regressive analysis. Sartre, like Parmenides, offers no clear account of the relation of the way of truth (being-in-itself) and the way of appearance (being-for-itself) other than to say that they are related. The falleness of the for-itself has an almost theological character. How the perfection of wholly positive being-in-itself could have generated the negative being-for-itself remains a mystery somewhat like the mystery that John Hick sees in traditional theology's version of the fall of creation from grace. Hick argues that in the traditional Augustinian theodicy the fall represents an ex-nihilo creation of evil by perfect creatures. Somehow "unqualifiedly good (though finite) creatures" were capable of evil that God did not create in them, otherwise we could blame

God who gave him his imperfect nature.[22] In the same sense there is no reason and no explanation for the "ex nihilo" creation or emanation of the for-itself from the in-itself. Sartre would argue, simply, that we are presented with the brute fact of the existence of these two categories of Being the one dependent on the other.

Sartre's descriptions of the activities of consciousness resemble Plotinus' attempts to explain the relation of Transcendent Being and consciousness through emanations out of the One, a descent into multiplicity conditioned by non-being, and the aspiration to reverse this descending movement and return to pure Being. This Neo-Platonic cosmology seems to haunt Sartre throughout *Being and Nothingness*. Being-in-itself, pure undifferentiated Being, emanates, for no reason, being-for-itself which is between Being and nothingness. At death the for-itself is reabsorbed into the in-itself, the One. What is lacking in this comparison is, of course, the possibility of mystic union with the One by consciousness. But in talking about the intentions of the for-itself and the apparent intentions of the in-itself, Sartre goes beyond the Plotinian similarities to a component that includes the false-hope pattern of development in Being similar to that of Jacob Boehme and the German idealists. Being seeks to become both in-and-for-itself. To consciousness it would seem that the fall is a positive occurrence because of the possibility of the illumination of the in-itself. But because of the ontological structures of Being and nothingness, such a projection is impossible. In the conclusion of *Being and Nothingness* Sartre discusses the metaphysical implication of the ontological structures of the in-itself and the for-itself in these very terms.

On the ontological level nothing permits one to affirm that, from the beginning and in the very womb of the in-itself, the for-itself means the project to be the cause of itself.. . . [And yet] everything happens as if the in-itself, in a project to ground itself, gave itself the modification of the for-itself. (The for-itself is the in-itself losing itself as in-itself in order to ground itself as consciousness).. . . Thus everything happens as if the in-itself and the for-itself were presented in a state of disintegration in relation to an ideal synthesis.[23]

The in-itself seems to emanate the for-itself in a project to ground itself. But Sartre rejects the possibility of reabsorption of the for-itself into Being in such a way that the opposition between the in-itself and the for-itself is aufhaben. The

---

[22]John Hick, *Evil and the God of Love* (San Francisco: Harper and Row, 1977) p. 174. Berdyaev sees the whole theological conception that the fall was possible as a proof that traditional theology must accept the independence of man's freedom from God. Nicholas Berdyaev, *The Destiny of Man* (New York: Harper and Row, p. 27.

[23]*EN*, pp. 715 & 717. *BN*, pp. 760 & 762.

completion of consciousness and Being in being-in-and-for-itself is rejected.[24] But Sartre maintains that the ideal of this totality constantly haunts the for-itself and even seems, at least to consciousness, to have originated in the in-itself.[25] Sartre tries to show that the for-itself, in its immanence, is a lack that tries to transcend itself, as a lack, toward itself as a totality: something it cannot attain.

This idea of a totality that is not attainable and yet somehow essentially present in the project of the for-itself is problematic. It is the formalism of Sartre's ontology which insists on the separation between the in-itself, as the massive material character of Being, and a for-itself consciousness, that introduces negation into the world through the character of its own nothingness, that excludes the possibility of movement toward totality. (Or, as we shall see in the analysis of being-for-others, it excludes the possibility of movement even toward other consciousnesses.) Consciousness, in *Being and Nothingness*, is necessarily an unhappy consciousness. Totality, the combination of the in-itself and for-itself, is an unattainable goal that is ever present as the ideal but ever denied in reality. If

---

[24]I think that the idea of Sartre as a kind of inverse Plotinian is somewhat strengthened if we accept the description of the problem of the desire to be god in two excellent recent studies of Sartre's ethics. David Detmer argues that the description of the desire to be God that permeates Sartre's description of humanity in *Being and Nothingness* only describes the bad faith of consciousness' attempt to become in-itself-for-itself. Detmer argues that the radical conversion passages in *Being and Nothingness* and the footnote where Sartre hints at avoiding bad faith through authenticity indicate that Sartre argues that freedom is the highest and only value and that man must forget the desire to be God and attempt to found all value on the fact of his freedom. Detmer sees the famous "man is a useless passion" passage as only referring to the impossible project of the desire to be God. If Detmer is correct then Sartre would think that the desire for a Boehmeian or Hegelian synthesis of being and nothingness that seems to be inherent in consciousness could be freely chosen against. In this case the analogy with neo-Platonism would be that Sartre proposes a kind of reverse picture of Plotinus. Consciousness is emanated by a "material" not ideal being-in-itself and is eventually reabsorbed into it. Also the "value" of consciousness is in its separate existence from that being that emanated it. Its reabsorption in that being represents that tragic finale of its freedom and its value. David Detmer, *Freedom as a Value: A Critique of the Ethical Theory of Jean-Paul Sartre* (La Salle, Illinois: Open Court, 1988) pp. 102-131.

[25]Sartre may have a problem here. If the desire to be God is inherent in each person then it would seem as though it may have originated in the in-itself because like the situation that conscious is thrown into it did not choose the desire to be god. In *Being and Nothingness* there are ample passages that indicate the desire to be god is a part of the structure and thus the in-itself character of consciousness.

this is the case then absurdity is the best word to characterize the philosophical anthropology found in *Being and Nothingness*; the for-itself, by nature, possesses an ideal that cannot possibly be fulfilled.


## God, the Ego, and Bad Faith

In the section, "The Origin of Negation," of *Being and Nothingness* Sartre argues that notions of God and the transcendental ego have all been efforts to combine characteristics of being-in-itself and being-for-itself. All have attributes of being-in-itself, such as permanence and necessity, and yet they also have the attribute of the for-itself: consciousness. They are "magical" creations of metaphysics. Sartre terms them "magical" because they are created to explain a reality that cannot be explained and to provide consciousness with a sense of totality that it, by its nature, lacks. In addition, their existence would involve the combination of characteristics that, according to Sartre's ontology, cannot be combined. They are examples of the psychological condition in man that Sartre calls bad faith.

Traditionally, the ego is based on a notion of the material presence of a self that does not change over time. The conception of an ego presupposes that every action is directed to the permanent self or the ego. The ego is a privileged, changeless "me" that has states of feeling but transcends all of those "states." Sartre argues that the ego is usually conceived as a permanent structure like a stone that lies at the bottom of a pool. The ego is pictured as unaffected by the currents around it and it radiates emotions in relation to objects outside of it. But to see the ego as transcendental is to reverse the order of reality because the ego is created. Rather, the emotions themselves are transcendental. Hatred, spite, etc. are not confined to the momentary experience. There is more to hate than is given at any moment. My hatred of someone is an ongoing experience, more than what is given at any particular time. The self is a transcendent object, but its transcendence is very different from the transcendence of the emotions. It is an object, and precisely, the object of the emotions. In fact, the ego is constituted by the emotions, it is the point toward which constitution moves. The ego is an object outside of the stream of consciousness that is constituted by the individual like other objects in the world. This is what Sartre means when he says we choose ourselves at each instant. At each moment we choose the kind of self that will be constituted. This is why Sartre insists that we only become what we are at death; at that moment we cease to be consciousness and become an object.

It might be argued that through the elimination of the static ego Sartre begins to eliminate the problem of other minds. He gets rid of all individual minds or transcendental egos in such a way that minds are not viewed as individual material monads, unaffected by their environment. But the problem of other minds returns under the guise of radically different points of view separated by internal negations.

So, although the Other is not regarded as a static center or soul resisting the influence of the world, he is still radically isolated from other consciousnesses. Each consciousness creates its own relation to the in-itself. There is still a strongly monadic character to Sartre's existentialism. If the ego is a projection and I am the flow of consciousness, what is the structure of the self and consciousness for Sartre? It might seem that by eliminating the static ego Sartre might avoid the problem of the self and the Other. But consciousness still possesses a monadic character because of Sartre's notion of the infallible character of perception (I have a privileged access to my perceptions and I perceive my own emotions). The non-positional character of consciousness gives a privileged place to me that no other has access to. I am my point of view, radically isolated from any other point of view. This is the non-positional character of consciousness.

There are no past acts of consciousness that cannot be reflected upon, but this is not the case with consciousness itself. Consciousness cannot be reflected upon because it cannot be turned into an object, it is always the non-positional point of view. Reflection distorts, it alters the fact of consciousness on which it is rendered precisely because it must lose the non-positional character of consciousness. Reflection needs an object and consciousness is never an object. It is constant change, never what it is. Non-positional consciousness is in constant flux, it is a point of view constantly changing its object. When consciousness reflects on itself it loses itself, or rather, only reflects on a past act of consciousness. Consciousness itself is the act of reflecting. This means that consciousness distorts and changes itself in the very awareness of itself.

Positional consciousness refers to the in-itself. The in-itself affects not only what consciousness knows but what it is. Consciousness always enters its world in a context, this context controls its freedom, nevertheless it is responsible for its facticity. As a consciousness, I am responsible because I can do what I can with the possibilities afforded by my facticity. Facticity and transcendence combine. "I am the transcending of a facticity." The situation into which I am thrown is a situation that I can modify to a certain extent. I always transcend what I am but because of this I can never be what I am. I am an event that takes place in a certain context over an extended length of time. Since I am non-positionally aware of myself, I am constantly aware that I am not the foundation of my own being. I am always dimly aware that I am gratuitous, a brute contingent fact with no foundation for my being. I am imperfect.

## God and Human Projects

Sartre appeals to Descartes' argument for the existence of God in the third meditation to show the nature of the human desire for totality and the impossibility of the existence of God. According to Descartes, I sense the existence of God because of the lacks in myself: I am imperfect but I still have an idea of perfection, of totality, that must have been instilled in me by God. This sense of perfection is the idea of God.

The idea of perfection requires the complementary idea of lacks. The imperfect being lacks the fullness necessary to bring about perfection. A lack involves three ingredients: the lacking or what is missing, the existing or what is and is missing something and the lacked or what there would be if the existing were perfect and had what it is missing. Sartre uses the example of the crescent moon. We see it as not whole in itself but as a part of a growing whole. To view it in this way is to give it the structure of a lack. Sartre applies this structure to consciousness. Consciousness is the existing that is aware of its lack of foundation. What is lacking is itself, its totality. Human beings, by their nature project both the totality and the possibility of consciousness's fulfillment. Human beings become involved in acts of bad faith because, as a negation, they are not and cannot be fully what they are. Still, to avoid the anguish that is created by the lack of any lasting essence, human beings engage in projects that aim toward the creation of an essence. Sartre uses the example of a waiter who attempts to become perfect, changeless, by reducing himself to the essence of a waiter. He would be no more or less than a waiter because as a waiter he is, at least, something. The attempt to give himself an essence, that he is not more nor less than, is doomed to failure because it is the nature of consciousness always to go beyond what it is, so it is never what it is. As with Heraclitus' stream, consciousness is never the same twice. Indeed Cratylus' modification may even be a more accurate characterization: consciousness is never the same once. There is a fissure in the for-itself; as its own negation, it is separated from itself. If consciousness could ever be fully itself it would be as God, completely self-sufficient, it would be both in-and-for-itself. But man can never ground himself because the idea of God is the idea of a magical entity. This is the meaning of Sartre's famous statement that man is a useless passion. The most basic desire of consciousness is guaranteed to be frustrated.

Consciousness is always colored by its facticity. It is always striving for the abstract structure, which is God, but is itself always a particular structure, a transcending of a facticity. God and the values that are associated with any Godlike magical entity, the Absolute, Being, etc., are human creations and as such they can function to give human beings what they desire, an essence. The religious experience of vocation is an attempt, repeated in many of Sartre's literary pieces to attain this essence. In *The Reprieve*, the character Daniel gladly accepts his vocation and new essence.

> I can easily describe that look: it is nothing; it is a purely negative entity: imagine a pitch-dark night. It's the night that looks at you, but it's a dazzling night, in fullest splendor; the night behind the day. I am flooded with black light; it is all over my hands and eyes and

heart, and I can't see it.. . . What anguish to discover that look as a universal medium from which I can't escape but what a relief as well! I know at last that I am.. . . I need no longer bear the responsibility of my turbid and disintegrating self: he who sees me causes me to be; I am as he sees me. I turn my eternal, shadowed face towards the night, I stand up like a challenge, and I say to God: Here am I. Here am I as you see me, as I am. What can I do now?--you know me, and I do not know myself. What can I do except put up with myself? and You, whose look eternally follows me--please put up with me. Mathieu, what joy, what torment! At last I am transmuted into myself. Hated, despised, sustained, a presence supports me to continue thus forever. I am infinite and infinitely guilty. But I am, Mathieu, I am. Before God and before men. I am. Ecce homo.[26]

Even though this confession of guilt before God may seem a long way from the desire to be the almighty Sartre's assertion that all human being desire to be God is still applicable here. Daniel is what he is, like God he is unchanging. And though his vocation is given him by God he has freely accepted it. He wills to be guilty before God. Daniel is still in bad faith because he cannot face the pure negativity of his freedom. For him it seems better to be infinitely guilty than be nothing in particular, a human being.

In *Saint Genet* Sartre argues that the Other or Others often take the position of God for us. The Other assigns us the meaning that we are so desperately seeking. The Other creates for us a substantial ego, which is a denial of the freedom and transcendence of consciousness and thus an act of bad faith. In my effort to be at one with the Other, and avoid my own freedom and transcendence, I create myself or accept an essence given me by the Other by "becoming" exactly what the Other wants me to be. Sartre illustrates this with the example of a woman who accepts the label of irascible from her husband.

> . . . if she accuses herself of having an irascible nature, if she projects behind her, in the darkness of the unconscious, a permanent predisposition to anger of which each particular outburst is an emanation, then she subordinates her reality as a conscious subject to the Other that she is for Others, and she grants to the Other a superiority to herself

---

[26]Cited in Thomas M. King, *Sartre and the Sacred* (Chicago: University of Chicago Press, 1974), p. 82. Also, in *Saint Genet*, Genet is told by the Others that he is a thief. He accepts the title and is free from the mental anguish of trying constantly to deal with the ambiguity of his existence. Jean-Paul Sartre, *Saint Genet: Actor and Martyr*, trans. Bernard Frechtman (New York: Pantheon Books, 1963), pp. 63.

and confers upon what is probable a superiority to what is certain. She endows that which had no meaning other than social with a metaphysical meaning, a meaning prior to any relationship with society.[27]

God, as the projected Other, represents the ultimate form of the reification of consciousness into a magical form or bad faith. Before the all seeing eye of God I am eternally created as what I am, I am always guilty. God grants me a permanent essence, this fulfills my project because the for-itself escapes its transcendence and "in God" becomes what it is. This is what Sartre refers to as a type of deification called Sainthood.

> The position of God is accompanied by a reification of my object-ness. Or better yet, I posit my being-an-object-for-God as more real that my For-myself; I exist alienated and I cause myself to learn from outside what I must be. This is the origin of fear before God.[28]

God and the Other are linked in Sartre's philosophy because the Other, who is beyond me (whether he is a projection of my desire to be like God or really another consciousness) is capable of objectifying my existence for me. This I both fear and want. I fear it because it is and is not what I am; it attempts to arrest the flow of consciousness; it robs me of my freedom. I want it for the same reasons, my objectification eliminates the anguish that I feel from my freedom.

In *Being and Nothingness* human reality is a dualism of facticity (determinateness) and transcendence (openness) the two oppose each other and the contradiction is not to be resolved. Bad faith, however is the art of affirming identity while preserving differences. In Bad faith a person refuses to see the contradiction of identity and difference that is inherent in consciousness. A similar scheme applies to being-for-itself and being-for-others. I see myself in the facticity of how others see me and as a transcendence of that facticity. Sartre claims that any fixation on an ideal is an act of bad faith because the very structure of man defies fixation. Consciousness both is and is not its determinations. This means that consciousness always exists in the ambiguous middle ground between them.

Sartre's description of the circuit of selfness and the creation of values illustrates once again the similarity of Sartrean existentialism to an idealist eschatology. Consciousness aims at the creation of a perfect self on the other side of facticity. Human beings are projects; all are attempting the ultimate project of founding themselves, of attaining fullness. Thus, all projects are based on the desire to be God. Consciousness desires to be both in and for-itself. All human

---

[27]Sartre, *Saint Genet*, pp. 33-34.

[28]*EN*, p. 350. *BN*, p. 355.

projects fit into this general pattern but all are uniquely different. The uniqueness of each project gives rise to the creation of different values; this is the ontological foundation of the beliefs in objective values, the traditional idea of morality, and the spirit of seriousness. For the waiter, all his activity takes on a certain value in the light of the project of becoming a perfect waiter.

Consciousness is a lack and this is the real meaning behind the traditional notion that God is the good. God is the totality, the lacked, the standard of value, the ideal. So God haunts the whole of life because he is the goal at which we are aiming. God could not serve the function of being the ideal goal if he existed. God is so good, so perfect (the combination of the in-itself and for-itself) that he cannot exist even as an ideal because even the ideal is a magical entity. The absence of God for Sartre is thus the absence of a regulative idea. Thus, Sartrean ethics is deprived of the function that God plays in Kant's Second Critique.[29] Any question of infinite progress is denied because the possibility of the fulfillment of will and desire, the lacking and the lacked, the basic project to be God, is ontologically impossible. God as a magical entity cannot even be consistently thought. But this denial of the possibility of God as a regulative ideal assures the absurdity of the Sartrean universe.[30]

Sartre claims that we arrive at the notion of the desire to be God through the description of particular projects. The particular is always at the level of the brute fact. The desire to be God is a dimension of the human condition rather than human nature. The desire to be God is not a psychological state all actions are reduced to. It does not determine the projects by which one attempts to become what one is. The notion of the desire to be God is the basic fact about the human condition and is based on the description of human activity. It can manifest itself in billions of different ways. There is a genetic relation between each basic human

---

[29]Hegel had already pointed to the difficulty with Kant's Idea of God and its relation to virtue in the sections on "The Moral View of the World and "Moral Duplicity" in the *Phenomenology of Spirit*. If God is perfect he is beyond the temptation of the inclinations, He has nothing to choose against. If He has nothing to choose against is he free? Hegel thought that Kantian morality with its emphasis on the free and autonomous moral consciousness and the performance of its duty done for its own sake demanded the existence of the resistance of the natural realm. God does not experience this resistance, so how can God function as a regulative ideal for the autonomous moral consciousness? G.W.F. Hegel, *The Phenomenology of Spirit*, trans. by A.V. Miller (Oxford: Oxford University Press, 1977) pp. 364-384.

[30]This is why Sartre can say in *Existentialism is a Humanism*, that existentialism feels the absence of God more sharply than other forms of philosophy. Jean-Paul Sartre, *L'Existentialisme est un humanisme* (Paris: Les Éditions Nagel, 1967), pp. 34-37.

project and momentary mental acts but it is not causal. There is no sense in which the desire to be God causes the particular project. But there must be a project for each consciousness and all of them reflect, to a certain extent, the desire to be God. It is on this point that Sartre differentiates "Existential psychoanalysis" from Freudian psychoanalysis. Freud's theory is based on a notion of human nature. He moves from a system of general principles about human drives to a explanation of all human behavior. For Sartre, Freud's theory is another case of the creation of a magical entity. It is based on a theory of human nature that freezes the reality of freedom. Sartre claims that his version of human projects as the desire to be God is a characterization of the human endeavor to endow life with some sort of meaning in relation to the frightening infinity of the possibilities of freedom. The desire of being-for-itself to found itself can be universally observed in human activity without resorting to some theory of hidden drives beneath everyday activities.

The human aim in creating morality is to create values that can be endowed with eternal status. Moral philosophy is an attempt to support this drive toward eternality. The creation of absolute values results from the particular type of project to be God and the subsequent effort to see everything in the light of the project, to interpret the whole of experience through the project. Sartre calls this the spirit of seriousness. The spirit of seriousness is an act of bad faith because it presupposes something to exist which by its ontological constitution would be impossible: God, or some first principle by which the rest of the totality of one's existence can be determined. (This could just as well be God or the ideal of the perfect waiter). It must be recognized, says Sartre, that absolutes, like all values and meanings, are the values that human beings create. They have no separate existence by themselves, nor do they inhere in the nature of things. Human beings will values to be absolute and, in so willing, implicitly will that they inhere in the nature of the in-itself. For the very reason that would make them absolute they constitute an act of bad faith. Human beings will the absolute but are not absolute themselves, neither can the absolute that they create be what they wish it to be. Man extinguishes himself that God might be. But God is a magical entity and an impossibility; so all basic projects reflect the general absurdity of the attempt.

It is true, writes Sartre, that values fly up in the world like partridges in a field, but this does not mean that they are ready-made and independent. Their springing up is a part of human projects. Consciousness is the source of values, nothing else. Consciousness creates values and then tries to endow them with absolute character. So from the point of view of values it makes little difference whether one becomes a "leader of nations" or quietly "gets drunk alone."

> Thus, it amounts to the same thing whether one gets drunk alone or
> is the leader of nations. If one of these activities takes precedence
> over the others, this will not be because of its real goal but because of
> the degree of consciousness that it possesses of its ideal goal: and in

this case it will be the quietism of the solitary drunkard that will take precedence over the vain agitation of the leader of nations.[31]

The discussion of bad faith, value, the necessary failure of the desire to be God seems to indicate a general pessimism about Sartre's form of existentialism that is impossible to overcome. This introduces what many critics have considered the one of the great problems of *Being and Nothingness*.[32] In this view Sartre promises an existentialist ethics at the end of *Being and Nothingness* and never provides one because an existentialist ethics based on the ontology present in that book is impossible. To follow the course that Sartre seems to have outlined here implies moral anarchy. The great existentialist virtue, authenticity, does not really seem much different than Gide's sincerity though Sartre also provides a searing critique of sincerity, where we realize our finitude and act accordingly, would not make any difference; one would just act and choose. In the process of doing this you are creating values but these values have no possibility of permanence. This forces the question why should one act authentically? Is not more comfortable and just as free to choose bad faith? Is the basis of ethical judgement really only a judgement dependent on taste? Should we act authentically because it is more beautiful to act authentically? If ethics is to be conceived of as action in relation to Others, does authentic action imply a more authentic relation with the Other? In this view Sartre's version of radical freedom is unable to provide a ground for making ethical choices, even for choosing the "solitary drunkard" over the "vain agitation of the leader of nations." The choice is either arbitrary or the result of individual preference. Sartre's version of freedom wrestles with the Kantian notion of a regulative idea but then undercuts the possibility of such by reducing the ideal to a magical entity. Sartre cannot escape the absurd universe that grows out of his ontological framework. Sartre himself is seen to have admitted the failure of *Being and Nothingness* and this is the reason the promised work on ethics never materialized. Sartre abandoned the existentialist project of *Being and Nothingness* for the Marxism of *The Critique of Dialectical Reason*.

---

[31]*EN*, pp. 617-618. *BN*, pp. 626-627.

[32]Detemter notes the following: Henry Veatch, *For an Ontology of Morals* (Evanston: Northwestern University Press, 1971), pp. 74-77; Mary Warnock, *Existentialist Ethics* (London: Macmillan, 1967), pp. 43-48; Richard Bernstein, *Praxis and Action* (Philadelphia: University of Pennsylvania Press, 1971), pp. 151-154; Wilfred Desan, *The Tragic Finale: An Essay on the Philosophy of Jean-Paul Sartre* (New York: Harper and Row, 1960) pp. 181-184; Alvin Plantinga, "An Existentialist Ethics," in *Review of Metaphysics* 12 (December 1958): 248-249; Risieri Frondizi, "Sartre's Early Ethics: A Critique" in P. A. Schillp ed., *The Philosophy of Jean-Paul Sartre*, pp. 370-391.

I think Jeanson, de Beauvoir, and, more recently, Anderson and Detmer have shown that this kind of an interpretation of Sartre may be too facile. Detmer points to five ideas in *Being and Nothingness* that seem to show Sartre's ultimate pessimism: 1) the unfulfillable desire to be God;, 2) the existential condition of bad faith that seems an unavoidable part of existence; 3) conflict is the original meaning of being for others; 4) Sartre thinks there are no non-arbitrary or objective values; and, finally, 5) the two famous quotes at the end of the work that see man as a useless passion and claim that it makes no difference whether one becomes a leader of nations or quietly gets drunk alone.[33] But he also claims, along with Jeanson, De Beauvoir, et al., that these passages and the bulk of *Being and Nothingness* is only and indication of the possibilities of consciousness when it involves itself in the hopeless quest of the desire to be God but that there is a possibility for consciousness, by nature free, can choose against the desire to be God. this is the possibility of radical conversion.[34]

## Radical Conversion

Both Detmer and Anderson admit that the radical conversion passages in *Being and Nothingness* are rare but they think they are significant in view of later statements by Sartre, the ethical theory that is found in the unpublished notebooks on ethic, and the ethical theories of Sartre's two disciples, De Beauvoir and Jeanson. Detmer asserts that Sartre was careful, even in *Being and Nothingness*, to point out that the theory therein propounded was not his final word on values, the other, or the possibilities of human existence. First, in the footnote at the end of the section on bad faith, Sartre asserted that it was possible to "radically escape bad faith. But this supposes a self-recovery of being which was previously corrupted. This self-recovery we shall call authenticity, the description of which has no place here."[35] Second, there is a footnote that concludes the section on

---

[33]Detmer, pp. 102-103.

[34]Detmer asserts that the most common reaction to The radical conversion passages of *Being and Nothingness* has been silence, most critics don't even consider them. This is understandable because they are relatively few in comparison with the texts that indicate a general pessimism. But in the mid-forties, even with his limited reading of Sartre, Berdyaev argued that the idea of freedom mediated Sartre's pessimism. But Berdyaev still thought that because of Sartre's conception of nothingness and its association with freedom Sartre could not escape the ultimate hopelessness of his position. Detmer, p. 105. Nicholas Berdyaev, *Truth and Revelation*, pp. 97-104.

[35] *EN*, p. 111 n 1. *BN*, p. 86 n 10.

concrete relation with others "these considerations do not exclude the possibility of an ethics of deliverance and salvation. But this can be achieved only after a radical conversion which we cannot discuss here."[36] Third, Detmer claims that in *Being and Nothingness* Sartre is only concerned with the implications of the universal project to be God. Detmer and Anderson both argue that the radical conversion is the realization that one has the possibility to reject the project of all projects which is the desire to be God. Even though the desire seems to be in us as a type of nature. Sartre writes there is an act "to makes manifest and to present to itself the absolute freedom which is the very being of the person."[37] Detmer claims if the for-itself **is** freedom and as Sartre has defined freedom as the ability to negate, to say no, certainly the for-itself has the possibility to say no to the desire to be God.[38] Sartre had asserted from very early in his career that seeing

---

[36]*EN*, p. 484 n 1. *BN*, p. 504 n 3.

[37]*EN*, p. 655. *BN*, p. 695.

[38]If this is the case then Sartre's idea of the freedom of the for-itself resembles Schopenhauer's description of the self and life. The self is able to assert itself contrary to the projects that it is tricked into by nature through the escape into art or acts of compassion. Schopenhauer suggested that the thing-in-itself was really an irrational and limitless urge which he called the "the will to live." This is not Sartre's in-itself but its effect on human beings is not unlike the idea of the desire to be god, or to be the foundation of one's existence. For if we interpret the desire to be god as, Detmer and Anderson do, as an inclination that exists in us almost as a nature then the desire to be God has some qualities of the in-itself. Sartre himself admits that, from the point of view of consciousness, separating the in-itself from freedom is difficult. So as with Schopenhauer the in-itself character of the desire to be god, like "the will to live," is free of the principle of sufficient reason and is a sheer striving without and end. For Schopenhauer it is only in art or acts of compassion that approach the noumenal character of the will and are also capable of negating it. This resembles Jeanson's, De Beauvoir's, Detmer's and Anderson's assertions that the radical conversion passages indicate the possibility of realizing the self as freedom and negating the desire to be god through a free choice. In Schopenhauerian terms, one could become a pure will-less subject of knowledge free from the burden of self-assertion through denying the impossible quest of becoming the foundation of one's being. Sartre would argue that Schopenhauer is too much a metaphysician when he imposes this will on all things in the world and not simply as a part of the being of consciousness and vehemently disagree with Schopenhauer's assertion that in art the mind comes to know the noumenal realm. (Though in *The Words*, Sartre admitted that he once saw his salvation as possible through writing, Roquetin thinks as much in *Nausea*.) Sartre would also see Schopenhauer's idea that the escape from will requires the

the possibility of escape from the world and its determinations meant that the possibility of a partial negation of all situations existed. "For a consciousness to be able to imagine it must be able to escape from the world by its very nature, it must be able by its own efforts to withdraw from the world. In a word it must be free."[39] And in *Being and Nothingness* Sartre argued that the possibility of "nihilating withdrawal" in questioning the world indicated that consciousness as questioner is not "subject to the causal order of the world; he detaches himself from being."[40] Anderson argues that the three pages on ethical indications at the end of *Being and Nothingness* indicate that Sartre saw the possibility of choosing against the desire to be God. Anderson contends that the famous passage that call man "a useless passion" etc. have only to do with the desire to be God. In this light one should see that only people who "still believe there mission of effecting the existence of the in-itself-for-itself is written things, they are condemned to despair; for they discover at the same time that all human activities are equivalent. . and that all are on principle doomed to failure.. . . Thus it amounts to the same thing whether one gets drunk alone or is a leader of nations."[41] The despair is linked only to one that is gripped with the spirit of seriousness. In connection with this last passage Anderson thinks "Less obviously, Sartre may be saying that despair and failure are inevitable only if one persists in taking God as his value and vainly pursues this unattainable goal."[42] Such an interpretation of these passages lessens considerably what has usually be taken for the harsh despair with which *Being and Nothingness* ends. But Sartre himself speaks explicitly in *Being and Nothingness* about a project of the for-itself that has freedom as its foundation and goal.

> This particular type of project, which has freedom for its foundation and its goal, deserves a special study. It is radically different from all others in that it aims at a radically different type of being. It would be necessary to explain in full detail its relation with the project of

---

abrogation of individuality to be in bad faith. Arthur Schopenhauer, *The World as Will and Representation* trans. E.F.J. Payne (New York: Dover, 1969), pp. 177-178, 194-200.

[39]Jean-Paul Sartre, *The Psychology of the Imagination*, (New York Philosophical Library, 1948) p. 240.

[40]*EN*, p. 65. *BN*, p. 34.

[41]*EN*, pp. 721-722. *BN*, p. 767.

[42]Thomas C. Anderson, *The Foundation and Structure of Sartrean Ethics* (Lawrence: The Regent's Press of Kansas, 1979), p. 28.

being-God, which has appeared to us as the deep-seated structure of human reality. but such a study can not be made here; it belongs rather to an Ethics and it supposes that there has been a preliminary definition of nature and the role of purifying reflection ( our descriptions have hitherto aimed only at accessory reflection); it supposes in addition taking a position which can be moral only in the face of values which haunt the for-itself.[43]

Finally, Detmer cites the questions that Sartre poses in the section on "Ethical Implications" in *Being and Nothingness* that aim at the possibility of a choice of consciousness that is free of the desire to be God and on which will be founded the existentialist ethics.

What will become of freedom if it turns its back upon this value [the desire to be God]? Will freedom carry this value along with it whatever it does and even in its very turning back upon the in-itself-for-itself? Will freedom be reprehended from behind by the value which it wishes to contemplate? Or will freedom by the very fact that it apprehends itself as a freedom in relation to itself, be able to put an end to the reign of this value? In particular is it possible for freedom to take itself for a value as the source of all value, or must it necessarily be defined in relation to a transcendent value which haunts it? And in case it could will itself as its own possible and its determining value, what would this mean? . . . All these questions, which refer us to a pure and not an accessory reflection, can find their reply only on the ethical plane. We shall devote to them a future work.[44]

---

[43]*EN* p. 655, *BN* p. 695.

[44]*EN*, pp. 721-722. *BN*, pp. 767-768. The key terms that appear in these sections are **purifying** and **accessory refection**. Jeanson clarifies the meanings of these two terms and how they relate to the desire to be god.
1. **Purifying reflection** reflects on the whole project of the desire to be God itself.

. . . its role to reveal man--by giving him access to the moral plane of authenticity--that his quest of being and his wish to appropriate the in-itself are merely possibilities among other possibilities. Pure reflection allows him to stop taking as irreducible the basic value that orients all his choices; it ceases to be the ideal presence of the self-caused being. He is then in a position to choose this value himself; to imbue it with value or to reject it.

Sartre here points to a distinction between ethics and ontology. *Being and Nothingness* is a work on ontology and not itself concerned with ethics but with the structures of being. Of course it is upon these structures that the existentialist ethics must be founded. Berdyaev argues that the description of freedom cannot begin with ontology because ontology, as the science of being, cannot describe freedom as prior to being and must make it dependent on being and thus unfree. Berdyaev thus sees ethics as prior to ontology. Sartre in making freedom the negation of being attempts to build an ethics that, although based on the ontology of *Being and Nothingness*, escapes the ontology through the negation of the desire to be God that is offered by being. The question is whether or not this escape is possible.

Detmer argues that the point of the radical conversion passages is that Sartre did not intend that the description of utter fruitlessness of the desire to be God in *Being and Nothingness* be taken as inescapable. That the ontology of *Being and Nothingness* is a description of the "eidetics of bad faith" but that Sartre saw the possibility of escape from bad faith and the formation of values based on freedom itself.[45] Sartre himself indicated as much in *Existentialism is a Humanism* in 1946, freedom is the foundation of all values.

> Besides, I can bring moral judgment to bear. When I declare
> that freedom in every concrete circumstance can have no other aim
> than to want itself, if man has once become aware that in his

Jeanson p. 208

2. **Accessory reflection** is only dealing with the day to day, with what is given, it see values of which the desire to be god is primary as given to it in being. Jeanson describes it in the following way:

> [it] bears only on the secondary structures of action, as in deliberation over the means to attain a certain end. While engaging in it, one refuses to ask oneself about the existence or significance of a supreme end or of a fundamental choice. Accessory reflection permeates day-to-day living, living which thinks of itself only to justify itself, which finds itself in the wrong only with regard to the use of this or that procedure, which finds one's basic failure not in a choice--which, being fundamental, it prefers to ignore--but in the unavoidable disappointments of "destiny."

Jeanson p. 180

[45]Simone de Beauvoir, *The Ethics of Ambiguity* trans. Bernard Frechtman (New York: The Citadel Press, 1948) p. 11.

forlorness he imposes values, he can no longer want but one thing, and that is freedom, as the basis of all values. That doesn't mean that he wants it in the abstract. It means simply that the ultimate meaning of the acts of honest men is the quest for freedom as such.. . And in wanting freedom we discover that it depends entirely on the freedom of others, and that the freedom of others depends on ours.[46]

Though Sartre's promised work on ethics never was published in his lifetime it is apparent that this is the direction that he took. In the posthumously published notebooks Sartre indicated that "every effort of the for-itself to become in-itself is doomed to failure. He calls for a conversion from the project and insists that only through modification of the project can alienation be overcome. After conversion the new goal is liberation or human liberty ". . . *but this Goal is not given it is willed.*" Unlike the desire to be God, the will to liberty is not given it is willed.[47] Thus Sartre thinks that the value of consciousness is not in its ability to become God but in its contingency, for it is in this very contingency that its freedom lies. Like Kant Sartre seems to believe that my freedom which is my value is the ability to choose against my inclinations and desires or my being. I can never eradicate the desire to be God but through my freedom I can refuse to act on the desire.

### God

Sartre thinks the idea of God is only possible because the ideal has the attributes of the in-itself and the for-itself. The examination of universals in the eidetic reduction is supposed to have shown this. Like Feuerbach, Sartre thinks that God is the projection of the desire for the human ideal. God is both absolute necessity and absolute consciousness. His being is grounded in Himself and not outside of Himself; He has no need of any Other outside of Himself. But, in Sartre's terms, to be conscious is to be intentional, to have an object, to be aware of the Other, and in that sense, to depend on the Other for at least a part of one's being. It is also to be capable of change and negation. These are not possibilities for the in-itself. Thus, under Sartre's definition of being and consciousness, God is an impossibility. But what is stunning about Sartre's conception of being-in-itself is the ways it resembles the traditional Christian interpretation of Deity. In fact the relation of the in-itself and for-itself is , in many ways, similar to

---

[46]Jean-Paul Sartre, *Existentialism is a Humanism*, tr. Bernard Frechtman (New York: Philosophical Library, 1947) pp. 53-54.

[47]Jean-Paul Sartre, *Cahiers pour une morale* (Paris: Gallimard, 1983), p. 486.

traditional theological conceptions of the relation of God and creature. Just as the creature is related to and dependent on God for its being but not its nothingness the for-itself is related to and dependent on the in-itself for its being for its being but not its nothingness. . And Just as God is not related to or dependent on the creature in any way the in-itself is neither related to nor dependent on the for-itself in any way. Traditional theology always has the difficulty of the relation of revelation but falls back on the on the unknowabilty of of the transcendent chararacter of God. Sartre makes the description perhaps more consistent in that he implies that no relation is at all possible. The in-itself is not conscious. It is only approached indirectly through the being of the phenomenon. If we accept the Sartrean framework, God as conscious being makes no sense. Revelation is impossible because consciousness implies a dialogical relation of the for-itself to the in-itself.

Sartre is famous for arguing that God is incompatible with human freedom. It would be difficult to imagine how the traditional philosophical notions of the divine in the East or the God of the West could be made compatible with Sartre's ontology and his explanation of human freedom.[48] The for-itself exists as the

---

[48]Francis Jeanson argues that a conception of God is not necessarily rejected in Sartrean existentialism. Jeanson thinks that for Sartre, the traditional notion of God either makes him transcendent and beyond me or immanent and the only thing that is important about me; the rest is simply an epiphenomenon. A god who exists independently of man is a guilty God; one that is responsible for all the evil that exists for man, the epiphenomenon. But this also means that man is the eternal innocent and that he is beyond all morality. Man ceases to be a moral agent himself. In this sense there is only true reality in God and none in man but it is only one step from here to Feuerbach's atheism. Descarte's doubt is understandable only in the human world where man is at least capable of self-transcendence. This would be the only authentic belief in God: "I hesitate: therefore, I can will that God exists." Jeanson, p. 206.

The hesitation that comes through doubt is necessary to human freedom and hence to moral freedom itself. Doubt, says Jeanson, allows us the possibility of willing the existence of God. The question is now one of our moral choice. In any case, whether I affirm or deny the existence of God, I, as a person, am involved in the choice. Thus, in a sense, God's existence does depend on me. Jeanson calls philosophy a human endeavor, "all philosophy is humanism," because it is solely on the level of the human that the invocation of God gets its meaning. On the level of human experience the metaphysical notion of God has no meaning; it is only on the level of engagement that the idea of God has meaning. This is related to Berdyaev's drama of the dialectic of the divine and the human. In the world it is only as man creatively turns toward the creation of being from chaos that God himself gets meaning. Indeed this is also the case for Martin Buber.

negation of positive being. Sartre moves to argue that the traditional Western explanation of the existence of God is impossible because of the in-itself's existence apart from any subjectivity. He says that the notion of creation cannot apply to the in-itself because a world created out of the subjectivity of God would remain intra-subjective and without the possibility of objectivity. By definition, the in-itself has to be independent. Consciousness requires a real object in order to be consciousness of something. Sartre would assert that the creation of being by God in traditional terms cannot make sense because Sartre assumes the existence of being already anterior to the act of creation. Creation ex nihilo is impossible, given Sartre's ontology.

---

Even for Buber God is dependent on man for the retrieval of the exiled Shekinah. Man is creative through counteracting chaos through the creation of relationships between human beings.

The fundamental problem with Jeanson's interpretation will surface in the analysis of Sartre's conception of the Other. From the point of view of the desire to be God in *Being and Nothingness*, any kind of real relationship with any other, whether it be one with the gods or human beings, is impossible. This is the case because of the monadic character of Sartre's ontology. But if we maintain, as Jeanson does, that relation may be possible, though difficult, because our choice gives us the freedom to reject the desire to be god and the responsibility to bring freedom to the Other. It is difficult to see what Jeanson could mean in speaking about the possibility of willing belief in God because almost any God imaginable would have to fit the Sartrean characterization of the for-itself in order to qualify for the position. There are not many actual theological descriptions of the divine that match this criterion for consciousness and thought. Any traditional ideas of deity do not. Neither is an ideal of God as a regulative ideal available for Sartre the way it is for Kant, because Kant's regulative idea depends on the possibility of its fulfillment. One last possible conceptions of God might be offered by something like the personalist, pluralist, idealism of the American philosopher George Holmes Howison who, like Sartre, also maintained that freedom is crucial to human existence and that freedom is untenable if the individual is dependent for his existence on a creator God or Absolute One. Thus, each human being stands in an individual relation with others and God. But even here God unites human experience. Although he is not to interfere with individual freedom, the system supposes the possibility of moral perfection and discussion of objective values which Sartre denies. On the other hand, any sort of conception of the divine ground that binds both gods and creatures seems also to fail because of Sartre's rejection of unity. For an explanation of Howison's thought see "The limits of Evolution and Other Essays Illustrating the Metaphysical Theory of Personal Idealism," in J.W. Buckingham and G. W. Stratten, *George Holmes Howison Philosopher and Teacher* (Berkeley: University of California Press, 1934).

Sartre's conception of human freedom as absolute in human beings is fundamentally incompatible with the Western idea of God. Sartre describes this incompatibility in his essay on "Cartesian Freedom." God, for Descartes and the West, is totally free and creates all that is ex nihilo without any restraint from facticity. In this version of God, says Sartre, human freedom can only be negative. Freedom is the purely negative ability not to conform to the absolute being, to the world created by God. Human freedom does not allow for creation and man only exercises his freedom in rebellion against God.

## Cartesian Existentialism

Sartre's relation to Descartes' philosophy is as important as his indebtedness to Hegel, Husserl and Heidegger. Sartre argued that the only suitable starting point for phenomenology was the Cartesian cogito. Just how important this statement is becomes apparent in Sartre's article on "Cartesian Freedom." Three Sartrean themes emerge from his relation with Descartes: the cogito as the starting point of knowledge, the radical aloneness of the cogito in relation to the outside world, and the negative character of freedom and consciousness.

There are three important steps in Sartre's interpretation of Descartes in "Cartesian Freedom." First, Sartre points out that Descartes, like the Medievals, reserved creative freedom for God. Second, for Descartes, Christian freedom is the conformity to the law of God, the negation of the negation that is human freedom, and hence, for Sartre, not freedom at all. Finally, Sartre discusses Descartes' conception of human freedom which is negative in character. It is in essence the denial of created being, based in the radical separateness of the Cartesian cogito.

Absolute freedom, for Descartes, is reserved for God alone; this is the freedom to create. The free act is "an absolutely new production, the germ of which could not be contained in an earlier state of the world and that consequently freedom and creation were one and the same."[49]

The important point to grasp in Sartre's discussion of Cartesian freedom is that he believes that, for Descartes, liberty and human autonomy only exist in the realm of the negative, of evil. The Christian Saint flees the world, aspiring to the realm of being, to the completely positive, and thus negates his own freedom and existence. In this way the Saint attempts to realize his desire to be God. Sartre indicates that the flight, however, is doomed to failure. It is impossible to escape

---

[49]Jean-Paul Sartre, "Cartesian Freedom," in *Literary and Philosophical Essays*, trans. Annette Michelson (New York: Collier Books, 1962), p. 195. Jean Paul-Sartre, "La liberté cartesienne" in *Situations I* (Paris: Gallimard, 1947), p. 332.

the anguish of human freedom which implies the negation of the in-itself. Thus, Christian freedom is an illusion.

> Christian saintliness is a negation of negation. It rejects only that part of ourself which comes from us, that is, from our nothingness: error and passions . . .. At the end of the renunciation there remains only being, absolute positivity without any negative counterpart, that is, the creature insofar as he relates to God alone.[50]

Sartre's idea of Christian freedom is similar to Augustine's description of it in the *City of God*; the human will is only free when it submits itself to God's law. But it seems clear that Sartre thinks there is not a significant difference between this form of Christian freedom and the freedom Spinoza speaks of: the human being is free only to conform to God's law. For Sartre this is an annihilation of the human. What is there left of the human will and freedom after it submits to God's law? Sartre says this is the meaning of the ideal of the annihilation of the self in all ascetic and mystical practices.

Freedom is one, but it manifests itself differently according to different situations. What is one about it is that it exists in a world that neither calls nor refuses it. Descartes, who is above all things a metaphysician, experiences at first not the freedom of creating ex nihilo but the experience of "pensée autonome" that discovers by its own powers the intelligible relationships between essences.[51] Sartre says that freedom is the act of independent judgement. This notion of freedom is in line with Descartes' original experience of doubt that leads to the discovery of the cogito.

Intellection is not the result of a mechanical process but has as its origin the will to attention. Descartes discovers autonomy in showing that intellection is not simply the mechanical process of pedagogy. It is the refusal to be distracted that leads to the radical exclusion of all exterior action, to the total autonomy of the individual thinker.[52] Before a doctrine of essences, freedom can never be more than the possibility to adhere to the truth. But, for Descartes, judgment is the decision to adhere to essences; this is, for Sartre, where Descartes includes the conception of engagement. For Heidegger, no one can die for me; death is radically my own. But, for Descartes, no one can understand for me; judgment and

---

[50]Jean-Paul Sartre, *Literary and Philosophical Essays*, p. 193. *Situations I*, p. 332.

[51]Jean-Paul Sartre, *Literary and Philosophical Essays*, p. 180. *Situations I*, p. 314.

[52]Sartre, *Literary and Philosophical Essays*, pp 180-81. *Situations I*, pp. 314-315.

understanding are all radically my own. Finally, I must decide what is true for the whole of the universe.[53]

As the moral man in Kant is the legislator of ends, Sartre says that Descartes, in his role as metaphysician, chooses the laws of the universe; he chooses his world. One can say "yes" or "no" to the world and the "yes" of man is not, for Sartre, different than the "yes" of God. Sartre quotes Descartes:

> Only the will do I perceive within me to be so great that I cannot conceive the ideal of anything wider or more far-reaching, so that it is chiefly the will which enables me to know that I bear the image and likeness of God.[54]

Freedom is not a quality among others, each human being (here human beings resemble some characteristics of Descartes' God) is freedom. In Descartes, the capacity to judge is the same for every human being. No human being can be more human than another because freedom is a quality not defined quantitatively, it simply is and is infinite in each one.

Descartes, like the Stoics, makes a distinction between freedom and power: to be free does not mean to be able to do what one wishes, but to want what one can. There is nothing that is entirely within human power except thought. Here the word thought is taken as all the operations of the soul, not only meditation and the will, but even seeing, hearing, and determination of movement from one place or the other. Inasmuch as these actions depend on the soul, they are thoughts. This does not mean that exterior events and things are in our power, they are, but only insofar as they follow our thoughts. They never do this absolutely or entirely because there are other powers, outside of us, that can modify the results of our plans.[55]

With fairly limited powers man has total freedom. But it is necessary to note the negative quality of this freedom. Clarity and distinctness are not different from divine grace; there is, in Descartes, little difference between divine clarity and natural clarity. The good and the true are the same, Being. The good is autonomous, but if the good is outside of us, to be really free we would have to conform to it. This is a crucial point in Sartre's interpretation of Descartes. Sartre goes on to say that the source of human freedom and autonomy, which are one and the same, is nothingness. It is through nothingness, because she deals with non-

---

[53]Sartre, *Literary and Philosophical Essays*, p. 183. *Situations I*, p. 317.

[54]Jean-Paul Sartre, *Literary and Philosophical Essays*, p. 183. *Situations I*, p. 318.

[55]Sartre, *Literary and Philosophical Essays*, pp. 187-188. *Situations I*, pp. 320-321.

being, evil and error, that man escapes God. God, if such a being were possible, is fullness in which there is no negative element, no nothingness.[56] As such, God cannot fathom or comprehend the nothing. Sartre follows Augustine's explanation for the existence of evil and the negative. God has put into me all that is. He is the author and bears responsibility for all that "is." But He is not responsible for that which is not. It is because of my limits that I am free; I can turn from God. I conserve my freedom of indifference because there are things that I do not know or, at least, that I do not know well, thus my stoic adherence to their positivity is not possible. The order of truth exists outside of me and I cannot affirm it because it is not in my power to encompass it; it is plenitude while I contain the nothing. According to Sartre, that which makes me autonomous is not creative invention, but refusal; my freedom is a negative activity. Thus, Descartes' method of doubt, of refusal to accept anything to the point where he finds he cannot refuse any further and there discovers the cogito, complete autonomy, is the primal act of freedom. Doubt is a rupture, a hole, a lack, an end of contact with Being. Through doubt man has disassociated himself from the universe.

Descartes' image of the Malevolent Genius demonstrates the autonomy of man. She may triumph over all tricks and traps because she is free.

> The hypothesis of the Evil Genius shows clearly that man can escape from all traps and illusions. There is an order of the true because man is free, and even if this order does not exist, it would be enough for man to be free for there never to be a reign of error, because man who is pure negation, a pure suspension of judgment, can, provided he remains motionless, like someone holding his breath, withdraw at any moment from a false and faked nature.[57]

But at the moment that man attains this pure autonomy she has become a pure nothingness, without body, memory, knowledge, or personality. It is at this moment that man apprehends himself in the cogito. Man's freedom does not come from what man is but from what man is not. Sartre thinks that Descartes, though he is inspired in this doctrine by the stoic doctrines of apathea and autarkeia, is the

---

[56]It might be argued that what Sartre says here about God is inconsistent with Sartre's description of God as the in-itself-for-itself. As in-itself-for-itself God would be both full and empty. But I think that Sartre's implicit point about the traditional theological idea God is a good one. It is impossible to talk about God as a Person without reference to nothingness. Even if the theological tradition describes God as fullness whenever it talks about him as a Person God must include nothingness. All traditional descriptions of God are examples of bad faith.

[57]Sartre, *Literary and Philosophical Essays*, pp. 190-191. *Situations I*, pp. 325-327.

first to really see that man's freedom is a negative act. Because man is finite, this liberty is in no way creative; it is in itself nothing.

Sartre thinks that when Descartes returns to the ontological proof for the existence of God Descartes shows the limits of his ability to push the Cartesian negation. Descartes, following the Stoics, not only asserted that man can refuse non-being but that he must embrace Being. Descartes reintroduces God into the picture. Descartes fails to see negativity as productive, and he turns to creating a constructivist picture of reality that is inconsistent with the earlier method of doubt. Here Sartre accuses Cartesian freedom of rejoining Christian freedom and becoming a false freedom in which man does not choose his world and is not autonomous. Man does not invent his own good and so is only nominally free. The Cartesian man is free only for evil and not for good, for error and not for the truth. God guides man toward the knowledge and virtue that is decided for him ahead of time. Man is called free, but only insofar as he refuses this world. Error and evil are non-being and man lacks the power to produce anything.[58] In the world he operates in the realm of Platonic appearances, of dreams and not reality.

But, claims Sartre, Descartes' introduction of radical doubt has shown that not even God could have complete power over man. God is limited; His liberty is no more complete than man's. In describing the freedom of God, Sartre indicates that Descartes, like Feuerbach, has projected his own idea of man's ideal freedom.

> If he conceived divine freedom as being quite like his own freedom, then it is of his own freedom, such as he would have conceived it without the fetters of Catholicism and dogmatism, that he speaks when he describes the freedom of God. We have here an obvious phenomenon of sublimation and transposition. The God of Descartes is the freest of the gods that have been forged by human thought. He is the only creative God. He is subject neither to principles--not even to that of identity--nor to a sovereign Good of which He is only the executor. He had not only created existents in conformity with rules which have imposed themselves upon His will, but He has created both beings and their essences, the world and the laws of the world, individuals and first principles.[59]

But although the idea of the freedom of the creator God is the human ideal of creative freedom it is a contradictory ideal that is inconsistent with freedom. Under Sartre's interpretation of the relationship of consciousness and doubt, which is based in part on the idea of the cogito that emerges in the *Meditations*, God

---

[58]Sartre, *Literary and Philosophical Essays*, p. 196. *Situations I*, p. 330.

[59]Sartre, *Literary and Philosophical Essays*, p. 194. *Situations I*, p. 331.

cannot be conscious because consciousness implies doubt and lack. Consciousness, like thought, is based on the ability to doubt, to experience the imperfection and finitude of human being that creates the ideal of perfection and infinitude Descartes sees as being "in the mind." For Descartes, God's consciousness must be radically unlike human consciousness; it is immediately one with its objects. But in Sartre's interpretation of consciousness (which may be implied in Descartes as well) this cannot be consciousness at all but only pure, positive, brute being-in-itself. Consciousness is negation and imperfection. God's perfection would not possess what Jeanson called the moment of hesitation that allows for deliberation and the moment of freedom that is in thought.[60]

Sartre maintains that Descartes, like himself, understood that individuals are radically free. A free act is a new creation that cannot be reduced to previous conditions. But the freedom of God, though it resembles the freedom of man, is unlike man's because it has lost the negative element completely. The freedom of God is pure productivity, it is not in time and it is eternal. It is in this respect wholly positive as is the in-itself.[61] With God there is no separation between will and intuition, between the good or the truth, and will. God invented the good, reason, etc. Human freedom is only limited by the divine freedom that is the creator of values and truth. According to Sartre's reading of Descartes, the world, values, truth, etc. have been created, however, by God's free act and do not exist by necessity in and of themselves. Therefore, the only impediment to human freedom is the divine freedom. But for Sartre, freedom does exist by necessity. It is the basis of being, its "secret dimension." It is the "true face of necessity."[62]

Sartre, like Feuerbach, argues that it is only a short step to eliminate God from the picture and see that Descartes has been following an intuition of human freedom. Descartes' cogito and his discussion of the isolation of each individual mind prefigures the radical individuality of Sartre's conception of the human condition. It is through man, as a freedom, that the world is founded. But Descartes has also shown the problem of human desire. God is the object of the human desire to be God, the desire to erase the disjunction between Being and will. In relationships with others this disjunction becomes all the more apparent because the others limit, and sometimes frustrate, the possibilities of my free

---

[60]Kockelmans, pp. 269-270.

[61]Sartre, *Literary and Philosophical Essays*, p. 196. *Situations I*, pp. 332-333.

[62]Sartre, *Literary and Philosophical Essays*, p. 197. *Situations I*, p. 334. But Sartre has much the same problem as Descartes in his discussion of the negative and freedom. Berdyaev will argue that Sartre's freedom is not real because it lacks the real ability to create. When all is said and done the for-itself merely collapses into the in-itself. The negative is totally dependent on the positive. The prevalence of the positive is at the basis of Sartre's ontology.

creation of a world. At the same time, because being-for-others is one of the basic modes of being, the presence of others allows me to constitute a world.

## II.  THE DESIRE TO BE GOD

Sartre's interpretation of the Cartesian cogito, and the isolated and negative nature of consciousness that it implies, is at the heart of his interpretation of freedom. The way he interprets the cogito through the ontological split of the in-itself and for-itself leads directly to his philosophical anthropology. Consciousness as negative freedom attempts to break out of its individual negativity toward a positive creation of totality. Consciousness aims to be both in and for-itself. This is the desire to be God. There are as many projects as there are human beings, but each project is the expression of the individual's desire for totality. The individual demonstrates her fundamental choice of how she desires to be and expresses this original choice in particular terms.[1] The desire to be God is never constituted as such. Only in each particular situation does the project reveal itself. The desire to be God always realizes itself as a desire to be in a certain manner and expresses itself in countless different projects that make up conscious life.[2]

Sartre, unlike Heidegger, does not wish to divide the infinity of human projects between authentic and inauthentic projects. Even though the very idea of bad faith seems to have already pronounced them inauthentic, Sartre would say that the projects themselves are not inauthentic. It is simply the fact that we refuse to recognize them as our choices, as our projects that makes them such. Neither inauthenticity before death or anticipatory resoluteness are to be viewed, says Sartre, as the fundamental projects of our being.

On the contrary, they can be understood only on the foundation of an original project of **living**, that is, on an original choice of our being. ... This fundamental project must not of course refer to any other and should be conceived by itself. It can be concerned neither with death nor life nor any particular characteristic of the human condition: the original project of a for-itself **can aim only at its being.**[3]

---

[1]Sartre, *EN*, p. 649. *BN*, p. 689.

[2]*EN*, p. 564. *BN*, p. 592.

[3]Sartre, *EN*, p. 651. *BN* p. 691.

The for-itself concerns itself with its own being in such a way that it seeks to become what it is in order to be the foundation of its own being. It desires to be as the in-itself is. It desires the stability of being what it is and not what it is not. The for-itself chooses its project because it is a lack, and the description of freedom has shown that freedom itself is negative. Freedom and lack are one and the same. Freedom is the concrete mode of being, of the lack of being. Man is essentially (if one can give him an essence in Sartrean philosophy) the desire to be; this is an a priori description of being-for-itself.

> . . . the for-itself chooses because it is lack; freedom is really synonymous with lack.. . . Freedom is the concrete mode of being of the lack of being.. . . Fundamentally man is **the desire to be**, and the existence of this desire is not to be established by an empirical induction; it is the result of an **a priori** description of the being of the for-itself, since desire is a lack and since the for-itself is the being which is to itself its own lack of being. The original project which is expressed in each of our empirically observable tendencies is then the **project of being**; or, if you prefer, each empirical tendency exists with the original project of being, in a relation of expression and symbolic satisfaction just as conscious drives, with Freud, exist in relation to the complex and to the original libido.[4]

Sartre insists there is not at first a desire to be that gets expressed later in all concrete desires. Rather, there is nothing but the symbolic expression. The desire to be never does and cannot manifest itself explicitly, but only appears symbolically as jealousy, avarice, love, cowardice, courage and a thousand other expressions. For example, for the romantics, Don Juan represents the constant effort of man to get past himself towards God. Don Juan is eternally unsatisfied in sin, but the place of God, the object of his desire cannot be filled. The élan toward God is heightened by the empty place of God. The search for God, says Sartre, is not less concrete in Don Juan's desire for a particular woman. The possession of a particular woman represents the constant search for the eternal feminine that is an in-itself-for-itself, a magical entity that can be possessed. But since no particular woman can be the universal eternal feminine, Don Juan can be faithful to none. The quest has no ultimate fulfillment.[5]

All human projects demonstrate that the for-itself is its own lack of being. What being-for-itself lacks is the in-itself-for-itself; a magical entity that would completely encompass both positivity, impassivity, and permanence on one side, and, freedom, negativity, relativity, and consciousness on the other. This magical

---

[4]*EN*, p. 652. *BN*, p. 692.

[5]*BN*, p. 689. *EN*, p. 649.

entity is a denial of the nature of the for-itself. The for-itself erupts as the negation of the pure positivity of the in-itself; but that negation defines itself as projection toward the in-itself.[6] The for-itself projects itself as a being-in-itself and it is just this effort at projecting being-in-itself that is the negation of the in-itself and the eruption of the for-itself. So the project that would create an in-itself nature in the very being of the for-itself, is doomed to fail. It is in the nature and structure of human projects to aim at an ontologically impossible fulfillment. We may say that, for Sartre, consciousness is that being which by its nature is concerned with its own being, but the project created by that concern is always and in every case doomed to failure.

"To be human, is to try to be God; man is fundamentally the desire to be God."[7] Sartre argues that to assert that all human strivings are symbolizations of the basic desire to be God is not a denial of human freedom because the desire is never explicitly constituted as the desire to be God. The goal of the desire is always the object of a particular empirical activity, in a particular situation. The desire to be, always realizes itself in the desire of a certain way to be. In whatever form the concrete goal of the particular aim is expressed, it is a value created by the individual. The value is always a symbol of the desire to be God. The structure of this desire manifests itself in at least three degrees: in each empirical desire, in the way I react in each situation, and in how I, as a person, exist in community with others. Each of these represents a symbolization of the way in which I wish to create myself as a person, which is the way I attempt to realize myself as an entity, a being-in-itself.[8]

---

[6]*EN*, p. 653. *BN*, p. 693.

[7]*EN*, p. 653-654. *BN*, 693-694.

[8]In *Being and Nothingness* Sartre indicates that these symbolizations show themselves in a least three degrees:

> Thus we find ourselves before very complex symbolic structures which have **at least** three stories. In empirical desire I can discern a symbolization of a fundamental concrete desire which is the person himself and which represents the mode in which he has decided that being would be in question in his being. This fundamental desire in turn expresses concretely in the world within the particular situation enveloping the individual, an abstract meaningful structure which is the desire of being in general; it must be considered as human reality in the person, and it brings about his community with others, thus making it possible to state that there is a truth concerning man and not only concerning individuals who can not be captured. Absolute concreteness, completion, existence as a totality belong then to the free

Sartre appropriates and reinterprets the Feuerbachian conception that God is a projection of the self as the desire to be God in every human being. For Feuerbach, even though humanity inevitably becomes more and more alienated by the projection of its own possibilities in an imaginary deity, humanity also moves toward the abolition of alienation in the realization that it has projected its own inner essence in a false deity. With this realization of human possibility, alienation is overcome. For Sartre, Feuerbach would represent an important advance in the history of thought but his atheism still retains the metaphysical character of the tradition of Western theism because of its eschatological belief that totality is possible. This is not the case for Sartre. God is the projection of the human desire, and human beings may even see him as such. But God is also simply a symbolization of the human desire to forge the magical compound of the in-itself and the for-itself. This activity will be repeated in countless other fashions even if human beings abandon their overt theology, because they always attempt to become the ground of their own being in totality. For Sartre, Feuerbach is correct in assuming that God is a projection of human desires but he is wholly wrong in thinking that those desires can ever be fulfilled by imagining that doing away with God will integrate man. Man can never overcome his contingency and lack of necessity and hence, his alienation.[9] Even in the passages where Sartre hints at the possibility of radical conversion this fundamental alienation only seems to be lessened. The for-itself never escapes the desire to be God, just as one never escapes the desire to overcome the lacking toward the lacked, but the individual can recognize and choose against the desire. In this sense he is partially liberated from it. But there can be no goal of total liberation as Kant foresaw in postulating immortality as one of the regulative ideal. Sartre rejects any idea of immortality

---

and fundamental desire which is the unique person. Empirical desire is only a symbolization of this; it refers to this and derives its meaning from it while remaining partial and reducible, for the empirical desire can not be conceived in isolation. On the other hand, the desire of being in its abstract purity is the **truth** of the concrete fundamental desire, but it does not exist by virtue of reality. Thus the fundamental project, the person, the free realization of human truth is everywhere in all desires (save for those exceptions treated in the preceding chapter, concerning, for example, "indifférents").

*EN*, p. 654. *BN*, pp. 694-695.

[9]In a way similar to Feuerbach, Jeanson attempts to soften and modify Sartre's position. He makes it possible for the believer to be engaged in an authentic activity as long as he remembers that God is not a proposition to be proven but a project in which man participates. Jeanson p. 206.

and thus would not admit the possibility of the infinite striving for perfection that Kant thinks is necessary for the fulfillment of the moral law.[10]

Sartre writes that the for-itself, as consciousness, wishes to have the impenetrability and infinite density of the in-itself. It wishes to avoid the contingency of its own existence by becoming its own foundation and thus to assure its position as a necessary being. That is why the aim of the for-itself is projected as that which the for-itself lacks in order to become in-itself-for-itself: the values projected by the for-itself are determined by this lack.[11] It is this ideal that is called God.

> This is why the possible is projected in general as what the for-itself lacks in order to become in-itself-for-itself. The fundamental value which presides over this project is exactly the in-itself-for-itself; that is, the ideal of a consciousness which would be the foundation of its own being-in-itself by the pure consciousness it would have of itself. It is this ideal which can be called God. **Thus the best way to conceive of the fundamental project of human reality is to say that man is the being whose project is to be God.** Whatever may be the myths and rites of the religion considered, God is first "sensible to the heard" of man as the one who identifies and defines him in his ultimate and fundamental project. If man possesses a pre-ontological comprehension of the being of God, it is not the great wonders of nature nor the power of society which have conferred it upon him. God, value and supreme end of transcendence, represents the permanent limit in terms of which man makes known to himself what he is. To be man means to reach toward being God. Or if you prefer, **man fundamentally is the desire to be God.**(my emphasis)[12]

God is felt in our hearts in the same way that Descartes argued that God must exist. We have the notion of perfection in our minds whereas we ourselves are not perfect beings. The Cogito proves, for Descartes, the existence of God because human beings exist in doubt, and this split in their knowledge implies imperfection. But they have within them at least an implicit understanding of perfection. According to Descartes, this idea of perfection cannot come from human beings alone, being imperfect beings, but must have come to them from without, from God. Sartre, on the other hand, uses much the same argument but

---

[10]Immanuel Kant, *Critique of Practical Reason*, trans. Lewis White Beck (New York: Macmillan, 1985), pp. 126-136.

[11]*EN*, p. 653. *BN*, p. 694.

[12]*EN*, p. 653. *BN*, p. 694.

maintains that God cannot exist. Consciousness is an imperfect form opposed to what it stands before, being-in-itself, and is even less perfect before its projection of the magical being that could be both in-and-for-itself, both consciousness and substance. Sartre maintains that human beings have an a priori conception of God. It is not the effort to explain the great spectacles of nature or the power of society that led man to invent God, but, as with Feuerbach, "God" is the symbol through which man gives voice to what he is.[13] The magical entity that human beings call God is the projection of consciousness' own desire for totality which is seen to lay on the other side of the circuit of selfness. The fundamental lack of totality in us intends some final unity. This lack announces God in our hearts as the fundamental human project: we try to imitate God; we try to be God. ". . . **man is the being whose project is to be God.**"[14]

### The Desire to be God and Possession

Man is the pure desire to be God and as such he is the creator of values. God is the repository of human value. Once again, Sartre's thought on this point is near Feuerbach's.[15] God is the reflection of what human beings hold important.

---

[13]Consider this passage from *The Essence of Christianity*.

The consciousness of the infinite is nothing else than the consciousness of the infinity of consciousness; or, in the consciousness of the infinite, the conscious subject has for his object the infinity of his own nature.. . . The divine being is nothing else than the human being, or, rather the human nature purified, --i.e., contemplated and revered as another, a distinct being. All the attributes of the divine nature are, therefore, attributes of the human nature.

Ludwig Feuerbach, *The Essence of Christianity*, trans. George Eliot (New York: Harper and Row, 1957), p. 3, 14.

[14]*EN*, p. 653. *BN*, p. 694.

[15]Feuerbach also associates our conception of value with the creation of our gods. The better we know our gods the better we really understand our own desires.

Such as are man's thoughts and dispositions, such is his God; Consciousness of God is self-consciousness, knowledge of God is self-knowledge. By his God thou knowest man, and by man his God; the

But he nevertheless attempts also to make these values eternal; he forgets that he was their creator. Values are purposes that we possess or desire to possess and make permanent. They give meaning to our existence. Like God, value is for Sartre a magical being-in-itself-for-itself. Desire, the lack of being, is directed toward that being of which it is the lack. The in-itself-for-itself, consciousness, that has become substance, that being that has become the cause of itself, is God or value.

> Desire is a lack of being. As such it is directly **supported** by the being of which it is a lack. This being, as we have said is the in-itself-for-itself, consciousness become substance, substance become the cause of itself, the Man-God.. . . Human reality is the pure effort to become God without there being any given substratum for that effort, without there being **anything** which so endeavors. Desire expresses this endeavor.[16]

Desire to be God is not only expressed by the effort to create the in-itself-for-itself, but is also always related to the brute existence which is the current object of desire. The desire is expressed as corresponding to the many objects in the world. We desire to possess an object. This object may be a bit of bread, an automobile, a woman. But the object of desire does not have to be a concrete object. Even an object that exists obscurely and has not yet been realized is still an object of desire as, for example, when an artist wishes to create a work of art.

It is not immediately obvious why Sartre maintains that the desire to create is reducible to the desire to possess and, thus, the desire to be God. If I create a

---

> two are identical. Whatever is God to a man, that is his heart and soul; and conversely, God is the manifested inward nature, the expressed self of a man,--religion, the solemn unveiling of a man's hidden treasures, the revelation of his intimate thoughts, the open confession of his love-secrets.

Also:

> To enrich God, man must become poor; that God may be all, man must be nothing. But he desires to be nothing in himself, because what he takes from himself is not lost to him, since it is preserved in God.. . .

Ludwig Feuerbach, *The Essence of Christianity*, (New York: Harper and Row, 1956), p. 13, 25.

[16]*EN*, p. 664. *BN*, p. 705.

painting it is because I wish to be the origin of its concrete existence. Its existence only interests me in the measure that I have created it and the link of creation that I have established gives me a particular right of property upon the creation. It is not simply that something is brought to exist, it is brought to exist by me.[17] Just as God has a particular right of property on his creation, I have a particular right of property over what I have made. The object owes its existence to me. Because the object exists by my act, my existence gains a type of necessity that it did not have before. I am the necessary being for that object that I have created. God's act of creation is the supreme example of possession because God has not only created the individual object but the very material that it was made from so the object is absolutely dependent on God for its being. God, again, is the symbol of the fulfillment of human desire, for God possesses His creation completely and his existence is necessary for the existence of all his creations.

Sexual desire, hunger, and desire for knowledge are also all reducible to the desire to possess. They reflect the effort to create a link between the inner I and the outside object. The desire for knowledge is like hunger. It is the desire to possess and digest the object that is before us and yet to leave it there in its entirety.[18] To possess the object it must be absorbed, digested, eaten, but continually to possess it, it must continue its independent existence. The image of Jonah in the whale marks the dream of assimilation without destruction. But the problem is that desire always destroys its object. In reaction against this necessity, the for-itself wants the assimilation but not destruction of the object. Then the object would still exist in its integrity, as an in-itself, while, at the same time, being a part of the for-itself. The impossible desire of possession exists in sexual relations. Here the ideal is that the body should constantly be possessed by the lover but also constantly new and opposite leaving no trace of possession. The beloved should cease to be another and become one and yet somehow remain the Other. Similarly, knowledge attempts to be both the penetration of the object and, at the same time, only the caress of its surface. It aims to digest the object yet contemplate it from a distance. The object is not endlessly malleable because it receives its being from the being-in-itself but it receives its status as object from the for-itself.[19] "This is why desire to know, no matter how disinterested it may appear, is a relation of **appropriation**. To know is one of the forms which can be assumed by **to have**."[20] Thus, sexuality, hunger and knowledge are all considered to be forms of possession and, as such, reducible to the desire to be God.

---

[17]*EN*, p. 664. *BN*, p. 705.

[18]*EN*, p. 667. *BN*, p. 708.

[19]*EN*, p. 668. *BN*, p. 710.

[20]*EN*, pp. 668-669. *BN*, p. 710.

The idea of property gets its meaning as something that belongs to or is a part of the person who owns it. Sartre uses the French phrase for possession, "être à," which has no English equivalent and which literally means "to be to the person who possesses it." In other words, the possession, appropriated by the person, becomes a part of his being; this represents a union of the in-itself and for-itself. Looking for an example, Sartre appeals to the phenomenology of religion and the conception of Mana. He cites Eliade's description of burial rites in primitive societies. A man's personal goods were buried with him, or his wife was entombed or thrown on the pyre with him. Sartre explains that the positivist explanation, that he may have them for use in the next world, is not adequate to explain what is going on in the burial ritual; the object was a possession and hence a part of the departed person and had to be buried with him because it possesses his being. In this same sense I try to meet the possessor through the objects that he has possessed to make his presence become somehow permanent for me. I visit a museum dedicated to some great person in the past and behold the articles that belonged to him. Through them I attempt to meet that person, remember him and perpetuate his being.[21]

Possession is an attempt to overcome the exteriorization of objects, to establish a subjective link between the object and me and yet to have the object maintain its exteriority. The mind is seen an intermediary relation between the absolute interiority of the me and the absolute exteriority of the not-me.[22] To possess something is then to appropriate it, to have created it "for me." Therefore, Sartre asserts that to have is, in the first place, to create. The links between myself and the object are links I have created; they must be constantly reestablished, continually created anew.

> To have is first to create. And the bond of ownership which is established then is a bond of continuous creation; the object possessed is inserted by me into the total form of my environment; its existence is determined by my situation and by its integration in that same situation.
> . . . Through ownership I raise them (my possessions) up to a certain type of functional being; and my simple life appears to me as creative exactly because by its continuity it perpetuates the quality of being possessed in each of the objects of my possession. I draw the collection of my surroundings into being alone with myself. If they

---

[21]*EN*, p. 677. *BN*, pp. 719-720.

[22]*EN*, p. 687. *BN*, p. 731.

are taken from me, they die as my arm would die if it were severed from me.[23]

What I create is an emanation from me. What I create is myself, the way I choose myself to be in the world, the meaning I want objects to have for me in the world I have chosen. By creation, Sartre means the way that I have chosen to make the formlessness of being-in-itself appear in my world as form. What I have created is myself or i have chosen how to exist alongside the in-itself for others. But creation must be renewed at each instant; it can only exist by its movement. If one ceases to recreate the links between oneself and the object, creation ceases; the ties are abolished. The relation between myself and the object can radically change because my world can be disrupted by the Other, so my relations to the objects that I possess through creation can also change. I can be left either with my own subjectivity or simply with the brute existence of the material object which is completely indifferent. Creation cannot conserve itself.[24]

The meaning of possession entails that in the same upsurge of activity the object be identified with me and yet totally separate from me. The object possessed, inasmuch as it is possessed by a person, is a continuous creation; but in itself the object is a brute existence by its character as an in-itself. This is especially made manifest in tools: Sartre uses the example of a pen. It is entirely mine in that I do not even distinguish it from my hand in the act of writing, that is, my act. But my action does not modify the physical character of the pen. I own it. But in itself the pen is not modified by my ownership because, in a realist sense, it is only an ideal relation that exists between myself and the pen. Thus, in possession the object is the link between myself and the in-itself. But this also reveals the point where possession, as a manifestation of the desire to be God, fails. I can enjoy my property only in the sense that I am not aware of it, that is if I use it as a tool, if I use it in striving toward another goal. The moment I stop and contemplate it as it is, I lose it and it becomes a brute and independent existence for me; it is, once again, indifferent to me.

---

[23]*EN*, p. 680. *BN*, pp. 723-724.

[24]*EN*, p. 881. *BN*, p. 724. Sartre's ideas on creation may have been influenced by Bergson. Bergson argued in *Creative Evolution* that creation takes place because of the relation between consciousness and matter. The élan of consciousness creates being and new forms in relation to matter which congeals the original conscious creative élan in material form. Of course, the major difference between Sartre and Bergson is that Sartre views the frustration of this creative drive as inevitable whereas Bergson argues for some kind of preservation of consciousness' creations. In addition, Bergson does not see possession as a structure of creation although he would consider that anything appropriated would be so through a creative relation to the world.

To possess something is fundamentally the desire to possess a world through the object that is possessed. Every project of possession aims at placing the for-itself at the foundation of the world. The for-itself possesses its world through the particular object involved in the act of possession. Thus, the point of possession is to reverse the ontological relation of the for-itself and the in-itself. It aims to place the for-itself at the foundation of the concrete in-itself instead of the other way around. Through the particular object one aims at the general, the whole of the in-itself, just as Don Juan would possess all women by possessing a single one.[25] In this way the desire to possess shows itself to be fundamentally in bad faith. Sartre argues that in possession, as in other instances of the desire to be God, I deny my contingency which is precisely my freedom.

The desire "to have" and the desire "to be" coincide. The desire "to have" is not irreducible; it can be reduced to the desire "to be" which is the desire to be God. Appropriation of an object is also a symbol of the ideal relation between the for-itself and its object. Each act of appropriation is, in its way, the creation of a value. Values are the products of the efforts of the for-itself to create concrete relations with objects and others; they are the solidifiations in rules of the efforts of the for-itself to possess its world.

We see that appropriation is nothing save the **symbol** of the for-itself or value. The dyad, for-itself possessing and in-itself possessed, is the same as that being which is in order to possess itself and whose possession is in its own creation--God.[26]

Possession is also a defense against the Other. It prevents the deterioration of my world before the Other's efforts to recreate the world in his image. In the act of possession I attempt to delineate my world, to create it in such a way that the Other cannot reinterpret it for me. The possession is mine already, the relationship is pre-established by and for me so it may not be altered by the presence of the Other.

Thus the possessor aims at enjoying his being-in-itself, his being-outside. Through possession I recover an object-being identical with my being-for-others. Consequently the Other can not surprise me; the being which he wishes to bring into the world which is myself-for-the-other--this being I already enjoy possessing. Thus possession is in

---

[25]*EN*, p. 688. *BN*, p. 723.

[26]*EN*, p. 682. *BN* p. 725.

addition a **defense against others**. What is mine is myself in a non-subjective form inasmuch as I am its free foundation.[27]

But possession is an ideal that cannot be achieved. Death always renders possession an unachieveable project. This is the realization of the ungodlike impossibility of completely possessing the object that leads to the violent desire to destroy it. Destruction, like eating, is an assertion of my power over the object, the reabsorption of the object into me. In one act I realize the relation of creation in reverse. The object now depends on me because I can destroy it.[28]  I can, in a sense, "take it with me."

The ideal being, be it the God of the believer or the highest value of the atheist, or even the ultimate object of the American consumer, is a being the need of which I feel within me at the foundation of myself. But, argues Sartre, that still does not mean, as it does for Descartes, Plotinus and Feuerbach, that such a totality exists--or even that it might be a possibility. Indeed, in Sartre's ontological framework, it is not even a possibility. Yet, for Sartre, God haunts human existence and the absence of God is sorely felt as the absence of the possibility for the completion of the human project. The for-itself is an anti-value. By its nature it is the destruction of all values. It is so because, by their nature, values pretend to have an independent existence above and outside of human consciousness. God is the symbol of all value and stands above the world of ambiguity. God possesses the character of consciousness and yet is what he is, he does not change. God is the possessor and creator of the world.

In Sartre's analysis of speed and the description the skier, the skier imagines that he possesses and is not possessed, by his object by sliding across it and so evades the possibility of reflecting on its brute existence, its otherness. In the description of slime Sartre writes that the human distaste for the viscous comes from its not being any object in particular and yet has characteristics of solidity and adhesiveness that symbolize the miring of the flight of consciousness. We abhor slime because it does not permit sliding across it, it sticks to us, it is not ordered. Slime is symbolically the death of water. And water is the symbol of consciousness in its flow across the in-itself. It is the fear of this disorder that haunts human beings.

Speed and flowing water are symbols for the flight of consciousness. The choosing of Sartrean freedom that forsakes seriousness entails flight from the spirit of seriousness. Consciousness also mires itself in the values that it regards as absolute. What is difficult is to see how this flight can point to any other value than the liberation of consciousness so it can participate in the flight. The negative anti-value character of the for-itself that both is and is not what it is and is the

---

[27]*EN*, p. 682. *BN*, p. 725.

[28]*EN*, p. 683. *BN*, p. 726.

negation of all that is closer to disorder that the order of value.[29]    Man is a useless passion because he endeavors to create a meaning that will have permanent existence, independent of him, to which he can appeal to give meaning to his world. At the center of human being is the desire for a permanent meaning that is in total contradiction with the nature of reality. Such values are magical entities with the characteristics of both the in-itself and the for-itself; as such, they are ontological impossibilities. But what about liberation or freedom itself as a value.

*Being and Nothingness* presents an ontology, and, as Sartre and his collaborators later claimed, it was also a discussion of the desire to be God which is a study in the eidetics of bad faith. Sartre infers in the radical conversion passages that the description of the types of activity that would escape bad faith cannot be described in this work on ontology but only in the promised work on ethics. This indicates, as Berdyaev maintains, that, as the activity of freedom, ethics cannot be discussed along with ontology. As beings with desires human beings are the fundamental desire to be God. Sartre indicated as much when he discusses the idea of value. "The fundamental value which presides over this project is exactly the in-itself-for-itself. . . It is this ideal which can be called God." But there is one very explicit passage where Sartre writes that this given value is not freedom. "If man on coming into the world is borne toward God, what becomes of freedom?"[30] Thus Sartre makes a distinction between reflective and pre-reflective values. The desire to be God is a pre-reflective value.[31] Breaking away from bad faith is only possible if a break from the pre-reflective idea that I have to fulfill some kind of objective value. Sartre argues that there are no objective values and that the spirit of seriousness arises from my unreflective acceptance of values that I find in the world as if they had some kind of objective status.[32] When Sartre says that the in-itself seems to have emanated the for-itself that it might complete itself he seems to say that by nature we cannot think about the in-itself in another way. It is only through reflection that we are capable of the free choice against what we by inclination desire. Thus although Sartre admits no ultimate objective value the discussion of the desire to be God indicates the possibility of salvation. There are two types of value in *Being and Nothingess* both imply the possibility of salvation. This first was the false hope of salvation engendered by the implied dialectical development of the in-itself to the fall that creates the in-itself and its negation the for-itself and the final union in God of the in-itself-for-itself. This is the eschatological dimension of bad faith. The second

---

[29]*EN*, pp. 702-703. *BN*, p. 748.

[30]*BN*, p. 566.

[31]*BN*, pp. 93-95.

[32]*BN*, p. 95.

dimension is now the possibility of the for-itself turning away from God to itself and to freedom.

If this interpretation of Sartre's project is correct then, more than Feuerbach and Schopenhauer, *Being and Nothingness* appears to resemble another of Hegel's idealist adversaries. In his work on freedom, *Of Human Freedom*, F.W.J. Schelling argued that, from the point of view of Being, the development of individual beings led to egoism and evil. Schelling sketches the development of individuals from a previously undifferentiated source, the Absolute. The development of the individual involves the negation of what it is not. Thus it is dependent on its unity with what it is not for its own identity. But as the individual discovers himself through the negation of all that he is not it develops a desire to be God itself. It can come to see itself as necessary while all others are dependent on it. It also desires to see itself as the source of its own being and unrelated and not dependent on any other beings. But to do so is the ultimate lie and ultimately results in the dissolution of the individual because the individual exists only in relation to others. Schelling argues, this drive toward the development of individuality demands that the individual see that his very individuality is derived from his dependence on others and God. This is the source of his freedom. It implies the Kantian moral law that commands respect for the Other. In the metaphysics of freedom that is found in *Of Human freedom*, freedom and the moral law may ultimately lead to something like the in-itself-for-itself; the forged unity of God, man, and creation that preserves difference. The vital difference between Schelling's and Sartre's descriptions of freedom is that Schelling's source is derived from the German mystic Jacob Boehme's intuition of the *Ungrund* or groundless, the undifferentiated abyss that is prior to Being. For Schelling, this is what makes possible the overcoming of the distance between the self and the Other, because they are not ontologically separated. Sartre at this point more closely resembles the Western theological tradition. Being-in-itself more closely resembles traditional accounts of Being than does Schelling's appeal to the *Ungrund*.[33]

In the preceding interpretation of Sartre's idea of freedom freedom becomes the ultimate value and the liberation the ultimate project. But I think it is still fairly unclear why my liberation necessitates that I should ever wish to work for the liberation of others. The absurdity of human desire for totality in Sartre's early thought reappears to frustrate the human desire for totality: Sartre's characterization

---

[33]F.W.J. Schelling, *Philosophical Inquiries into the Nature of Human Freedom*, trans. James Gutmann (La Salle, Illinois: Open Court, 1936). Berdyaev, though he claims not to be directly influenced by Schelling, admits the sources of his thought to also be found in Boehme and Kant. Berdyaev was also one of a group of Russian idealist philosophers profoundly influenced by Vladimir Soloviev who was, in turn, influenced by Schelling and had attended his Berlin lectures on the philosophy of mythology and revelation.

of being-for-others. Jeanson, de Beauvoir, and Sartre's more recent commentators like Detmer and Anderson have shown that Sartre's point is that ethics is to be based on the idea of freedom as a value. It is to be based on the free choice of contingency against the desire to be God. But it is unclear that the ontology permits much more than my individual choice for myself. The imperative to work for the liberation of others is unclear because it seems that I may be ontologically removed from them.

# III. THE DESIRE TO BE GOD AND THE OTHER

## Sartre's Conception of the "For-Others"

The frustration of the desire to be God is plainly illustrated in relations with other consciousnesses. The Other represents the frustration of my desire because through his "look" he changes me into an object. My world is lost to me. It becomes his world and I am an object in it. In order to regain my world I must objectify the Other and give him a place in my horizon. This being the case, relationships between consciousnesses are necessarily conflictual. Sartre insists that the existence of the Other cannot be proven, that the Other's existence is closer to me than something that could be proven--the Other is immediately present. This presence can be disclosed in certain privileged emotions, such as the experience of shame. Here I become aware of myself as the object of the Other. I am ashamed of what I am.[1] Yet shame is not, at least not originally, reflective. I become aware of myself as an object only because I see myself as an object for another. Shame presupposes the presence of someone else. It is a recognition that I am as I appear to the Other. Thus, the for-itself refers to the for-others.

Sartre criticizes modern and contemporary philosophers' attempt to give an explanation for the relationship with the Other in "The Existence of Others" in *Being and Nothingness*. In his efforts to avoid what he calls "The Reef of Solipsism," Sartre criticizes five positions: realism (Descartes), idealism (Kant), Hegel's absolute idealism, and the phenomenological positions of Husserl and Heidegger. Against Descartes, Sartre argues that realism provides no real explanation of our knowledge of "other minds." According to realism, I hypothesize another mind to account for the behavior of another body, on analogy with my own mind. This is where realism fails. In fact, it becomes its opposite, idealism. When it faces the question of the existence of others, if it is to be consistent, it would be forced to concede that our "so-called" knowledge of others

---

[1]*EN*, p. 354. *BN*, p. 352.

is only an ideal mental construct which we fabricate as a hypothesis to explain the behavior of bodies.[2]

Sartre writes that Kantian idealism constitutes objects, including others, out of phenomena. He asserts that the problem of the Other is not the same as Kant's problem of knowing the noumenon.[3] The problem is not how my experience of the Other could be produced by some hidden Kantian thing-in-itself, an Other-in--itself lurking behind the phenomena. Rather the problem is how it comes about that the phenomenon of the Other--my awareness of the Other's mind, of its presence--is a phenomenon that refers to further phenomenon in a special way. In perception, the sides I see of the cube refer to or promise others that I could see if I turned the cube around. But my experience of the Other refers to further phenomena--the Other's own private consciousness--that on principle could never be my phenomena, but must remain her own. The experience of the Other is like perception and unlike imagination in that it makes promises that are not guaranteed to be true. But it is unlike perception, and this is crucial, in that these promises can never, in principle, be tested by me. This is the real nature of the problem. Sartre thinks that the concept of the Other cannot be a category because concepts or categories, like causality, serve to link some of *my* phenomena with other of *my* phenomena to form a coherent phenomenal world. But the concept of the Other links some of my phenomena with other phenomena that on principle can never be mine. Neither can the concept of the Other be a regulative concept. A regulative concept, for Kant, is not a category in terms of which we "constitute our experience." It is a kind of hypothesis that is useful, not insofar as it is supposed to be true, but insofar as it serves to guide our investigations of phenomena.[4] A regulative idea is a hypothesis, even one we automatically and inevitably make, that serves to motivate and guide our investigations of phenomena. It does not "constitute" our experience, and all attempts to prove it to be true are futile. But all such concepts refer to my phenomena, my experiences, and serve to regulate them. The concept of the Other, on the other hand, refers to phenomena that can never be mine.

Therefore, claims Sartre, Kantian Idealism must take one of two routes: either solipsism, or the acceptance of a real but non-empirical connection between real consciousnesses. Solipsism is opposed to our deepest inclinations. But to affirm the existence of others anyway is to return to realism in the sense that our experience of the Other is not something we constitute; it comes from outside, in the same way that, for Descartes, our perceptions of things come from external

---

[2]*EN*, p. 277-282. *BN*, pp. 273-278.

[3]*EN*, p. 281-282. *BN*, pp. 276-277.

[4]*EN*, p. 281-282. *BN*, p. 277-78.

objects.[5] We have therefore come full circle in respect to the relation with the Other, idealism becomes realism and realism becomes idealism.

The fundamental assumption that underlies both realism and idealism is that I and the Other are related by an external negation. When we say that A is not B, we have an external negation, provided that the negation does not originate in either A or B and does not affect either A or B. Thus, the table is not the ashtray. The table is the way it is, and so is the ashtray. The table is just a table. Its not being the ashtray is not a constitutive ingredient of the table. The negation does not arise there. Neither is its not being the ashtray something that profoundly affects the table. Even if the ashtray never existed, the table would remain exactly what it is. An external negation requires a witness because, as Sartre points out earlier in the "Origin of Negation," consciousness is the source of negation, of differentiation between things.[6] The ashtray is separate from the table because consciousness interprets it in its existence as an ashtray. In the in-itself, the brute being separate from being-for-itself, there is no separation, no differentiation. For differentiation there must be a witness, a consciousness that differentiates one thing from another. An external negation is performed by a witness on *his* world. The Other as subject Other, not a simple physical object, is outside of the world of the witness and cannot be explained by an external negation.[7]

Sartre now turns from idealism and realism because they do not see that the negation between the self and others cannot be an external negation but must be an internal negation. Husserl, Hegel and Heidegger have all made this move. They all accept the conclusion that the relation between myself and the Other must be an internal negation. When I am conscious of myself, I am conscious of myself in relation to the Other, as not being the Other: I am I, and no one else. It is only in terms of Others that I am conscious of who I am: not them. This is an internal negation and does not require a third party to establish the relation. In an internal negation the self sees itself in relation to the Other, and recognizes itself through the Other by seeing itself as not being the Other.

Sartre adopts some of Husserl's theory of the Other. But because he attempts to discard, or in Sartre's words, transcend Husserl's theory of the transcendental ego, upon which hinges Husserl's notion of intersubjectivity, he must also abandon the theory of intersubjectivity. For Sartre, empathy, as a way of approaching the Other toward the creation of community of meaning, becomes an impossibility. So, even though Sartre claims to have discovered a way to describe the immediate presence of the Other to consciousness, the Sartrean for-

---

[5]*EN*, pp. 284-285. *BN*, pp. 281-282.

[6]*EN*, p. 284-288. *BN*, pp. 283-285.

[7]*EN*, p. 285-287. *BN*, pp. 283-285.

itself is absolutely isolated. Consciousness exists as a monadic stream, unrelated to any Other.

Even though Husserl's theory includes the transcendental ego, Sartre thinks the problem reemerges: how to explain and ground the relation of one transcendental ego to another? One might reply that my ego constitutes the phenomenal world in such a way that it refers to other egos in somewhat the same way as the three perceived sides of the cube refer to three more sides. But this in effect makes "the Other" a Kantian category which will not work for Husserl for the same reasons it wouldn't work for Kant. Furthermore, Husserl defines being in terms of an infinite series of phenomena, measuring being by knowledge. Knowledge is the relation positional consciousness has to its phenomenal object. So the ego of the Other, which on principle can never be a phenomenon, cannot be a being.[8] Thus, Husserl cannot, for Sartre, escape solipsism any more than Kant could.

Sartre next moves to Hegel, whom, he thinks, has made some progress towards a characterization of the Other. For him, the Other is needed not for the constitution of the "world" but for the very existence of consciousness itself.[9] The self needs recognition from the Other. The self, in its very determination as selfhood, is established only by an internal, necessary relation to the Other. The stages, or "moments," in the Hegelian dialectic indicate a progressive realization of the self precisely as that which is not the Other. The very being of consciousness as self-consciousness is constituted by consciousness thrown back upon itself as not the consciousness of the Other. In order for there to be the truth of my identity with myself (I am I), I must discover myself in the Other as an object. I can become myself only to the extent that I recognize the Other as a me-as-an--object. Thus, in the master-slave relationship the Other must become the slave, an object without a unique interiority, in order for me to discover in him the content of my own consciousness and in order that I can regard the Other only insofar as he is aware of me. But I need his recognition of me in order to become a self. And for this I need the recognition of an equal Other, but I have reduced the Other to an object, a slave. Thus, my own value depends on, and is constituted by, the value the Other gives me: he must recognize in me a value as a self that is not tied to empirical existence, and I must thus manifest myself as one who is willing to

---

[8]*EN*, pp. 290-291. *BN*, pp. 287-288. It seems that Sartre may have misinterpreted Husserl's theory of the transcendental ego, making it seem more like the personal human ego that Husserl wants to transcend. Husserl's community is intermonadic but the source of the community of consciousnesses in Husserl is the transcendental subjectivity itself. Maurice Natanson, "The Problem of Others in *Being and Nothingness*," in Paul Arthur Schillp, ed. *The Philosophy of Jean-Paul Sartre* (La Salle: Open Court, 1981), p. 326-344.

[9]Hegel's Master-Slave dialectic seems to have become the basis of much of what Sartre says about human relationships. *EN*, p. 292-293. *BN*, pp. 288-289.

risk my life. But simultaneously I wish the death of the Other, for I do not wish to depend on his acknowledgement of me. Although I recognize that the Other is a self-conscious being in his own right, I also realize that I can establish my right only in opposition to him. Thus, I reduce the Other to an object-Other, one who is not a self but an object in my world. Indeed, the self can never truly face the self-as-an-object, and the subject-object dichotomy is now formed by impure reflection.

Hegel's insistence that the Other is related to the self by an internal, necessary relation is, Sartre maintains, an advance, but the problem still remains on the level of knowledge rather than being. For Hegel, there is an identity of being and knowledge. But even granting this identity, we are led to serious problems. Hegel's view of knowledge, and thus of reality, is of a consciousness as a subject-in-itself opposed to an object-in-itself, and that which separates the subject from the object is a given void or nothingness. The subject and the object are presented as definite "givens."

It is Sartre's position, however, that to the extent that the subject-object relation ("I know myself") represents determination, it is the result of a secondary act of reflection and not the pre-reflective awareness of self. In fact, whatever the relation of man to other people, this relationship (just as any relationship to himself) is not a subject-object relation. The for-itself cannot conceptualize its primary being-for-others, and it cannot conceptualize the Other as a for-itself. We must recall, Sartre notes, Kierkegaard's insistence that Hegel has forgotten the true, unique interiority of each individual. The for-itself and the for-others are prior to any conceptualization and therefore the relation to the Other is not on the level of knowledge but prior to it. Sartre charges Hegel's idealism with leading to an epistemological and ontological optimism. First, Hegel optimistically assumes that the knowledge the Other has of me can correspond to how I see myself as an object for him. Second, although I may recognize in the Other myself as an object, this cannot be his view of me as an object. To "know" how the Other sees me would be to "know" him as a free subject. But I "know" the Other only in the light of my own free subjectivity.

There are some problems with Sartre's interpretation of Hegel's theory of the Other that I will take up more fully in the next chapter but they should be mentioned briefly here. Klaus Hartmann disagrees with Sartre's accusation that Hegel is guilty of epistemological optimism. He argues that Sartre's version of the Other cannot really give the Other to me because I do not see myself in the Other; I have no access to the Other as subject but only the Other as object. In Sartre's ontology what is given to the cogito can only be objective being and not being-for-itself. Thus, Sartre's theory of the Other may not be a great advance on the classical theory in which the Other is given to me as a body.[10]

In relation to the dialectic of the master and slave relationship Sartre seems to discount the relation of the slave to the world, which is so important in Hegel's development of the relation, and only sees the immediate interpersonal relation. For Hegel, the self revelation in the master-slave dialectic only takes place after the risking of life by the master and the work relation of the slave to the objects that he transforms; it is thus not an immediate relation but a mediated relation. In fact the immediate relation is the foundation of the original alienation. For Hegel, the recognition of one of the parties in the relation of the other only takes place after the transformation of the two in relation to the world has taken place. The lord and bondsman must cease to confront each other as immediate existents.[11]

---

[10]Hartmann notes the basic inaccessibility of the Other which is one of the fundamental tenets of Sartrean existentialism. Access to the Other is ontologically barred from the self.

> For Sartre, negation and negatedness, answering to subject and object, constitute a contradictory opposition. Accordingly, recognizing oneself in the Other involves the contradiction that a subject is available to itself as object, that in the object a subject has access to itself qua subject. We can appreciate this view as a transformation of the epistemological insight, that a cogito only refers to phenomena, to the more radical ontological thesis that what is given to a cogito can only be being-in-itself and not being-for-itself. The for-itself is non-identity; as objectified, however, it assumes the status of identity. This idea, which for Sartre is self-evident in terms of structure, runs parallel to the more explicit classical theory according to which the Other is given as a body credited with an inferred subjectivity. The Other turns into a construct, a conceptual object, so that the cogito is barred from ever reaching the Other's subjectivity. This antagonism between subject and object, which makes it impossible to have cognitive access to the Other as a subjectivity, or to recognize oneself in the Other, forms one of Sartre's basic convictions. It contrasts with Hegel's basic conviction that the progress of the dialectic mediates the subjective and the objective, a conviction which makes Sartre regard Hegel as guilty of "epistemological optimism." Hartmann, pp. 115-116. *EN*, p. 296. *BN*, p. 293.

[11]Hartmann writes that, for Hegel, the overcoming of immediacy precedes the self-recognition of self-consciousness in the Other.

Sartre says that Heidegger solves the problem of the Other and meets the requirements of relationship by means of a simple definition: the being of human reality is "being with": *mitsein*. For Heidegger the question of the existence of the Other is a false problem. The relation is part of a synthetic relation, being-in-the-world, and is related to the instrumentality of things and the world only through a more primary relation to other human realities. This ontological relation to the Other is conditioned by our freedom and consequent responsibility for how we are related to the Other.

Sartre thinks that Heidegger has defined, rather than justified, the human reality as a part of a synthetic unity. Heidegger, like Husserl, maintains that Dasein primordially constitutes the world; it bears within itself the possibility of "transcendental constitution." Dasein projects the world; it throws the projected world over what exists. The self is consolidated around the project of Being-in-the-world. For Heidegger, the Other is the entity that is in the world and it is encountered as being in the manner of Being-in-the-world.[12] So, with Heidegger, even the Other, in the transcendental sense, has to be aligned with "me;" she is the projection of my project and is not to be distinguished, in this respect, from the ready-to-hand. Accordingly, being-with-one-another is essentially represented by the model of my relation to the Other and not by the model of the relation of the Other to me.

Sartre argues that Heidegger has merely pointed toward the solution to the problem, rather than given it. Heidegger's approach remains on the level of the universal and not on that of the concrete and does not offer an explanation of my concrete relations with others. For, while freedom and the possibilities of the self can be seen as constituting the world in part, the freedom and possibilities of the self can in no way be seen as constituting the existence of other selves, other freedoms. So, in essence, Heidegger's problem is the same as Kant's. Sartre concludes that the basis for this failure is that Heidegger's concept of transcendence is in bad faith. In Heidegger's view of the self, we remain on the level of

---

. . . what he says is that the immediate "having" of the Other in intuition would not constitute the "determinate negation" required on the level of self-consciousness. Self-recognition of self-consciousness in the Other presupposes a sublation of immediacy; e.g., the master has to risk his life, and the slave has to work away his stubbornness. Once immediacy is sublated in this way on either side, self-recognition, in view of the identity achieved on either side, is already granted. Hartmann, p. 118.

[12]Martin Heidegger, *Being and Time*, trans. John Macquarrie and Edward Robinson (New York: Harper and Row, 1962), p. 154.

selfhood. There is no intrinsic, immediate relation to a reality other than the self, no true transcendence, as in the for-itself's relation to the in-itself.[13]

## The Relation to the Other

Sartre thinks that the study of Husserl, Hegel and Heidegger has revealed the necessary conditions for a theory of the Other. Such a theory would have to consist of the following points: First, we cannot prove the existence of others.

Thus since the Other on principle and in its "for-Itself" is outside of my experience, the probability of his existence as Another Self can never be either validated or invalidated; it can neither increase nor decrease, it cannot even be measured. . ..[14]

Existence is always a brute given, it is either there or not. The existence of the Other cannot be demonstrated like our own through the Cartesian Cogito. But as a matter of contingent fact, the Other exists and I cannot doubt it any more than I can doubt my own existence. Second, a description of the Other must not seek reasons for the Other's existence, but, show how the Cogito exhibits the a priori presence of ". . .the concrete, indubitable presence of a particular concrete Other, just as it has already revealed to me my own incomparable, contingent but necessary, concrete existence."[15]   Third, the only point of departure is the Cartesian Cogito. The Cogito must not merely reveal the Other as an object but as a being that interests our being. Fourth, the Other is not, at least at first, an object; it is not an object of my positional consciousness. Fifth, we must accept the fact that our relation with the Other can never be established by an external relation. The multiplicity of others can never be a mere collection but is a synthetic totality. We can never adopt the point of view of the whole.[16]   The existence of the Other is always established by an internal negation which, for Sartre, represents an even more radical separation of the self from that which is outside of it. Because in this negative relation the self sees itself as not the Other.

---

[13]*EN*, p. 301. *BN*, p. 297.

[14]*EN*, p. 308. *BN*, p. 307.

[15]*EN*, p. 308. *BN* p. 308.

[16]*EN*, p 309. *BN*, p. 309.

This negation can be conceived in two ways; either it is a pure, external negation, and it will separate the Other from myself as one substance from another substance--and in this case all apprehension of the Other is by definition impossible; or else it will be an internal negation, which means a synthetic, active connection of the two terms, each one of which constitutes itself by denying that it is the other. This negative relation will therefore be reciprocal and will possess a twofold interiority: This means first that the multiplicity of "Others" will not be a **collection** but a **totality** (in this sense we admit that Hegel is right) since each Other finds his being in the Other. It also means that this Totality is such that it is on principle impossible for us to adopt "the point of view of the whole." In fact we have seen that no abstract concept of consciousness can result from the comparison of my being-for-myself with my object state of the Other. Furthermore this totality--like that of the For-itself--is a detotalized totality; **for since existence-for-others is a radical refusal of the Other, no totalitarian and unifying synthesis of "Others" is possible.** [emphasis in last sentence mine][17]

On these points Sartre develops his own description of relation with others in the analysis of "the Look."

The purpose of Sartre's analysis of "the Look" is to reveal the existence of other persons as free and independent subjects. This fundamental relation to the other person is not to be understood as esoteric or as a kind of mystical relationship; it is a part of our everyday experience. Although the Other can appear as an object to me, this is not my basic or direct relation to him. Sartre maintains that the awareness of the Other is directly given to me as another subject and yet in connection with me. The experience of the Other, as an object, is a reference to that direct relation.

In Sartre's description of seeing a man in the park, the man, if he is perceived as a thing, is only externally and inessentially related to the things around him. But when we perceive him as a man, he is the center of a "grouping." Things are oriented to him, and not to me.[18] When I see the man as a man, suddenly things regroup themselves, arrange themselves according to his point of view, not mine. The appearance of the Other brings about a disintegration, and so, poses a threat to my world, to the totality that is the aim of my project. The Other is a new center toward which things group themselves. I am no longer free to constitute the world in the manner I would desire to. With the apprehension of the Other a hole in the universe seems to be created towards which things are flowing.

---

[17]*EN*, p. 309. *BN*, p. 309.

[18]*EN*, pp. 311-312. *BN*, pp. 311-312.

The world of my creation, which reflects my effort to create a foundation of my being, disintegrates.

An important part of the description is Sartre's admission that at this point we are still on the level of "knowledge," and we may thus be mistaken about the existence of the Other. We first apprehend the Other not as an Other but as an object. Then we apprehend a new totality, in which he is a new center toward which things turn. But this apprehension of a new totality is based on my feeling of the disintegration of my world in relation to the Other as a new center of the world.

In looking at the Other-as-object we see him as someone who is subject for the objects that surround us. But we also see that we too can be an object for the Other. The Other as object refers to the Other as subject, to the permanent possibility of my being seen, of my being an object for the Other; the object-Other that I see may become the subject that sees me.[19] I can only be an object before the Other as subject, before the Other's look.

The look comes from a "sensible form" ( i.e., a perceptible object), but not necessarily a definite one.[20] When I apprehend the look, I cease to perceive the eye and I become aware of myself. The look is the intermediary between me and myself. The phenomenon of the look does not immediately refer to the organs of sight. It is rather my consciousness of being looked at, of having a body, of finite location in space and time. I am vulnerable, I am conscious of being seen. The Other reminds me of the link between the flight of consciousness and the in-itself character of the body.

As long as consciousness is considered in isolation, there is no "self" (ego) in consciousness. Now, however, the "self" haunts unreflective consciousness as an object in the world, not as an object for me (that would be reflection), but as an object for the Other. But the Other is no longer an object for me. While I know, as a being-for-itself, that I am this "being" only in the sense of not-being it, only as surpassing myself toward future possibilities, I now, simultaneously, recognize an "outwardness" of my possibilities: my immediate presence before the Other. Further, insofar as the Other is looking at me, not I at him, I recognize myself as an object transcended by his possibilities. I have become a transcendence-- transcended. A freedom is engulfed by another freedom. The Other refers me to the being which I am not; I am an object, a thing, which is for the Other a being-in-itself. This is a limit to my freedom because it is an attempt to limit my possibilities of becoming. My possibility has become a probability which is outside me. The situation has escaped from my grasp I am no longer the master of it. The recognition of myself as having an objective character does not take place on the level of knowledge. If it did, the Other would be known only as an object and

---

[19]*EN*, p. 315. *BN*, p. 315.

[20]*EN*, pp. 316-318. *BN*, pp. 316-318.

therefore only as a probable other mind and thus would not have the threatening power associated with the look. It is through the immediate awareness of the Other as subject that I become aware of my own status as object. This awareness touches me on the level of the pre-reflective cogito. The cogito reveals my own existence; it also reveals my consciousness as essentially modified by the presence of the Other. I experience the Other, as Other, not an object in the world but an essential modification of my consciousness. The Other is first experienced as the alienation of my possibilities and the objectification of myself.

My objectification by the Other Sartre calls solidification. Being an object means being being-in-itself. The Other makes me into an object by bestowing predicates upon me. The qualification "wicked" would characterizes me as an in-itself. In Sartre's literary works there are many examples of solidification before the look of the Other. The Other is the enemy. It is the Other who defines me, who gives me an ego, who turns me into an object, that reifies my being. In *Saint Genet*, Sartre discusses the creation of a substantial ego, which is a denial of the freedom of consciousness and thus an act of bad faith, by "becoming" exactly what the Other wants us to be. The person who accepts the a label from another grants to the Other a superiority to herself. She gives to that which had no meaning, other than social, a metaphysical meaning, a meaning prior to any relationship with society.[21] This is the creation of God inasmuch as God is the archetypal Other. Kafka's novels display this God as ". . .only the concept of the Other pushed to its limit."[22]

For Sartre's notion of the Other, the return to self, as a center, results from the recoiling or recovering myself from the Other. I recoil from the grasp of the Other's freedom into my center which is myself. The Other, for Sartre, is only on the fringe of my being, never in my center. So the Other constitutes me only negatively when I differentiate myself from him. I reject the freedom of the Other because he has rejected me as a freedom in his attempt to reduce me to an object. I only get myself back from the Other when I perform the same operation on him. In the rejection of the Other I grasp myself as the not-Other and it is thus that I come to know myself. I reject the object-I that he has made of me and thus I reject the Other as well. But the price that I have to pay for the recovery of myself is necessarily the loss of the Other, the loss of his original presence. My objectification by the Other is turned into my objectification of him. This is the second moment of my relation to him.[23] It is therefore I who make the Other be, in that the negative relation gives me the Other as an Other.

---

[21]Sartre, *Saint Genet*, pp. 33-34.

[22]*EN*, p. 324. *BN*, p. 326.

[23]*EN*, pp. 346-350. *BN*, p. 351-353.

Therefore in so far as I am conscious (of) myself as of one of my free possibilities and in so far as I project myself toward myself in order to realize this selfness, to that extent I am responsible for the existence of the Other. It is I who by the very affirmation of my free spontane- ity cause there to be an Other and not simply an infinite reference of consciousness to itself. The Other then finds himself put out of play: he is now what it depends on me to not-be, and thereby his transcen- dence is no longer a transcendence which **transcends me** toward himself but a purely contemplated transcendence, imply a **given** circuit of selfness. [author's emphasis][24]

But it could be asked, "Is the Other's look simply the meaning of my objectivity-for-myself, as the whole cube is the meaning of the sides facing me?" If this is so, then solipsism is possible after all.[25] Sartre wants to avoid this and thinks that I am not an object for myself in that way. The Other does not make me an object for myself but for him. The me that is revealed for me in the look is not the me of my own possibilities; it is the me essentially modified by the Other. The me is "out there." I both acknowledge the image as mine and yet, at the same time, am alienated from it because it is not totally under my control or my understanding. Sartre uses the example of being labeled "evil" by the Other. If my awareness of myself is an awareness of myself as evil, this is a modification of my consciousness brought about by the factual awareness of a freedom that is not my own. Sartre's description of human reality as the desire to be God presented in *Being and Nothingness* makes human relationships are basically sado-masochistic. The possibility of experiencing a "we" relationship is contrary to the given situation of the ontological structure of reality.

In opposition to Heidegger, Sartre argues that there is no true mitsein as a given. Being-with does not represent one of the fundamental categories of human reality. In *Being and Nothingness*, the we exists in two ways: as the we-object or "Us" and as the we-subject. The Us is created in relation to a third. For, example if I am with another the appearance of the third can turn both the Other and myself into objects. I am aware of my conflict with the Other in the eyes of the third. I form a totality with the Other's behavior before the third. Thus, there is a kind of unity between us. This is the way that Sartre will talk about class consciousness of the oppressed before the look of their oppressors.

My relation with the Other forces me to be outside of myself. Because of the freedom of the Other, I am no longer "master of the situation."[26] The

---

[24]*EN*, p. 348. *BN*, pp. 352-353.

[25]*EN*, pp. 332-336. *BN*, pp. 335-337.

[26]*EN*, p. 322. *BN*, p. 325.

situation is not, as Sartre usually puts it, circumscribed by my possibilities, but by those of the Other. I am, through the look of the Other, dragged into the situation, that is, welded in it together with my surroundings and the others in my surroundings. The relation of myself with others is no longer in me but outside of me.

> Thus the appearance of the look is apprehended by me as the upsurge of an ekstatic relation of being, of which one term is the "me" as for-itself which is what it is not and which is not what it is, and of which the other term is still the "me" but outside of my reach, outside of my action, outside of my knowledge.[27]

I am always alone in relation to the we-object just as in relation to the object-Other. It is only a pluralistic modification of the situation. But in relation to the we-object the possibility of the third emerges and, as indicated above, this is for Sartre in *Being and Nothingness* the only possibility for solidarity, for the union of the I with Others. When the third looks at us we withdraw into a community in which the I no longer has priority over the Other because, for both of us, our possibilities have been alienated from ourselves. The alienation here, says Sartre, is even more complete because the third does not differentiate between me and the Other. He sees the whole situation in which I am thrown together with the Other and he forces me to see myself as someone who is fundamentally like the Other.[28] This means that it is only in this alienated relationship, under the look of the Other, that I experience myself as one among others.[29] But this is not the same as Husserl's intersubjectivity or Heidegger's mitsein. It is a negative assembly and the conflict situation of the encounter excludes the possibility of the constitution of a community.

We are also aware of Others as subjects through the relation which we have to artifacts that are not our creation, such as maps, telephones, the objects of human creation. This awareness of the Other through his creations does not modify our ontological situation in the way that the "us-object" or the phenomenon of the look does. Here our freedom does not become entangled or involved, in any major respect, with the freedom of the Other. This "we" relation is a subjective experience on my part. I choose how I react to the material before me. For example, in reading an article on starvation in Africa I can adopt two stances: I either regard the situation impersonally as something "interesting" or I can choose to become personally involved in famine relief. In both cases Sartre would call these subjective decisions on my part. My being-in-the-world has not been

---

[27]*EN*, p. 327. *BN*, p. 329.

[28]*EN*, p. 492-493. *BN*, p. 515.

[29]*EN*, p. 496-497. *BN*, p. 519.

fundamentally altered by the presence of the Other the way it was in the "Us" relation. The experience of the we in the sense of a positive experience of involvement and community is only a subjective experience.

God, as the projected Other represents the ultimate form of the reification of consciousness into an object. This object is granted an eternal status that I supposedly am not free to transcend, because before the all-seeing eye of God I am eternally set as what I am; I am always guilty.

> The position of God is accompanied by a reification of my object-ness. Or better yet, I posit my being-an-object-for-God as more real than my For-myself; I exist alienated and I cause myself to learn from outside what I must be. This is the origin of fear before God.[30]

God and the Other are linked in Sartre's philosophy because, like our idea of God, the Other is beyond me and is capable of objectifying my existence for me. This I both fear and want, I fear it because it is and is not what I am, and it robs me of my freedom. I want it for the same reasons. My objectification eliminates the anguish that I feel from my freedom. The fact that I both fear and want the objectification, the vocation that is offered me by the Other, is indicative of the ideal of God that is present within me. The contradictory desires to free myself from objectification by the Other and also to have a vocation reflect the magical entity, God, who possesses both an unchangeable essence and the ability to create a new one.

The Other takes the position of God in the moment I am objectified by her. She mediates me through myself as the concrete condition of my being. In being-for-the-Other my factical being arises in being-for-myself. I am always beyond my factical being but because I am an object for the Other I must confront my factical being; what I am and am not. "In order to be what I am, it is sufficient for the Other to look at me."[31] The Other drives me into being an object, into being what I am, and compels me to tear myself away from her to negate myself.[32] The Other compels me to transcend my present state of being but she also represents the destruction of my project to be being-in-and-for-itself. Were it not for the Other I might even be able to be God, at least to imagine myself as God. But the presence of the Other will not allow me to continue to see myself as that magical entity. It is in my relation with the Other that I am also forced to assert that I am not that being-in-itself that the Other has reduced me to. I must transcend her objectification of me.

---

[30]*EN*, p. 350-351. *BN*, p.355.

[31]*EN*, p. 320. *BN*, p. 321.

[32]*EN*, p. 359. *BN*, p. 365.

Sartre's analysis of the Other emphasizes the radically subject-oriented perspective of his philosophy. There is a strong sense that even though, in *Being and Nothingness*, Sartre has striven for the immediate experience of the Other, what has resulted is a more radical isolation than is present in any of the philosophical theories that have considered the problem. Sartre's theory attempts to escape the "reef of solipsism," but in so doing actually creates an ontological barrier between the self and the Other. In Sartre's descriptions of concrete relation with the Other he maintains that all relations between the self and the Other are necessarily conflictual. This is so because each consciousness represents a monadic center of negative freedom, an anti-value that strives for the creation of totality that is by its nature impossible to create.

The reason Sartre sees the explanations of intersubjectivity, dialectic and Mitsein, that are offered by Husserl, Hegel and Heidegger, as examples of bad faith is based on one of the fundamental tenets of *Being and Nothingness* and is also the basis of the frustration of the basic human project which Sartre calls the desire to be God. This basic tenet is Sartre's idea of negation: that negation is the for-itself's action on the negated in-itself, the action of a subject on an object. It is impossible in the Sartrean ontology to see the self in the Other because this would involve the contradiction that a subject is available to itself as an object, that in the object the subject sees itself reflected. For Sartre the self is only aware of the presence of the Other but never glimpses the Other in itself. This is apparent in Sartre's reference to the impossibility of God and Leibniz's discovery of the internal negation. Here Sartre argues the impossibility of God's both being in and outside the creature.

> If God is I and if he is the Other, then what guarantees my own existence? If creation is held to be continuous, I remain always suspended between a distinct existence and a pantheistic fusion with the Creator Being.[33]

The relation to the Other is the same as the relation with God. When Sartre emphasizes the radical separateness of consciousnesses who are individually related not to each other but to objects, he sets up a static structure that refuses any mediation between distinct existence and pantheistic fusion. Such efforts are made in Husserl, Hegel and Heidegger. All three in some way attempt to reconcile the radical plurality of beings and Being. Berdyaev will attempt to offer yet another solution to the same problem. In the next section we shall consider the problems with the Sartrean theory of the Other and the desire to be God in relation to Sartre's Cartesianism and his characterization of freedom, in order to see if a

---

[33]*EN*, p. 288. *BN*, pp. 284-285.

radical characterization of human freedom requires the radical autonomy and the ultimate absurdity that Sartre's seems to require.

# IV. PROBLEMS WITH SARTRE'S ONTOLOGY

## Part I: Sartre's Explanation of the Other: Some Implications and Problems

There are several difficulties with Sartre's assertion that his philosophy offers a description of the immediate presence of the Other. But the most important question is whether the Sartrean characterization of the Other ever breaks out of the subjectivism of its Cartesian framework. Sartre certainly seems to think that it does. This is why he writes "The Other is by nature out of the world."[1] The initial experience of the Other is the experience that the world has an extramundane dimension. Because the Other does not belong to my world, he can never fall prey to the phenomenological reductionn This is what Sartre thinks separates his explanation of the Other from those offered by Husserl and Heidegger. There is no initial Mitsein. The relation of being and nothingness in Sartre is fundamentally different from even the early Heidegger. In *What is Metaphysics*, Heidegger writes that "In the Being of beings the nihilation of the nothing occurs" and, he quotes Hegel, "'Pure Being and pure Nothing are therefore the same.' For Heidegger this proposition of Hegel's. . .is correct. Being and the nothing do belong together. . .."[2] Nothing's nihilating does not represent the discreteness of being and nothingness but that Being and nothingness are together in a single event. This allows for Mitsein, because the origin of the ground of Being is the same for every being; they are not ontologically separate. For Sartre the for-itself is the nihilation of the in-itself, but the purely in-itself is not affected by the nihilating activity of the for-itself. The in-itself and the for-itself remain distinct. The for-itself is related to and dependent on the in-itself for its being but the in-itself is not, in turn, related to the for-itself. The for-itself is not in the very Being of beings. This somewhat resembles the distinction in traditional theology between God and creature. Thus, the negative character of the for-itself is radically individual.

---

[1]*EN*, p. 290. *BN*, p. 287.

[2]Martin Heidegger, "What is Metaphysics," in *Martin Heidegger: Basic Writings* (New York: Harper and Row, 1977 ). p. 106, 110.

86

Consciousnesses are radically separate from each other. Being-with-others is an ontological impossibility.

In *Being and Nothingness*, the experience of the Other is not the experience of an alien being-in-the-world, but that of an alien being-beyond-the-world. The presence of the Other is not mediated through the world but it is rather an immediate presence and this is the meaning of its extramundanity.[3] If being-for- -itself constitutes the world in relation to being-in-itself, the meeting of another subject is beyond all possible knowledge; it must be an unmediated presence. But what is given must be only the extramundanity of the Other, a hole, a nothing through which my world is destroyed.

Sartre thinks the encounter with the Other is unmediated and can only be characterized negatively. The Other is present to me without mediation. The mediator that is excluded is the world. This is because the world is the world that I project; but, between myself and the Other, the medium of my world-horizon vanishes. In order for me to experience the Other in my world, the Other must be experienced in some other way than as the Other; it must be looked at as an object in the world and not as an independent freedom. But the Other will constantly destroy this kind of order. The Other cannot be integrated into my inner-worldly project for the reason that it is present but outside my world. For Sartre, the Other is supposed to be as originally evident as the cogito, but it is evident, like the for-itself that it is so as a negation.[4]

Both Hartmann and Theunissen have pointed out that there is a basic dualism throughout *Being and Nothingness*; Sartre binds together the method of an objective ontology of totality and a subjective transcendental philosophy. Sartre hangs his theory about the relation of the self and the Other on his distinction between being-in-itself and being-for-itself.[5]

Sartre wants to remain a phenomenologist and not become a metaphysician (at least in the traditional sense). The dualistic conception of being as being-in-itself and being-for-itself reflects the split between his objective ontology and subjectivism. And although Sartre's subjectivism usually receives the priority as far as explanation is concerned, it is the objective ontology founded on his description of being-in-itself that provides the reason for the primacy of subjectivism in the explanation of the world. The for-itself is completely dependent on the in-itself, but it is the for-itself that discloses the in-itself because the for-itself

---

[3]*EN*, p. 316. *BN*, p. 316.

[4]*EN*, pp. 344-345. *BN*, p. 349.

[5]Michael Theunissen, *The Other: Studies in the Social Ontology of Husserl, Heidegger, Sartre and Buber* (Boston: MIT Press, 1984) p. 206. Klaus Hartmann, *Sartre's Ontology: A Study of Being and Nothingness in the Light of Hegel's Logic* (Evanston: Northwestern University Press, 1966), pp. 137-138.

is the center of interpretation. But it is the positive ground of being, the Parmenidean in-itself, that provides for the existence of the for-itself. The similarity with traditional theological discussion of the relation of God and world are striking here. Being-in-itself is the basis of the existence of consciousness which exists only as the negation of being. Being itself is beyond the capability of the for-itself to understand, even in part, and yet it is the basis of the for-itself. The for-itself is completely dependent on a being that it is not, and that being is so totally beyond the power of the for-itself to penetrate that there is really nothing that can be said about it.

Like his disagreement with Heidegger's Mitsein, Sartre's criticisms of Hegel's dialectic show that Sartre's subjectivist position hinges on his ontology that eliminates any kind of negativity from being-in-itself. Since the in-itself is totally positive, positive Being is not one of the moments of Being, but, "the ground on which the characteristics of the phenomenon will manifest themselves."[6] What Sartre rejected in *Being and Nothingness*, is, in Hegelian terminology, the "ingredience of negation in being." He thought that negation has to leave a "nucleus" of being untouched; "being is and nothingness is not." Sartre takes Hegel to mean that being and non-being are coeval contraries whereas non-being is the contradictory opposite of being and thus posterior to being (as the positive). Non-being presupposes an act of the mind. Yet, as we have already noted, Sartre admitted that it was extremely difficult to locate the in-itself and to distinguish it from the for-itself. "It is . . . impossible for me to distinguish the unchangeable brute existence from the variable meaning which it includes."[7] Though the in-itself and for-itself are Hegelian terms the distinction between is not arrived at dialectically the in-itself is seen to be a necessity following from the ontological argument and the exigencies of Sartre's interpretation of intentionality.[8]

---

[6] *EN*, p. 49. *BN*, p. 16.

[7] *BN*, p. 498.

[8] Once again Sartre himself admitted the interview for the Schillp volume that he never seriously considered Hegel until after *Being and Nothingness* and that *Being and Nothingness* was not a truly dialectical work.

**P.** Did you also read Hegel then. (at the Ecole Normale)

**Sartre** No. I knew of him through seminars and lectures, but I didn't study him until much later, around 1945.

**R.** As a matter of fact, we were wondering at what date you discovered the dialectic?

Sartre's criticism of Hegel is that nothingness is implicit in the being which serves as his starting point.[9]  But Hegel's point in *The Science of Logic* is that pure, immediate, and positive being results or passes over into nothingness.  This passing of being over into becoming is one of the most important moves in the early portion of the *Logic*.[10]  Sartre seems to miss the motion of the dialectic that is present in the *Logic* which posits the determinations that result from the mutual passage of the opposites into one another.  This facet of Hegel's thought about being is similar to the Boehmian position, the absorption of being and nothingness in the *Ungrund*, and to Berdyaev's assertion that nothingness as indeterminacy or meonic freedom is already present at the heart of or as the ground of being. Sartre's objections to Hegel's position reflect the Cartesian standpoint of Sartre's existentialism.  Ontology is viewed in the light of the subject-object opposition. Being is brute existence, the totally positive in-itself.  Being totally transcends the subjective for-itself which is a combination of being and nothingness which performs a negation on, or at being.  But because of this opposition, Sartre's being, as Berdyaev noted, can only be thought about in the abstract.  Sartre must think of

---

**Sartre** Late. After *L'Etre et le Neant.*

**P.** [Surprised] After *L'Etre et le Neant.*

**Sartre** Yes. I had know what the dialectic was ever since the Ecole Normale, but I did not use it.  There are passages that somewhat resemble the dialectic in *L'Etre et le Neant*, but the approach was not dialectical in name and I thought there was no dialectic in it. However, beginning in 1945 . . .

**R.** There are one or two of the contributors who maintain that you were a dialectician from the start. . .

**Sartre** That is their affair.  I didn't see things that way.

**P.** But isn't there , after all, a dialectic of en-soi and pour soi?

**Sartre** Yes.  But then, in that case, there is a dialectic in every author's work; we find everywhere contradictions that oppose each other and are transformed into something else, et cetera.

Schillp, pp. 9-10.

[9]*EN*, p. 50. *BN*, pp. 16-17.

[10]*Hegel's Science of Logic*, pp. 82-108.

being in this way because in his exposition being cannot determine itself; it is the basis of, but, also like some theological representation of Diety, it is totally beyond thought.

For determinateness and plurality to arise nothingness must emerge. If plurality and determinateness do not exist in being-in-itself they must come into being through the for-itself. This only occurs with the emergence of consciousness, and so the relation of being and nothingness in Sartre's existentialism is based on the subject-object relation. The for-itself is the negation and determiner of the in-itself. It is through the for-itself that all determinations of being, that all objects make their appearance. The appearance of objects is an immediate occurrence. In *Being and Nothingness* there is no provision for an appearance of determinations in stages as there was in Hegel's or in Boehme's description of the theogonic process.

It is self-evident for Sartre that the only possible experience of freedom is in the subject alone. The experience of my freedom and genuine experience of consciousness is always the subjective experience of my consciousness.[11] So even objective ontology has to be revealed to us out of an inner experience by which we have special access to the outside; whether this is one of the privileged emotions such as nausea or boredom the very procedure of "objective ontology" is granted to us through an extremely subjective experience. The Other is always initially for me. I experience the Other as the not-I, as the hole through which my world vanishes. The Other is another negative element that is beyond my world. Where we encounter the Other or others we do not experience them as several individuals but only as the not-I or as the Other in his relationship to me. There is no real plurality of others but only the not-I, the negation of my world and my project. There is no reverse side in the relationship; I cannot bring it before me as a totality.[12] This impossibility is rooted in my fundamental inability to step out of my own being, the interiority of the cogito.[13]

This is the importance of Sartre's insistence that the relation to the Other must arise out of his interpretation of the interior negation. For the realist the basis of the negation is set by the existence of a third that presupposes that we are two impenetrable bodies. For both the idealist and the realist this is a purely spatial relation. Sartre, on the contrary, maintains that the interior negation is immediate and does not require the abstraction of the third person looking on from the outside. It is also an active relation in that it is something that we do and it is reciprocal; it lies in our being-for-itself. I am only myself in that I project myself as not being the Other and that the Other is only the other in that he projects

---

[11]*EN*, p. 329-330. *BN*, p. 332.

[12]*EN*, pp. 362-363. *BN*, pp. 369-370.

[13]*EN*, p. 298. *BN*, p. 299.

himself as not being me.[14]   But there is no experience of this reciprocity; I only experience my own feeling of not being the Other.   Sartre's separation of the I from the Other is much more pronounced than the spatial separation proposed by the realist or the idealist because it is more than just an ontic separation; it is an ontological abyss that shuts us off from the being of the Other.[15]   It can never be circumvented like the mere separation of physical units. Nevertheless, there is still a relationship between the I and the Other.   When the Other and the I see each other as separate they affect the basic projects of each.   Their projects are determined in the relation of the one to the other. Sartre believes the relationship of their projects makes their separation a part of their belonging together.[16]

Hartmann argues that, opposed to Hegel, Sartre does not think that I recognize myself in the Other though he does agree that I am myself only in distinguishing myself from the Other. The subject-other is only available to me in negative terms, as a sense of the negation of my world.   As the object-other he cannot be the one from whom I distinguish myself.   I cannot seize myself as objectified by him; to do that he would have to be another subject.   I experience the Other as a reference to myself; his intentions toward me appear objectified in my world.   But I only apprehend myself internally and not in the Other.[17]   In the alternative case I am the object of the Other and thus cannot appear to him, neither can he appear to me because at this moment I cannot negate the Other.   The Other is not me and not an object.   I do not recognize myself in the Other but only in negating the Other.   As Hartmann puts it "As in the case of my negating being-in-itself, my reference to the Other is a negation of exclusion."[18]

In the dialectic of the master and slave relationship Sartre seems to discount the relation of the slave to the world (which is so important in Hegel's development of the relation) and only sees the immediate interpersonal relation. For Hegel the self revelation in the master-slave dialectic only takes place after the risking of life by the master and after the relation of the slave to the objects that he transforms; it is therefore not an immediate relation.   In fact, the immediate relation is the foundation of the original alienation.   For Hegel, the recognition of the one for the Other only takes place after the transformation has taken place.   The one self-consciousness and the other self-consciousness must cease to confront each

---

[14]*EN*, p. 362-363.  *BN*, p. 368-369.

[15]*EN*, p. 363.  *BN*, p. 369.

[16]*EN*, p. 299.  *BN*, p. 298.

[17]*EN*, pp. 299ff.  *BN*, pp. 298ff.

[18]Hartmann, p. 115.

other as immediate existents.[19]  For Sartre, the world is not the opposite or the Other of the self, but rather something that the self constitutes.  The relation with the world is merely formal, it is not the dialectical opposite of the self.  Its relation with the world runs parallel to its own structural moments.  Whatever my determination happens to be I project myself toward its completion but I am the negation of myself and of all the determinations of myself that I achieve.  I cannot achieve the complete totality that I attempt to create.  There is always room for the projection of new possibilities and hence also of a new ideal for the totality that I wish to become.  For Sartre, in *Being and Nothingness*, the for-itself is, by nature of its being, a creator of metaphysical systems that reflect its desire to be God, but, ironically, also by nature it destroys them.  There is an unavoidably nihilistic character to *Being and Nothingness*.

Sartre's theory of the Other emasculates Hegel's dialectic of the master and slave.  It is precisely the point of the master-slave dialectic that the self recognizes itself in the Other.  This is quite different from Sartre's conception of awareness of the Other through my own feeling of objectification by him.  Hartmann disagrees with Sartre's accusation that Hegel is guilty of epistemelogical optimism.  He thinks that Hegel's optimism is justified within the system.  Hegel described the meeting with the Other as one in which I see myself in the Other.  One rises beyond the conflict to the death and the master-slave dialectic because of this.  Sartre's version of the Other cannot give the Other to me because I do not see myself in the Other as I have no access to the Other as subject, except in the awareness of a presence, but only to the Other as object.  In Sartre's ontology what is given to the subject can only be objective being and not being-for-itself.  Thus, Sartre's theory of the Other may not be a great advance on the classical theory in which the Other is given to me as a body.[20]

The analysis of the Other is supposed to provide Sartre with the answer to the fundamental problem of *Being and Nothingness*: the relation of being-for-itself and being-in-itself.  Sartre writes at the end of the section on the for-Others that the objectification of the for-itself by the Other is way that the for-itself participates in the in-itself.  The flight of the for-itself from Being is recaptured and frozen as soon as the Other appears.

> At the end of this long description of the relations of the for-itself with others we have then achieved this certainty: the for-itself is not only a being which arises as the nihilation of the in-itself which it is and the internal negation of the in-itself which it is not.  This nihilating flight is entirely reprehended by the in-itself and fixed in in-itself as soon as the Other appears.  The for-itself when alone

---

[19]Hartmann, p. 118.

[20]Hartmann pp. 115-116. See Sartre, *EN*, p. 296. *BN*, p. 295.

transcends the world; it is the nothing by which **there are** things. The Other by rising up confers on the for-itself a being-in-itself-in-the-midst-of-the-world as a thing among things. This petrification in in-itself by the Other's look is the profound meaning of the myth of Medusa.

We have, therefore, advanced in our pursuit: we wanted to determine the original relation of the for-itself to the in-itself. We learned first that the for-itself was the nihilation and the radical negation of the in-itself; at present we establish that it is also--by the sole fact of meeting with the Other and without any contradiction--totally in-itself, present in the midst of the in-itself. But this second aspect of the for-itself represents its **outside**; the for-itself by nature is the being which cannot coincide with its being-in-itself.[21]

Being-for-others is the way the for-itself participates in the in-itself. But how is this possible? According to Sartre's original thrust, how can being-in-itself which is transphenomenal and the being of things also be my being or the for-itself? Sartre's answer is that worldliness is brought to me by the Other. The relation with the Other robs me of my transcendence; it is the death of my possibilities. But this explanation does not seem to touch the real issue--what happens, by Sartre's own admission, is never a loss of my transcendence but only a temporary loss of its potency. If it were to be a total loss that would amount to a loss of my being. If this is the case then Sartre has still failed to show how the for-itself is present in the heart of the in-itself.

Through the privileged emotions like fear and shame which are aligned with pride, I experience myself as an object for the Other. Fear is the feeling of being in danger with respect to the freedom of the Other.[22] My Being for the Other is my transcendence transcended, but this is only a temporary condition. My transcendence is not destroyed but only temporarily stunned by the Other.[23] This is why the conflictual element of human relationships is unavoidable according to Sartre's ontology. One gets the impression of two fairly evenly matched boxers who alternately stun each other with stiff blows but are each incapable of "putting the other away." The Other is ultimately always my adversary because I must regain my transcendence in relation to the Other. The Other wishes to cut off my possibilities, make them his, make me see them in his light, not in mine. This cutting me off from my transcendence would have the effect, according to Sartre, of making me an in-itself object for the Other. My relation with the Other

---

[21]*EN* p. 502. *BN*, p. 525.

[22]*EN*, p. 326. *BN*, p. 328.

[23]*EN*, pp. 320-321. *BN*, p. 322.

represents the subtle death of my possibilities and this includes the possibility of the Other's subordination to me. As an object-other, the alien presence is included in my world. But when he becomes the subject-other I am subordinated to him; my world ceases to be my world. In Sartre's description of the relation with the Other there is no equal ground that can provide for a meeting between an I and a Thou. The Other brings about my fall from grace. I cease being the pure flow of consciousness, the determiner of being, and become at least temporarily an object. Even if I accept a vocation from the Other/God, he attempts to make me see that vocation in his light and not mine. ". . . the **Other's look** as the necessary condition of my objectivity is the destruction of all objectivity for me."[24]

In the alien world of the Other, I am not the center but I am somewhere out on the periphery. I am located at a particular point. I, the spatializer and temporalizer, from whom the world used to go out in all directions, am now spatialized, the look of the Other confers both spatiality and temporality on me.[25] All encounters with the Other involve a degradation in the being of either the I or the Other. One loses power over the world so that he/she falls into the world and becomes something worldly, an object in the world of the Other. Sartre says that my being for the Other comes upon me as being-in-the--midst-of-the-world-for--Others; I have become a piece of the world.[26] My entrance into the world of inert beings represents my fall from grace, the temporary disruption of all my projects to be God. But this fall from grace is never permanent. The relation between the self and the Other is reciprocal and alternating, and thus a constant conflict. As soon as I recover myself from my own feeling of objectness, I go about turning the Other into an object in my world. "Conflict is the original meaning of being-for-others."[27]

For Sartre, the Other decenters the world for me, he steals the world from me. The very same objects that had oriented themselves toward me now do so toward him as well, so the Other decenters the world centered on me. This is why Sartre represents the Other as a hole that is bored in my world and drains it away from me. For Husserl, we could get the world back on the basis of empathetic understanding of the Other through which I make the Other's relations to the world my own. Sartre thinks that this is not a possibility. I cannot place myself in the center of an alien world. The world of the Other is even more alien because of Sartre's ontological stance. Empathy, as described by Husserl, is unthinkable for Sartre because there is an ontological gulf between the self and the Other, and the

---

[24]*EN*, p. 328. *BN*, p. 330.

[25]*EN*, p. 325-326. *BN*, pp. 326-327.

[26]*EN*, p. 502. *BN*, p. 525.

[27]*EN* p. 431. *BN*, p. 444.

awareness of the alien presence of the Other is prior to any reflection. The basis of the impossibility of empathy is in the ontological difference that exists between myself and the subject other. This is the fundamental point of Sartre's version of the interior negation based on a conception of centers of consciousness that is Cartesian and monadic. Although the Other's alien nature is present immediately to us in the phenomenon of the look via privileged emotions, the interior of the Other is ontologically removed from my world. The Other is not and never can be present to me in his subjectivity. He is always outside. I experience my own objectness because of him. As Sartre admits in the example of the keyhole the Other need not even be present, only my memory of the experience of alienation.

When one is trapped peeking through the keyhole or has the feeling of the presence of the Other, one may be deceived; it may be that there is no one there. Sartre retreats at this point to say that it is only the probable presence of the Other that we feel and that the very fact that we can feel this is because we have come into contact with others in the past. The Other is transformed into a universal presence that is always and everywhere present, "the presence of a reality that cannot be enumerated."[28]

Because the Other need not be present to be another for me, it is possible that what Sartre calls the immediate experience of the Other is no more than a subjective experience. If this is the case, does Sartre avoid the reef of solipsism? Sartre also maintains that there is not, for me, a plurality of Others. This reveals once again the formal structure of Sartre's ontology. As far as the formal structure is concerned there is not a plurality of Others for me but only the in-itself, the for-itself, and the for-others. There may be a plurality of object-others in the world. But, for me, they, as subjects, are not numerically a plurality, but only that which is the not I. True to his methodological principle that all relationships to the Other are brought about by an interior negation, Sartre maintains that it is the feeling of my own objectness for the Other that grants me the Other as subject other. I suffer the Other coming to me so it is not the experience of an alien Other but rather my own interior experience, the experience of my own objectness that the subjectness of the Other is revealed to me.[29]

---

[28]*EN*, p. 338-341. *BN*, pp. 342-344.

[29]In the formal ontology the object-other and the subject-other seem to bear no relationship to each other. The conversion of the object-other into the subject-other is a radical conversion. The subject-other, who destroys my world, appears only on the basis of the destruction of the object-other, who is an object in my world. Hence there can be no analogy between the two; one does not indicate the presence of the other. The object-other refers only to itself and not to the subject-other. The object-other cannot be as independent as the subject-other because the subject is in no way an object for me. Finally the subject-other is given to me only in my own feeling of the existence of the Other through the privileged emotions of fear

Sartre's description of the relation with the Other maintains that it is not an empathetic experience that grants to me the subjectness of the Other. Sartre maintains that it is the feeling of my own objectness before the Other that grants me the Other as object-other. I suffer in the presence of the Other, he turns me, subject of my world, into an object in his. So the subjectness of the Other is revealed to me not in the experience of an alien Other but rather in the interior experience of my own objectness. Finally, Sartrean theory of the for-others is an interpretation of the meaning of my own objectness.

Ultimately Sartre's analysis of the for-others reveals a good deal of Sartre's theory of the development of consciousness in relation to the Other, but it also shows the theoretical meaning behind such Sartrean literary phrases as the famous "hell is other people." The Other is ultimately always an object for me. Though he is not an object that occupies my world, he is never immediately present to me as the subject other but only in my experience of my own objectness before him. Hence, in the ontology of *Being and Nothingness* universe where my project is to be God, the creator of a stable metaphysical ground, I am always ultimately alone. The felt presence of the Other, along with the transcendent character of the for-itself, makes the realization of my project impossible.

## Part II: The Theological Nature of Sartre's Critique of Theology

### The Problem of the Desire to Be God and Traditional Metaphysics

When Sartre says that the impossible desire to be God is the basic human project he has ultimately committed himself to a type of heroic nihilism. And though He seems committed to the absurdity of the human condition, defining the desire to be God as the for-itself's desire to be the ground of its own being but denying any possibility for the for-itself to achieve this goal. In *Being and Nothingness* he offers, as the only alternative to bad faith, a rather unclear notion of authenticity and creativity. Sartre denies the possibility of permanent meaning and consigns all efforts at its creation or discovery to the desire to be God which is always in bad faith. He describes the desire to be God as the object of traditional metaphysics and theology. Sartre thinks that his ontology represents a

---

and shame. But Sartre admits the Other need not be present to trigger these emotions that are supposed to grant the immediate presence of the Other.

significant break with this tradition which builds its meanings upon a "magical ground." He sees the efforts of Western metaphysics as denying the reality of becoming, which is the nature of consciousness, in the attempt to mix Being and becoming in a magical entity: God. But on examination of Sartre's existentialism it will become apparent that not only is he not able to escape the problems of the theological/metaphysical tradition he criticizes, he does not, in *Being and Nothingness* or his other existentialist writings, offer a structurally different system.

Sartre and his proponents have argued that Sartrean existentialism does not lead to the conclusion that human existence is absurd. Rather Sartrean existentialism is the philosophy that stresses the ambiguity of the human condition and attempts to be sufficiently objective to adapt itself to its object: human subjectivity.[30] In one sense human beings have no defined essence or rather that essence is always ambiguous, it is never, at least until death, once and for all decided. Human subjectivity is a continually free creator of meanings that are constantly exhausted and replaced. All philosophizing, all creating, all living, is done out of a situation--there is no stable ahistorical ground to which one can appeal for meaning.

The problem of the Western theological/metaphysical tradition is that it has attempted to discover the ahistorical ground through which it interprets the changing character of human consciousness. But a philosophy that takes the ambiguity of the uncertainty as inherent in the human situation must take change and historicality seriously and not attempt to find some unchanging ahistorical ground. According to Sartre, classical metaphysics does not comprehend the limitations of the human situation because it is intoxicated with the desire to be God. The metaphysician wishes to philosophize outside of a situation. He wants to find the ahistorical ground of meaning. In this way the classical philosopher imagines that he rises above all situations. The philosopher wishes to take God's point of view for himself. But, for Sartre, God's point of view is a contradictory or magical position because it excludes all situations and consequently all attitudes while the nature of consciousness is to be in a situation. God is a magical entity--a being with all perfections, who lacks nothing, is thus unchanging, is beyond space and time, and yet is conscious and is capable somehow of relation to a dependent temporal and spatial reality which he is not.

Not only theists but atheists have attempted to take God's point of view: the theists by appealing to the person of God as a metaphysical postulate, the atheists by attempting to establish permanent definitions of human essence. Sartre argues that the basis of existentialist philosophy is the non-exitence of such a consciousness. The chief metaphysical error of classical philosophy is that it thinks that a creation of the activity of consciousness is the essence of consciousness itself and so can fully explain consciousness. Consciousness can never get outside of a

---

[30]Jeanson, pp. 209-210.

situation; it can never situate itself in the impersonal. It is impossible to find the ahistorical ground of meaning.

The desire to be God represents the impossible ideal of consciousness: the aim for totality, a uniting of the in-and-for-itself. Sartre rejects the possibility of this totality. But there is still a type of totality that exists in Sartrean philosophy. The for-itself is not really a member of an ontological dualism, it is completely dependent on the in-itself and is eventually reabsorbed into it at death. Thus, Sartre's dualism and pluralism ultimately relapse into the monism of the in-itself. The subjective-idealist element (the for-itself) of Sartre's philosophy projects its annihilation and reabsorption in the objective-realist element (the in-itself). Consciousness collapses into the brute unconscious reality. But the relation between the two parts of Sartre's thought is highly problematic. The very existence of the for-itself is magical; it is the opposite of the in-itself and yet somehow generated by the in-itself.

This position is similar in structure to Neo-Platonism. For Plotinus, plurality emerges through emanation out of the One, a descent into multiplicity conditioned by non-being. There is no reason for the One's emanation of beings and its emanation in no way affects the perfection of the One. The soul aspires to reverse this descending movement and return to pure being. This cosmology is similar to Sartre's discussion of the for-itself's effort to strive for totality. In fact, Sartre stands Plotinus on his head, with consciousness, as being and nothingness, emanating from Being which is something akin to brute matter, while for Plotinus brute matter is something akin to non-being and pure Being to consciousness.

From the point of view of consciousness Sartre, like Christian-Neo-Platonism, explains the break up of the totality of being in terms of a fall, a decay, or a degradation in the existing perfection. Although pure, brute, being-in-itself is not affected, it seems as if non-being had crept into that totality to break it up, just as non-being in Leucippus' atomism creeps into the Parmenidean totality of being to make it burst into atoms. In describing consciousness' interpretation of its emergence from being-in-itself and the subsequent desire "to be" (or "to be God"), Sartre goes beyond Plotinus and traditional Christian theology to a Hegelian position that sees the longing for a conscious totality present in the in-itself. But this is impossible for Sartrean existentialism because, by definition, there can be no striving, no development in the in-itself.[31] Yet to the for-itself it always appears as though the in-itself has given a modification of itself toward the eschatological realization of an ideal synthesis of the in-itself-for-itself.[32]

---

[31]*EN*, p. 715. *BN*, p. 760.

[32]*EN*, p. 717. *BN*, pp. 764-765.

## Sartre's Objective and Subjective Ontologies

The problem that is implied by the relation of the in-itself and the for-itself is related to the fact that there are really two starting points to Sartre's ontology. Sartre attempts to move beyond both realism and idealism and his thought contains both realist and idealist elements. He attempts to create a philosophy with an objectively realist ontological perspective, in terms of brute positive Being, on the one hand, and a subject-oriented perspective, in terms of his version of phenomenology, on the other. The conflict between these two orientations--one subjective and the other objective--is reflected in the two types of being: the in-itself and the for-itself. Sartre's ontology is based on the subjective negation of positive Being. The question that follows from the realist ontology of the in-itself is how, given Sartre's description of the for-itself, does being-for-itself ever come to be? Why is there an original upsurge of consciousness at all? As with Parmenides, in *Being and Nothingness* there is something unreal about negation, and hence consciousness. Being-in-itself can only be described in positive terms. In being-in-itself there is no change, reality is stable. Being-in-itself does not come to be, there is no becoming, no time, and no differentiation. Sartre, like Parmenides, offers no clear account of the actual relation of the in-itself and the for-itself: of the way of being and the way of appearance. Instead he creates a philosophy with a subject-oriented perspective in terms of phenomenology that is based on a completely objective positive Being. Being-in-itself is ontologically prior, but at the same time nothing can be said about it, consciousness, always seen as the Cartesian cogito must always be the starting point. But the two orientations of the ontology are in no sense equal. Sartre always gives precedence to the positive element. The for-itself is described as absolutely dependent on the in-itself for its being (though not for its nothingness). The subjective, negative element is the focus of most of the discussion but negation is talked about as a degradation, a decay in the perfection of being. Negation is an aroma that hovers over being-in--itself but never really affects it. But, importantly, the only being the for-itself negates is its own. How it draws this being from the in-itself is not clear. The in-itself is a presupposition of intentionality and thus for Sartre a presupposition of phenomenology. Hence the in-itself is not demonstrated phenomenologically but through the ontological proof that phenomenology points to, but also, upon which it depends. So Sartre grounds his notion of the being of the phenomenon in a logical proof similar to Descartes' ontological proof for the existence of God. The phenomenon is. Its material content is dependent on being in-itself. Consciousness is by its nature oriented toward a being which it is not. Sartre's demonstration of the existence of the in-itself through the ontological argument intends to show that consciousness, intentionality, implies the in-itself or the being of the phenomenon in the same way that Descartes' discussion of doubt as a lack and imperfection was to prove the existence of certainty and perfection. Except, for Sartre, the "God" that is proven by the ontological proof cannot be conscious because consciousness implies imperfection and lack.

Freedom enters being through the for-itself and is negation for Sartre. But as with the in-itself, he abandons phenomenological analysis in positing the existence of the for-itself. The regressive analysis aims to start with concrete examples and move back to the origin of negation as the only possible explanation for the phenomenon of negation. Sartre endeavors to offer a meontological proof. The objective negative is the original starting point from which he works back toward the original negation in consciousness. Not nothingness, but consciousness is the opposite of being-in-itself because consciousness is a combination of being and nothingness. Nothingness is encountered in the world of objects but it cannot be referred to as being-in-itself because being-in-itself is pure positivity. Neither can it proceed from nothingness, for nothingness is not; therefore, it must proceed from a being which is concerned with its own nothingness, a being that "must be its own nothingness."[33] This being is the very opposite of being-in-itself. How this nothingness emerges from being, upon which it depends, is not clear but the regressive analysis is supposed to show there is no other possible explanation for negation and negativities. Sartre does not really consider other possibilities. It is because of its own nothingness that the for-itself negates being. There is no effect on being-in-itself. But the analysis of the for-itself seems to be conditioned by the already established existence of the in-itself as wholly positive. Once again, this is the basis of the idea that consciousness must be contradictory: the for-itself is both being and nothingness, it draws its being from the in-itself and its nothingness from itself. What Sartre refuses to entertain is the possibility of Being as both positive and negative, as possessing both characteristics.

But Sartre's version of the for-itself may be unnecessarily paradoxical. Sartre claims that the nature of the for-itself is to be contradictory, the for-itself both is and is not what it is. Hartmann correctly argues that, from a Hegelian point of view, Sartre tries undialectically to accomplish something that is only possible in dialectical thought and therefore must retreat to a paradoxical nature of the for-itself. Thus Sartre offers an abstract synthesis of being and nothingness that cannot explain the opposition of subject and being. For Hegel, the subject passes through a development of assimilating a being which is opposed to it and yet already united with it. Negativity integrates itself successively into Being. It is present in the very structure of Being itself.[34] If negation could be traced to being-itself, as it is in Hegel, Heidegger, and Berdyaev, the extremely paradoxical nature of consciousness Sartre ascribes to it would not be necessary.

Sartre maintains that a subject in its immanence is a lack and transcends itself toward an idea of itself as a totality that it cannot attain. It is just this idea of

---

[33]*EN*, p. 59. *BN*, p. 27.

[34]Hartmann, pp. 67-68.

totality that is not attainable and yet somehow present in the project of the for-itself that is problematic. For Sartre, as well as Hegel, transcendence occurs dialectically through the relation of a subject over against an object. But Sartre's dialectic really excludes the object because the negation of being in Sartre's ontology does not aim at the identification of subject and object but rather the continual motion of the subject. Even in the description of play, one of the most important images in the radical conversion passages in *Being and Nothingness*, the static structural character of consciousness in relation to Being. This motion is a continual circle because there is never a change in the status of the for-itself or Being.

Sartre's ontology thus adopts the static character of which he accused traditional metaphysics. The being of the for-itself is not developed in a dialectical double negation that moves itself toward totality or toward relation with the Other. As was the case in Plotinus, there is in no way a development in Being, but, for Sartre, it remains static, with a presupposed end point that the for-itself can see but not reach because of the ontological gulf which separates it from its destination. The for-itself and the in-itself exist as permanent structures, one without the possibility of change, the other as constant change that has no bearing on its way of being. Thus, despite all the talk about motion in Sartre's existentialism, it has a static ontological structure. The two starting points of Sartrean ontology collapse into one because of the priority given to the positive element. As is the case in Plotinus and traditional theology, the apparent dualism of the in-itself and for-itself collapses into the monism of the One, as the for-itself returns, in death, to the in-itself.

## Sartre, Metaphysics, and Theology

Sartre states that the conflicts between the self and others cannot be resolved from the outside because there is no superior viewpoint. The appeal to another viewpoint invokes the idea that there is a vantage point that encompasses the totality of being. The viewpoint would be either outside the totality, but this is an impossibility because then the totality would not be a totality and would suppose a higher totality, or a part of the totality, and hence, unable to achieve the absolute viewpoint. So again, for Sartre, the personal, conscious God of the Western tradition is an impossibility because the idea of a higher viewpoint of the whole always results in an infinite regress. If God is consciousness, then consciousness must be integrated with the totality. And if by his nature he is beyond consciousness, as his own foundation, the totality of being would appear to Him as an object. But this presupposes a new totality of God and his object and even another God to mediate the relation between them. This is the meaning of Sartre's famous statement that human consciousness sacrifices itself to the value, God, that cannot be realized: God is a projection, be it the God of traditional theology or the God of the mystics, of the human desire to reach totality. Reaching the totality always remains an impossibility for consciousness because the only totality is the in-itself and not consciousness.

I have repeated Sartre's description of being-in-itself several times but its resemblance to traditional theological and metaphysical ideas in the in the West bare repeating. Sartre sees Being as uncreated; it does not depend causally on anything else; it is without essence. Being-in-itself is simply there, overflowing, superfluous, absurd. There is no reason for its existence. It simply is. It is a violation of the principle of sufficient reason. As previously indicated, the in-itself is solid or "massif," "filled with itself," "opaque to itself." The in-itself has no inner and outer and no reference to what it is not. The in-itself is identical because it is only what it is and has no relation to another. It is completely positive. There is nothing negative about it. There are no distinctions within it. The in-itself does begin to sound like traditional accounts of God, albeit a God who is not conscious. With this description, despite Sartre's very creative modifications, he inherited a problem from the tradition. He must establish a relation between the in-itself and for-itself. But unlike traditional theology he cannot maintain that the for-itself is created **ex nihilo** by a willful, though unnecessary, free act on the part of the in-itself.

As traditional theism and pantheism have been beleaguered by the problem of the relation of creator and creature or ground and manifestation, Sartre's ontology is beleaguered by the problem of the relationship between the in-itself and for-itself. It seems simple enough to say that the in-itself is immovable, impenetrable, massive and totally positive. But when he passes to the description of the for-itself and how it is dependent on the in-itself for its being, Sartre runs into the same difficulties and admits the impossibility of distinguishing between unchangeable brute existence and variable meaning.[35] As in Parmenides and the metaphysical tradition, when Sartre posits the dependence of the way of appearance on the way of truth he cannot show why there should ever be a way of appearance. Sartre attempts to skirt this issue by saying that the for-itself is also a brute existent, it is simply there but posterior to and dependent on the in-itself. But this description of the for-itself runs into great difficulty when the for-itself relates to its past where it takes on the qualities of the in-itself. If the past is a humanized actuality, is there not a sense in which man adds to the plenitude of being? If so, can it still be maintained that the for-itself adds nothing to being? In becoming past, which is an objective in-itself, the pure possibility of the for-itself, the nothingness of Being and Nothingness, becomes something. If it is the case that the past has become something, an object for the for-itself that has a certain character of immutability, has not the for-itself added something to being, something that is not possible in Sartre's static ontology? Nor does it help to assert

---

[35]*EN*, pp. 579-580. *BN*, p. 610.

that the past is always merely reinterpreted by me because, like the brute in-itself, it still possesses the obstinate objective character of a brute existent that somehow limits the possibilities of my interpretation. Once again we are before the problem of the exact relation between the for-itself and the in-itself. Now at the most basic level, how does the in-itself limit the negating and interpretative capacity of the for-itself when Sartre's ontological monism-dualism contends that the for-itself is completely dependent on the in-itself for its being?

Sartre seems to try to get around this problem in a "magical" way. In *Being and Nothingness*, he does not always use being-in-itself in the usual sense. In fact, as Hartmann notes, there seem to be four forms of being-in-itself for Sartre: (i) the fundamental interpretation, being-in-itself containing qua plenitude, undifferentiated determinateness. The other three ways deal with the character of objects: (ii) being-in-itself as the ground for changes in our world and thus, as the ground not only for qualitative contents but also their discreetness; (iii) being-in-itself as a phenomenon available to me qua concrete consciousness; (iv) being-in-itself as featuring discreetness, place and temporal location "objectively" and "in truth," or as it appears for science. But the in-itself is supposed to be an "identity of being regarded as non-otherness."[36] Being-in-itself cannot be a thing differentiated from another thing. But if it cannot be differentiated from what it is not, then the ground of making such differentiations is lost.[37] Once we posit discreetness in being-in-itself, negation cannot be due to the subject exclusively; Sartre's reinterpretation of Hegel's opposition of being and nothingness in terms of being and subject breaks down. But if Sartre does not posit some kind of ground for discreetness in the in-itself, he cannot make clear the limiting capacity of the in-itself for the for-itself. If he does, his dichotomy between subject and object

---

[36]Hartmann, p. 41.

[37]Hartmann thinks there are several problems with talking about discreetness in the in-itself. This following objection is important to our discussion because the inconsistencies that Sartre sees in the metaphysical-theological tradition of Western thought reemerge in his philosophy in a new way.

> ...But the identity of being regarded as non-otherness, that which is not differentiated from another what, and so discreetness, the basis for a place and condition of a what is, is lost again. On the other hand, once we posit discreetness in being-in-itself, negation cannot be due to the subject exclusively; the reinterpretation of Hegel's opposition of being and nothingness in terms of being and subject breaks down. Hartmann, p. 42.

breaks down and with it the grounds for his interpretation of human freedom. Freedom is then determined by the in-itself.[38]

If being-in-itself is undifferentiated and differentiation comes to the in-itself only through consciousness as negation, how can being-in-itself also be the ground of differentiation? If consciousness is to be a revelation of what is, then the object and its qualities must not be merely ideal. If consciousness is to reveal a difference between objects, whether they are other humans, cats, slime, marshmallow, stones, gold, or iron pyrite there must be an actual ground for this revealed difference. If there is an actual ground for differentiation, the in-itself is involved in differentiation. Otherwise one relapses into idealism. But Sartre ascribes negation strictly to consciousness, and all determination to negation. Furthermore he ascribes all possibility or potentiality to negation; he does not recognize the possibility of an element of negation in being. Thus Sartre cannot, in the Hegelian manner, think of Being as an actualizing of its own potential determinateness. Phenomena are different realizations of the actual, but are in no way actualizations of Being. As Being is a non-temporal plenitude, it always "is what it is" or is fully actual. Potentiality or possibility comes to Being from the for-itself, and is only an external addition; it does not realize parts of being and does not stick to it. Sartre cannot say that things or objects are real. What he calls "thises" and their qualities are only sketched on Being by the for-itself. As with Parmenides, so with Sartre, there is an unreality about negation. But if Sartre is not to make a complete break with phenomenology, as the effort to return philosophy to "the things themselves," he cannot treat the phenomenon as less real than its ground. But the very nature of Sartre's characterization of the in-itself denies the fundamental reality of the phenomena, creating a chasm between the two components of Sartre's ontology: the realist, brute fullness of Being and the monadic, Cartesian, subjective centers of consciousness.[39]

---

[38]Both Fell and Hartmann recognize this problem in Sartre's ontology. Joseph P. Fell, *Heidegger and Sartre: An Essay on Being and Place* (New York: Columbia University Press, 1979), pp. 79-82. Hartmann, p. 43.

[39]Fell recognizes the depth of the problem and the impossibility of reconciling being and consciousness, the realist and idealist components of Sartre ontology. Fell argues that Sartre must maintain that the phenomena is a revaltion of what is and consciousness adds nothing to this relvation. Consciousness only brings differentiation out of the undifferentiated. Because of its identity with the determinate, it being-in-itself cannot be indeterminate so being-in-itself is both determinate and indeterminate. This problem is insoluable in Sartrean terms. As Fell puts it: "*So long as the ground of phenomena is fully actual prior to the intervention of understanding, the phenomenological program cannot be completed.*" What results is that either understanding is reduced to a passive role which brings with it the problems of realism, or understanding interposes itself between itself and the actual

And so, despite the brilliance of Sartre's phenomenological descriptions of life situations, the result of his inability to overcome the dilemma of idealism and realism toward an explanation of freedom is the development of a metaphysics that is as static as he felt were the theories of Being in the tradition of Western metaphysics. His protestations to the contrary, in the establishment of the in-itself-for-itself dichotomy, Sartre has created a conception of the in-itself that resembles the metaphysical first principle that he attacks. In establishing the for-itself, the relation between man and God that exists in traditional theology is recreated in the relation between consciousness and Being. Sartre's atheism cannot appeal to one of the trump cards of the theistic tradition, because it does not have the advantage of an appeal to the inscrutable nature of an all-powerful deity that wills the existence of a less perfect creation through which negation enters the world.

## The Problem of the Negative and Freedom

Sartre's dualistic conception of Being as being-in-itself and being-for-itself reflects the split between his desire to create an objective ontology and a transcendental subjectivism. Sartre's transcendental subjectivism receives priority in all his explanations of consciousness because all its activities are radically subjective. But it is the objective ontology, founded on his description of being-in-itself, that provides the foundation and explanation for the "primacy" of the transcendental subjectivism in the explanation of the world. It is the objective priority of positive being-in-itself over the negative for-itself that is the basis of the subjectivism of Sartre's philosophy. Sartre's criticisms of Hegel in *Being and Nothingness* show that the monadic character of consciousness hinges on Sartre's elimination of any kind of negativity from being-in-itself. If it were possible to maintain the Hegelian negation in Being itself, then consciousness, the for-itself, would not have to be interpreted as radically subjective and monadic as Sartre does. Rather consciousness would have its origin in being itself; as a moment in being, not outside and opposed to it, and not merely a negation of being.

Unlike the Hegelian idea that being and nothingness interpenetrate each other, in *Being and Nothingness*, positive Being is not one of the moments of Being, but "the ground on which the characteristics of the phenomenon will manifest themselves."[40] Positive being-in-itself is totally unaffected by negativity. Negation must leave the "nucleus" of being untouched; "being is and nothingness

---

and we have all the problems of idealism.
Fell, pp. 80-81.

[40]*EN*, p. 49. *BN*, p. 16.

is not." Sartre interprets Hegel to mean that Being and non-being are coeval contraries; whereas Being is primary and positive, non-being, the negative, is the contradictory opposite of Being and thus posterior to Being. Non-being presupposes an "irreducible act of the mind," and consciousness is not present in Being. This is the mistake Sartre thinks Descartes makes in the "Third Meditation." He says Descartes is correct in arguing that an idea of perfection or totality precedes consciousness but is wrong in thinking that this feeling of totality is an intimation of the existence of God. For Sartre, following Descartes' thinking, consciousness implies the ability to doubt. It is, thus, a negation of being, an absence of totality. Therefore, totality, by definition, cannot be conscious but is a brute positive being of which consciousness is a negation. Sartre does not really consider any other possible description of perfection or God than the standard one offered by the Western theological tradition.

Sartre criticizes Hegel's attempt, in *The Science of Logic*, to move from Being to nothingness without having nothingness implicit in the Being which serves as his starting point.[41] But Hegel's point, made early in the *Logic*, is that pure, immediate, and positive Being passes over into nothingness; hence, nothingness is present in Being at the very beginning. The very thought of pure abstract being renders nothingness: the passing of Being over into becoming.[42] Perhaps because in *Being and Nothingness* Sartre's though had not yet become sufficiently dialectical he seems to miss the motion of the dialectic present in Hegel's *Logic* which posits the determinations that result from the mutual passage of the opposites into one another.[43] Sartre's objections to Hegel's position reflect the Cartesian standpoint of Sartre's existentialism. Ontology is viewed only in the light of the subject-object opposition with Being totally positive, in-itself, and totally transcending the subject for-itself. But because of this opposition, Sartre's Being, as Berdyaev has noted, can never actually be thought about except in the abstract. Sartre must think of Being in this way because in his exposition Being cannot determine itself. For determinateness and plurality to arise, negation and nothingness must emerge. If plurality and determinateness do not exist in being-in-itself, it must come into being through the for-itself. This only occurs with the emergence of consciousness. And so the relation of Being and nothing-

---

[41]*EN*, p. 50. *BN*, p. 17.

[42]George Wilhelm Frederich Hegel, *Hegel's Science of Logic*, trans., A. V. Miller (New York: Humanities Press, 1969), pp. 82-108.

[43]This facet of Hegel's thought about Being is similar to the position taken earlier by the German mystic Jacob Boehme, described in the myth of the *Ungrund*, and later in Berdyaev's assertion that nothingness as indeterminacy or meonic freedom is already present at the heart or the ground of Being.

ness in Sartre's existentialism is based on the subject-object relation. The for-itself is in opposition to the positivity of the in-itself and it is only through the appearance of the for-itself that all determination of objects, of things in the world, make their appearance. The appearance of the objective world is an immediate occurrence, there is no provision for an appearance of determinations in stages as there was in Hegel's dialectic or in Boehme's description of the theogonic process. The ontology of *Being and Nothingness* is not sufficiently dialectical and this accounts, in part, for the rejection of the possibility of God. Sartre is correct in viewing God in terms of traditional ontology as a "magical" being that combines an ideal of static perfection with consciousness that is only possible with relation and change. But he does not consider alternative ideas of God which would combine both Being and becoming. This would require an ontology that would, like Hegel's, make some provision for negation in Being.

When Sartre rejects negation in Being he also rejects the possibility of any development of Being, and change becomes, like negation, unreal because negation leaves the nucleus of Being untouched.[44] The appearance of negation is only possible through a subject-object orientation. Through consciousness, negation comes into being. Consciousness, the for-itself, is the union of Being and nothingness. Because of this Sartre's conception of Being can only be thought of in the abstract, whereas Hegel's, Boehme's or Berdyaev's conception of Being, containing an ingredience of negation, is thought of in terms of determinations. In development Being becomes determinate. It is only abstract when it is not yet determined. Although Sartre adopted the terms in-itself and for-itself from Hegel, the Sartrean framework is very different. It entails a dualism separating the permanent of the Parmenidean being-in-itself as a basis and the errant, contradictory for-itself. But the dualism is really a monism because consciousness is wholly dependent on Being-in-itself. The Hegelian system, in which Being passes over into determinate Being, calls for the determination of Being by stages of the dialectic. But in *Being and Nothingness*, Sartre's ontology lacks this dialectical dynamism and remains at the level of positive Being.[45]

Sartre's placement of negation and consciousness outside of Being is also the basis of his interpretation of the meaning of human freedom. The creation of the radical differeniation of the for-itself from Being guarantees the absurdity of the human condition because it ensures the frustration of the creation of any permanent meaning. All human projects which symbolize the desire to be God are doomed to failure because of the impossibility of movement and development within Being itself. The creation of totality with the Other is impossible even though this creation of totality is the basis of human desire and of what consciousness sees as

---

[44]*EN*, p. 50. *BN*, pp. 17-18.

[45]Hartmann, p. 39.

the meaning of Being. Sartre seems to approach Schopenhauer's idea that life perpetrates a deception on creatures, luring them into perpetuating life because the for-itself, by its nature, desires a conscious totality it can never achieve but constantly strives for.

PART TWO


FREEDOM, *UNGRUND*, AND THE DESIRE TO BE GOD


BERDYAEV'S EXISTENTIAL PERSONALISM

# V.  BERDYAEV'S ALTERNATIVE INTERPRETATION OF FREEDOM

## The Difficulties of Berdyaev's Thought

Berdyaev is difficult to understand, not because of highly complex argumentation or a technical vocabulary, but rather because of the lack of sustained arguments and shifting usage of certain key terms.[1]  Berdyaev is, by his own admission, an unsystematic thinker.  His style is so easily read he seems to be simple to understand.  A casual reading might bring one to think that this is a man with good literary capabilities, but who unfortunately holds some rather superficial philosophical points of view and who cannot keep to a line of close argumentation.  It seems as though Berdyaev is too eager to arrive at conclusions for which he has not prepared the philosophical groundwork.  In many of his books he simply seems to assert a conclusion that needs to be supported by much more extensive argumentation or description.  But this problem is not as serious as it first appears because Berdyaev usually has supplied the argumentation elsewhere, perhaps in an earlier chapter, or more likely, in an earlier book.  There is an elaborate first philosophy that underlies Berdyaev's statements about history, religion, and human freedom.  It is this metaphysical background that must be understood in order to capture the originality and importance of Berdyaev's interpretation of freedom that is the basis of his metaphysics.  Several of Berdyaev's works must be read to be able to see just how he explains his philosophical position.  Berdyaev is an unsystematic thinker.  He is not an "aphoristic" philosopher like Nietzsche or his friend Lev Shestov but is what one of his commentators has called an "episodic" thinker: his works have a topical or thematic unity but there is no sustained

---

[1]For example Berdyaev uses "Being" differently at different times.  Sometimes he understands it as the abstract concept of Being that is the subject of ontology.  In this case "being" is the product of thought.  At other times he uses the term being to mean nature or the objectified world.  This is the world in which the categories and particularly causal determinism hold true.  And still at other times he talks about a true and original being created by God by ordering the potentialities of primal *meonic* freedom.

attention to individual problems.[2] They are written as meditations and reflect the process of Berdyaev's thinking. In this respect his style somewhat resembles Gabriel Marcel's *Metaphysical Journal*.[3] That Berdyaev always declared himself an unsystematic philosopher is consistent with his stance that will or freedom is prior to Being and system. For Berdyaev, philosophy, the thinking about reality, arises from an intelligible, but still mystic, vision.

> I can only repeat what I have said on other occasions, namely, that my vocation is to proclaim not a doctrine but a vision; that I work and desire to work by inspiration, fully conscious of being open to all the criticisms systematic philosophers, historians and scholars are likely to make, and, in fact, have made.[4]

As one of the few self-proclaimed existentialists, Berdyaev thought that philosophical writing and thinking must express the concrete experience of the thinker. When a thought develops it is created in a process of doubt, conflict, and contradiction. A philosophical style that develops an idea in the fashion of a continuous and consistent argument is a falsification of concrete experience, because it fails to convey the process which is a part of the truth of the idea. Berdyaev aimed at existential and not logical unity.

Coupled with this conception of the existential development of ideas Berdyaev believed that the spiritual impulse which animated his thought could never be completely expressed in writing. He said that none of even his best works adequately conveyed his "inmost idea," and this is why he returns to the same ideas again and again in most of the major works; looking at them each time from different perspectives, seeking after a fuller, more cogent explanation of them. This manner of writing can easily lead to misunderstanding, but within the meandering paths of Berdyaev's thought lies one of the most complete and original metaphysical systems offered by a religious existentialist. Indeed, for all Berdyaev's rage against system there emerges from within the existentialist dialectic of his thought a metaphysical system of freedom as complete and profound as that of the German Idealists.

---

[2]James Wayne Dye, "Nicholas Berdyaev and His Ideas on the Fundamental Nature of All Entities," in *Ultimate Reality and Meaning*, vol. 2, no. 3: pp. 109-135.

[3]The title of the French translation of *Solitude and Society* is *Cinq méditations sûr l'existence*.

[4]Berdyaev, *Dream and Reality*, trans. Katherine Lampert (New York: Collier Books, 1962), p. 289.

A fair appraisal of Berdyaev's metaphysics must take account of what he is trying to accomplish. Berdyaev bothers little with some of the problems that many contemporary philosophers have held to be the whole business of philosophy. The presuppositions of science, neutral descriptions of phenomena, the analysis of language, or even something like Sartre's meticulous descriptions of existential situations have little part in his thought which has more affinities with the metaphysical systems of the history of philosophy. In a way similar to the great metaphysical systems Berdyaev creates views of morality and politics that are consistent with his chief metaphysical principle: the ultimacy of freedom.

Berdyaev claimed Kant as his first master in philosophy and he bases his thought on Kant's separation of the cognitive and moral realms of experience. But it is through his adoption of Boehme's image of the *Ungrund* and its elevation of freedom to metaphysical primacy that he tips the Kantian balance in favor of the moral realm and builds a metaphysics on the Kantian moral postulates (God, Freedom, Immortality). He is then able to derive the objects of cognition as special effects of the activity of free subjects. It is this insistence on the metaphysical ultimacy of freedom centered in the person that leads Berdyaev to reject Sartre's version of existentialism as a traditional effort to derive freedom from a static category of Being.

## Berdyaev's Objections to Sartre's Existentialism

One approach to understanding Berdyaev's existentialist version of radical human freedom is to compare it with Sartre's very different version. In making the comparison I will consider the same three questions that were considered in relation to Sartre: first, the problem of Berdyaev's criticism of ontology as the foundation of freedom; second, the desire to be God and the question of the creation of meaning; finally, Berdyaev's version of the relation between the Self and the Other. To introduce these three themes I will start with Berdyaev's exposition of them in his article on Sartre, "Sartre and the Future of Existentialism" and a section on Sartre his the posthumous work *The Divine and the Human*.[5]

Berdyaev, along with his countrymen and contemporaries, S. L. Frank and N.O. Lossky, creates a philosophy based in a conception of the importance of the person. In a way similar to Sartre and Leibniz they describe the person as being monadic in character. But the person is not, as with Leibniz, a windowless monad but a substantial agent. Both Frank and Lossky emphasize an ultimate reality from which the plurality of monads arose, but Berdyaev's description of the ultimate

---

[5]Nicholas Berdyaev, "Sartre and the Future of Existentialism" in *Toward a New Epoch* (London: Geofrey Bles, 1949), pp. 95-105.

differs greatly from theirs.    Berdyaev forsakes ultimate Being for freedom. Berdyaev's position is anti-ontological. He takes any description of appearance as arising from Being as an attempt to derive becoming from a static ground.  This ends, in theism or pantheism, with a reduction of the individual and freedom to essential unimportance, to being completely inessential.  It does so in the impersonal ground of pantheism because of the denial of the reality of freedom, change, and individuals.  But the same is true of the personal God of theism because the freedom of the creature makes no essential difference to God who is the only essential being and not related to the creature.  In fact, in his autobiography Berdyaev declared this focus on individual freedom to be the center of existentialism, with the "emphasis on the subject as against the object, on the will as against the intellect, on the concrete and individual as against the general and universal."[6]

Berdyaev's objection to other existentialist philosophers, and particularly Sartre, is that they claim to speak about the importance of individual freedom but do so in the framework of ontology, an ultimate concern with the meaning of Being.  Berdyaev argues that ontology, the science of Being, can only lead to determinism and is ultimately incompatible with human freedom.  As a result, though he greatly admires Sartre's literary and philosophical work, he refuses to accept Sartre as an existentialist philosopher.[7]   Freedom is the primal datum about man and is prior to all other considerations, including the mind-matter distinction. It is a spiritual element: the ground of human creativity of Being and relation to the world and to others.  Berdyaev affirms this spiritual element as something that is experienced and beyond the ability of reason and the categories to prove.  Thus, he argues that a true existential philosophy cannot be an ontology.  For this reason Berdyaev thinks that Sartre's thought cannot be considered existentialist.

> Sartre should in no way be considered as a representative of existential philosophy, any more than Heidegger, who confirms this fact himself when he distinguishes one sort of existential philosophy from another.  Both of them want to construct an ontology by going back to the phenomenological method.  However, a true existential

---

[6]Berdyaev, *Dream and Reality*, p. 102.

[7]In some respects it may be Berdyaev who could be refused the title of existentialist as vague as that title is.  Like Buber, Berdyaev does not give a primary role to angst.  Contrary to other existentialists for whom angst is primary existential experience, Berdyaev's philosophy is not angst-ridden.  Nothingness is the beginning for his thought, not the end.  And Berdyaev's conception of nothingness contains not the traditional idea of radical non-being but the presence of endless possibility.  It is closer to the netti-netti or not this not this of Hindu thought than to the nothing of Western philosophy.

philosophy could not be an ontology, the latter always consisting of a doctrine of "being" built up by means of concepts. Ontology is always objectifying knowledge, but existence cannot be an object without being destroyed. Being is not a primary reality, a primary existence: it is already the product of a rational and objective knowledge, a product of thought.[8]

Berdyaev points out that there is a difference in the conception of nothingness in Heidegger and in Sartre. Sartre's idea of nothingness diverges radically from the conception of nothingness found in the German tradition whereas Heidegger retains elements of this tradition in his discussion of Being. Berdyaev thinks that this is significant because the German tradition has seen that the negative element is present in the positive Being, and this points to the primordiality of freedom. But Sartre's idea of nothingness is rooted in the Cartesian-/Augustinian tradition that equates freedom only with the negative imperfection of being. Freedom and the negative are an aroma that hovers over but does not affect being-in-itself.

In the former [Heidegger] one catches from time to time certain reminiscences of the old type of German mysticism, of the "undetermined" [Ungrund] of Boehme. Nothingness here acquires a deep meaning, but there is nothing like this in Sartre, rather he shows their corruption and falling-away of being while at the same time he wants to save it and to affirm freedom. The world has no sense. It is incoherent and absurd; human nature is low, yet man possesses the freedom which he can oppose to all else. He has the power of choice, can assume responsibility, can create for himself and make a better life in general.[9]

Berdyaev, though he agrees with Sartre that freedom is rooted in nothingness and not in being, thinks that Sartre has misunderstood non-being. Sartre has made non-being not only dependent on but posterior to Being. Berdyaev thinks that Sartre's idea of freedom is incoherent. Freedom dependent on Being is, for Berdyaev, not freedom at all. Freedom involves possiblity, including the possible creation of meaning. Berdyaev argues that this is unacceptable for then freedom is dependent on Being in the way that the creature is dependent on the creator who provides all meaning in traditional theological descriptions, or, in the ultimately meaningless ontology of *Being and Nothingness*. Implicit in Berdyaev's position is the contention that the even accepting the idea of radical conversion Sartre's idea

[8]Berdyaev, *Toward a New Epoch*, p. 96.

[9]Berdyaev, *Toward a New Epoch*, p. 98.

of freedom cannot ultimately work because it draws limits too strict for possibility. It also dooms to ultimate failure the efforts of the creature or consciousness to create meaning.

> (For Sartre) The freedom of man has its roots not in being but in non-being, it is not determined by anything at all. This is a true thought and I myself have often developed it, but here it is associated with a false metaphysics. . . . the néant in Sartre is of a different kind from the néant in Heidegger and again in Hegel. In Boehme's teaching the *Ungrund* precedes being and it is fecunding. It is the same in Hegel's thought, where the negative gives birth to becoming. But Sartre compares the néant to the worm which is the cause of the apple's becoming rotten. This means that non-being in his view comes after being and is a corruption of it. On that account it is incapable of giving birth to anything positive.[10]

The conception of nothingness that Berdyaev refers to is dialectical, the conception of Being and nothingness in which Being and nothingness are interdependent. Nothingness is within Being and it is this relationship that initiates the dialectic. Berdyaev thinks that Sartre's idea, which describes nothingness as a corruption of brute positive Being which arises from Being and is completely dependent on it but which in no way affects it, cannot explain the human capacity for creation unless it insists that all human creation is meaningless. For Berdyaev, Sartre the novelist thinks that he is describing existence in *Les Chemins de la Liberté* when he talks of Chamberlain sleeping or Daldier puffing a cigarette or people engaged in the sex act. But in Sartre's fashion of describing these everyday activities there is only the alienation that comes from the objectification of human existence. The root of this preoccupation with alienation, says Berdyaev, is in Sartre's failure in *Being and Nothingness* to be able to say what he means by nothingness and hence develop a satisfactory explanation of human freedom and creativity.

> In his great philosophical work (L'être et le néant) Sartre's use of the word 'nothingness' remains ambiguous. It can mean either that which precedes being or that which follows it. Consequently, the meaning of the term changes. Nothingness in Sartre means the corruption of being, whence, so it seems to him, comes nausea. . . The word, has,

---

[10]Berdyaev also mentions Sartre's description of nothingness as a corruption of being (as a worm gnawing at an apple), with the implication that nothingness in Sartre's philosophy is always a degradation of the ideal structure of Being. Berdyaev, *Truth and Revelation*, pp. 104-105.

however, another meaning. It is with nothingness that the possibility
of creating something new is connected . . .I am afraid that his
creative work springs from an already rotten being and not from the
freedom of nothingness![11]

What Sartre's idea of nothingness as the origin of freedom cannot explain
is the birth of the new. Berdyaev's criticism returns us to Sartre's Cartesian
interpretation of freedom. In Sartre's description of Cartesian freedom, human
freedom is differentiated from divine freedom by the fact that divine freedom
brings positive new existences into being while human freedom, on the other hand,
is manifested through the negation of what is. This is where Berdyaev fundamentally disagrees with Sartre's conception of nothingness and freedom. For Berdyaev,
nothingness is pure potentiality, thus what is brought into being is, in a sense, an
ex nihilo creation in that it is something more than had existed previous to its
appearance. Man and God share in this capacity for the creation of new meaning.
Contrary to Sartre's characterization of the ultimately meaningless character of the
in-itself and hence of existence, Berdyaev thinks that meaning transcends the
present state of the world and becomes a part of reality. Berdyaev argues that
Sartre cannot explain man's creative power. He recognizes that Sartre talks about
the importance of human creativity as a way to give life meaning, but says that in
Sartre's characterization of freedom and meaning this makes no sense. If the
meanings created by man all pass into nothingness, they are ultimately meaningless.[12] In addition, he thinks that Sartre, consistent with his Cartesianism, cannot

---

[11]Berdyaev, *Toward a New Epoch*, p. 98.

[12]Sartre, of course, admits that he thinks human creations are ultimately
meaningless. For example, in *Situations II* he writes that human creations are not
very important and man even less.

> . . . the collectivity passes the reflection and mediation by means of
> literature, it acquires an unhappy conscience, a lopsided image of itself that
> it constantly tries to modify and improve. But, after all, the art of writing
> is not protected by immutable decrees of Providence; it is what men make
> it; they choose it in choosing themselves. If it were to turn into pure
> propaganda or pure entertainment, society would wallow in the immediate,
> that is, in the life without memory of hymenoptera and gastropods. Of
> course, all this is not very important. The world can very will do without
> literature. But it can do without man still better.

Jean-Paul Sartre, *What is Literature?*, trans. B. Frechtman (New York: Philosophical Library, 1949), p. 297.

explain how man is able to create something "higher" than himself. So even if we accept the possibility of radical conversion in *Being and Nothingness*, Berdyaev would argue that the structure of the explanation of human freedom offered by Sartre is ultimately pessimistic.

But Berdyaev anticipates the "radical conversion" interpretation of *Being and Nothingness* because he sees that freedom does set a limit to the gloom of Sartre's philosophy. But, insists Berdyaev, this freedom is empty and futile, It leads to no result and has no aim in view, it represents a fall and a corruption of the perfection of the in-itself. This unwillingness to admit the possible eschatological fulfillment of wholeness is also the rejection of the possibility of meaning, including any meaning that is created by humans. But Sartre wants to stop short of the denial of the possibility of the creation of meaning when he admits the possibility of authenticity and infers that it is better than bad faith. But since Sartre thinks freedom only bears a negative character and does not admit the existence of any permanent meaning, it is hard to imagine how creation of authentic new values is possible. And yet, writes Berdyaev, Sartre is ultimately an optimist. ". . . . he sees paltry little man sunk in the mud rise up and change himself into a divinity, a creator of authentic meaning in the very recognition of the meaninglessness of the universe." But in Sartrean philosophy it is difficult to understand how this could happen. The fact that Sartre does say it reveals to Berdyaev that "a consistent and thoroughgoing godlessness carried through to the end is impossible." God represents ultimate meaning, the goal of human striving; as with Whitehead, also for Berdyaev God represents the possibility of any form of intelligibility. Sartre's atheism attests to this because Sartre does not consistently deny the possibility of meaning.

> But Sartre himself is not fully consistent in his atheism for even he finds himself limited precisely by liberty and the possibilities lying before it. Divine sparks are found unexpectedly in man. An even more consistent atheism would have recognized the absurdity of it all, the irremediable existence of man, the absence of any way out and of any future possibilities.[13]

Berdyaev says that the weakness in Sartre's philosophy lies precisely in the inability to admit the possibility of lasting meaning even though meaning is implied. Sartre's view of ontology is finally a static one. It lacks an eschatology

---

In our critique of Sartre's seeming Neo-Platonism we have already alluded to the fact that the for-itself does seem to add something to the in-itself in the creation of the past which seems to be a serious problem with Sartre's ontological division of positive being and negative consciousness.

[13] Berdyaev, *Toward a New Epoch*, p. 102.

that gives it meaning.[14] The world, says Berdyaev, is not meaningless and absurd, but no meaning is final. The world is the sphere of the creation of meaning.

> Deeper truth lies in the fact that the world is not meaningless and absurd, but is in a meaningless state. This world, the world as it appears to us, is a fallen world: in it death, absurd and meaningless, triumphs. Another world, that of reason and freedom, is revealed only in spiritual experience, something modern existentialists deny.[15]

Berdyaev, like Hegel and to this extent like Sartre's pattern of the projection of the for-itself toward completion, wants to create a philosophy that eschatologically sees the development of history toward meaning. This is the difficulty Berdyaev has with Sartre's characterization of human freedom and the capacity that it gives to human beings to create meanings. For Berdyaev, eschatology reveals the presence of meaning in human history, meaning which is also an ethical norm. The cosmos is only a partial reality, it is not complete, whole. This is opposed to Sartre's ontological notion of the brute perfection of the in-itself. For Berdyaev both Being and nothingness are in process. They form one stream that is projected toward completion at the end, in the eschaton. This is what Berdyaev calls prophetic or messianic mysticism. The world only escapes objectification at the end of time.

> The end of history is not only a truth of religious revelation but also a moral postulate of existential philosophy. That is why it is so important to grasp the fact that the objective world does not exist as a whole, as a cosmos; it is partial. The cosmos is a regulative idea. The cosmos is still to be created. It will make its appearance as a result of the transformation of the world.[16]

The crucial points in the argument between Sartre and Berdyaev about human freedom reside in each thinker's acceptance of the possibility of meaning. This attitude determines how they interpret the possibilities of human beings in the creation and understanding of meaning or what Sartre calls the desire to be God and the possibility of bridging the gap between the self and the Other. The foundation of their responses to these questions lie in their respective interpretations of human freedom which for both hinge ultimately on their attitudes toward the question of ontology. Berdyaev claims that Sartre's philosophy is not ultimately

---

[14]Berdyaev, *Toward a New Epoch*, p. 102-103.

[15]Nicholas Berdyaev, *The Realm of Spirit and the Realm of Caesar*, trans. Donald Lowrie (London: Victor Gollancz LTD, 1952), pp. 28-29.

[16]Berdyaev, *The Beginning and the End*, p. 147.

existentialist because its main thrust resides in a conception of freedom that calls freedom a negation of and a product of Being. It is completely dependent on brute Being-in-itself which is not affected by it. For Berdyaev, because the unity of Being and non-being characterizes freedom and reality, the question of the desire to be God is reinterpreted in the dialectic of the divine and the human and the desire to create meaning. Thus the creation of meaning and the creation of being are essentially the same thing. Berdyaev puts his description of the desire to create meaning in such a way that it overlaps with the question about the relation to the Other and the creation of community. The two questions of meaning and the Other are interdependent in Berdyaev's thought because it is in the creation of unity between the self and the Other that meaning comes to be. In this Berdyaev gives a different interpretation of what Sartre called the desire to be God. Human beings, like God, are creators of meaning and participate in the creation of cosmos.

Berdyaev's contention that Sartre's mistake is not to see anything positive about freedom that Sartre cannot see freedom as an affirmation but only as a denial, a negation. This contention is founded in the is the major difference between Sartre and Berdyaev's conceptions of freedom. Sartre's theory is derived from Descartes and the tradition of Christian theology that goes bamck to Augustine. Human freedom is only conceived in the negative as the negation of being. Berdyaev's idea of freedom is derived from Kant and Boehme. Freedom and negation are located in Being itself, better, prior to being and thus there is something postive about freeom itself it is prior to being the source of everything.

Berdyaev's entire philosophical enterprise hinges on the creation of a metaphysics in which freedom and creativity can be given a metaphysical priority and yet maintain the possibility of the creation of order and intelligibility and not the simple disintegration of the effort into sheer irrationalism. In an effort to talk about his metaphysical first principle Berdyaev draws on the symbolism of Boehme's *Ungrund* myth.

## The Boehmian Tradition and Berdyaev

Berdyaev is openly Christian and uses Christian images in conveying his thought. But he always insisted he was not a theologian but a philosopher. I believe that Berdyaev is justified in this claim for several reasons. First, he breaks with the theological tradition. Even though he is sympathetic to the Eastern Christian tradition, Berdyaev's main concerns are freedom and the person. He believes that these concerns are best explained in a religious context. Second, he is primarily concerned with providing a new metaphysical explanation of reality, though his explanation is couched in Christian terminology. Berdyaev took the discovery and creation of meaning within transitory human lives to be the heart of philosophy. Berdyaev walks the ridge between philosophy and theology. His philosophical point of view is informed by his Christian faith, but not over determined by it. In addition his philosophical point of view also informs theological perspective.

Berdyaev drew his theological inspiration from the Eastern fathers, particularly Origen and Gregory of Nyssa. His philosophical point of view derives partially from Dostoevsky, Ibsen, Nietzsche, Soloviev and the other members of the Russian religio-philosophical reawakening of the late nineteenth and early twentieth centuries. But the most profound source of his thought are in his relation to German idealism and from the writings of the seventeenth century German Lutheran mystic Jacob Boehme. Berdyaev created a di-polar conception of ultimate reality through the use of Boehme's image of the *Ungrund*. The polar opposites of unity and multiplicity, identity and difference, passivity and impassivity, positivity and negativity, Being and nothingness etc., are all present in an undifferentiated state in the *Ungrund*. There is no ontological difference between human beings and God as there is in traditional metaphysics, or between consciousness and Being as there is in Sartre's ontology because all of reality is contained in the primal unity of the *Ungrund*. The poles are held to be harmonized in God. Human beings, like God, also contain the polar opposites but they are not continuously harmonized in them.

The major component of Berdyaev's thought is his insistence on the metaphysical priority of freedom. "Abstraction and the hypostatizing of abstraction created both spiritual and materialistic metaphysical systems."[17] The keys to understanding how Berdyaev can insist on the ultimacy of freedom are found in the two principal intellectual sources of his thought: the philosophy of Kant and the mysticism of Jacob Boehme, particularly Boehme's image of the *Ungrund*. Berdyaev's first efforts in philosophy were through his reading of Schopenhauer, Hegel and Kant. The rejection of ontology has its roots not only in the voluntaristic mysticism of Berdyaev's interpretation of Jacob Boehme, but also in Berdyaev's reading of Kant whom he called his first "master in philosophy."[18] It was Kant who was to be the most important to the development of his thought. He called Kant the "metaphysician of freedom."[19] Kant's emphasis on priority the

---

[17]Nicholas Berdyaev, *Freedom and the Spirit* (New York: Books for Libraries Press, 1972), p. 1.

[18]Berdyaev, *Dream and Reality*, p. 93.

[19]This appreciation of Kant is also the key to Berdyaev's preoccupation with objectification. He accepts fully Kant's contention that the categories by which we interpret the phenomenal world do not necessarily have anything to do with the things themselves. So Berdyaev contends that the science of ontology cannot describe reality because of the rationalist's faith that reality must conform to the categories of his rational system. Thus, he objectifies living realities that exist

practical reason over the phenomenal was equivalent in Berdyaev's mind to the primacy of freedom over being and objectification. For Berdyaev, Kant disclosed the creativity of the subject in all modes of experience.

Freedom is the first principle of Berdyaev's philosophy. He wrote, "I have put Freedom, rather than Being, at the basis of my philosophy. I do not think any other philosopher has done this in such a radical and thorough-going way."[20] Freedom cannot be derived from Being because the concept of being includes the possession of objective and determinate character. Freedom, if it is to be taken seriously, is the absence of external determination. Any derivation of freedom from something more ultimate gives it determinateness and destroys its reality. So freedom must be metaphysically ultimate. If freedom is taken to be metaphysically ultimate it cannot be a mode of Being. It is what Berdyaev, coining his own term, called *meonic*, non- or not-being. Berdyaev develops this idea through the use of an image he appropriates from Jacob Boehme. This is Boehme's myth of the *Ungrund*, the pre-existential abyss out of which all things come into being. The *Ungrund* is not Being, it is the no-thing, pure potentiality, freedom that is as yet undetermined.

Through his appropriation Boehme's image of the *Ungrund* Berdyaev is able to take what could be termed an anti-ontological position in which freedom is regarded as prior to Being. Berdyaev's fundamental insight is that freedom is primarily, ultimately real, and as such its essence lies outside any kind of external determination. It cannot be derived from any more fundamental kind of reality. It cannot be subordinated to Being qua Being, because freedom refuses all determination. Berdyaev would accept the objection from traditional metaphysics that it is impossible to conceive anything more ultimate than Being since anything must be in order to have attributes and it would appear to the traditional metaphysician that freedom is an attribute of a being. Berdyaev agrees that for any thing to have attributes it must first have Being But he would object to the idea that freedom is some kind of an attribute of a Being. Beryaev's Kantianism is exemplified in this freedom which is beyond the categories of objectified thought. Freedom is no-thing. Berdyaev seeks to explain this idea through an appeal to Jacob Boehme's image of the *Ungrund*. Strictly speaking, the *Ungrund* is not anything, the idea of it is not a concept but a myth, a symbol whereby is expressed a fundamental truth about existence that is incapable of being expressed in an objective conceptual arrangement.[21] This incapacity is not due to the limitation of the knower, but concerns knowledge itself. All novelty, all uniqueness, is

---

outside of the pale of his categories. Berdyaev, *The Beginning and the End*, trans. R. M. French (New York: Harper & Brothers, 1952), p. 9.

[20]Berdyaev, *Dream and Reality*, p. 46.

[21]Berdyaev, *Freedom and the Spirit*, p. 73.

inexplicable unless freedom is prior to being. And Freedom is nothing. It is the undetermined.


## Jacob Boehme and the *Ungrund*

The basic choice that Berdyaev sees at the heart of any conception of freedom is inspired by Berdyaev's Kantianism, but the framework of that choice is put forward through his interpretation of Boehme's image of the *Ungrund*. In the *Ungrund* the antinomies: (positive and negative, being and nothingness, good and evil) are all pure potentialities that emerge with one another and are known through each other. In *The Meaning of History* Berdyaev described the image of the *Ungrund* that he had taken from Boehme as one of the most important discoveries of German thought.

> I am thinking of Boehme, who is not only a great German mystic, but also one of the greatest mystics of all time; and particularly of his *The Dark Nature of God.*... In fact, I believe it is one of the most important discoveries of the German spirit, where it has not ceased to be applied and developed in the spheres of art, philosophy and culture in general. This spiritual culture is founded upon an apprehension of primal Being as a dark and irrational force of obscure origin (not in the sense of evil, for this darkness goes deeper than the distinctions between good and evil). Somewhere in immeasurably greater depths, there exists a state which may be called *Ungrund* or "groundlessness" to which neither human words nor the categories of good and evil, nor those of being or non-being, are applicable. *Ungrund* is deeper than anything else and is the primal source of what, according to Boehme and Schelling, constitutes the *Dark Nature of God*. In the nature of God, deeper than Him, lies a theogonic process or that of divine genesis. This process is secondary when compared with that primal "groundlessness" and inexpressible abyss which is irrational and incommensurable with any of our categories. There is a primal source and fount of being from which an eternal torrent pours and in which the divine light shines everlastingly, while the act of divine genesis is taking place.[22]

---

[22]Nicholas Berdyaev, *The Meaning of History*, trans. George Reavy (London: Goeffrey Bles, 1945) pp. 54-55.

124

Boehme's dialectical voluntarism is based on the image of groundlessness which is the beginning of the development of Being. The *Ungrund* contains within it all of the antimonies, but they are unrealized and only potential: Boehme calls the *Ungrund* the "eternal silence." It is the actualization in being of these potentialities that is the source of life. Whatever the influences on Boehme may have been it is important to note, as did Hegel, Berdyaev and Koyré, that Boehme's thought was an important new departure in the history of Western thought.[23] Boehme's ideas came into this tradition as mainly original creations of an independent and non-academic mind, largely uninfluenced by the Greek and Latin traditions.[24] The basic difference between Boehme and the previous Christian mystics of the Neo-Platonic tradition is that he did not regard the

---

[23]Though opinions vary on Boehme's importance and place in the history of Western thought, he has earned the acclaim of some of his most important successors. He was hailed by Hegel as the founder of German Idealism. G.W.F. *Lectures on the History of Philosophy*, vol. III, trans. E.S. Haldane (London: Routledge and Kegan Paul, 1955), p. 188. In his study on Boehme, Alexandre Koyré also calls attention to his influence on Fichte and Hegel as well as the second philosophy of Schelling and Boehme's disciple Franz von Baader. Alexandre Koyré , *La philosophie de Jacob Boehme* (New York: Burt Franklin, 1968), p. 506-508. Koyré also points out that Boehme was read by such divergent minds as Newton, Comenius, Milton, Leibniz, Oetinger and Blake. See also Rufus Jones, *Spiritual Reformers of the Sixteenth and Seventeenth Centuries* (Boston: Beacon Press, 1959), and M. L. Bailey, *Milton and Jacob Boehme: A Study in German Mysticism in XVII Century England* (New York: Haskell House, 1964, Reprint). Nicholas Berdyaev points to the importance of Boehme's influence (via Schelling) on the Slavophiles and says that the metaphor of sophia is found in the second generation of Russian philosophers beginning with Soloviev and including Bulgakov, Frank, the Symbolist poets Blok, Beyli and Ivanov. He also acknowledges his own debt to Boehme. Nicholas Berdyaev, "Deux études sur Jacob Boehme" in Jacob Boehme, *Mystérium Magnum*, Tome I (Paris; Aubier, 1945), p. 39.

Boehme is one of those figures whose life is obscured by legend. It is true that he was a shoemaker by profession in the Silesian village of Gorlitz, but his doctrine was not created completely ex-nihilo; although he was unacquainted with Platonic and Neo-Platonic thought, the ideas of many of the mystics and alchemists of his time were familiar to him. Another source of Boehme's doctrine may have been the Kabala. But the extent that any of these sources may have determined the content of Boehme's theosophy is subject to speculation.

[24]Hegel, p. 188. Koyré, pp. 502-508. Berdyaev, *Essai de métaphysique eschatologique*, trans. Maxime Herman (Paris: Aubier, 1946), p. 122.

Absolute primarily as Being but as will. In the beginning is pure undetermined will; this gives Boehme's thinking a voluntaristic character new in Western thought. What follows is a brief description of Boehme's "system" which maintains much of the mythical language of Boehme's description and more closely resembles the chaos myths of creation than the traditional Western theological explanation of ex nihilo creation.

Boehme claimed not to have based his "system" on reason.[25] He regarded reason as a mere fragment of the unity of man's intelligence that existed before the fall and still exists deep within him.[26] In Boehme's version of the myth of the fall, Adam, for the most part, lost his intuition of the immediate presence of reality within him and thus lost the unity of his intelligence which became dominated by reason. But man still retains the divine force of intuition, though it is hidden in his

---

[25]Boehme felt that what he wrote he wrote through the direct influence of the spirit of God. The preface of *Aurora*, his first major work, he wrote, "for this book comes not forth from reason, but from the impulse of the Spirit." Jacob Boehme, *Aurora*, iii. pp. 1-3, cited in Rufus Jones, p. 152. Boehme is famous as the unschooled shoemaker, mystic philosopher of Gorlitz. Actually Boehme was quite well read in the wisdom of the period. He seems to have been influenced by Paracelsus and Valentine Veigel and his theories are at times extremely difficult to follow because they are often expounded in the archaic terminology of Alchemy. This difficulty is enhanced by Boehme's effort to write as his thoughts are dictated to him by the spirit of God.

> "I am only a layman, I have not studied, yet I bring to light things which all the High Schools and Universities have been unable to do... The language of Nature is made known to me so that I can understand the greatest mysteries in my mother-tongue. Though I cannot say I have learned or comprehend these things, yet so long as the hand of God stayeth upon me I understand." Boehme, *Third Epistle*, p. 22, cited in Jones p. 152.

Aldous Huxley once wrote that reading Boehme was like going to a picnic where Boehme brings the words and the reader the meaning. But this statement is too extreme for although Boehme is difficult reading, the general lines of his thought come through clearly, clearly enough for his influence to have spread quite quickly from Gorlitz throughout Germany to England and Russia. My interpretation of Boehme's *Ungrund* is based on Koyré's, Jones', and Berdyaev's readings of him.

[26]Boehme, *Mystérium*, vol. I, p. 50.

depths. It is by intuition alone, and not by reason, that one can understand the hidden world of God.[27]

## Ungrund as the All and Nothing:  Bliss

The *Ungrund* itself is envisioned as the undifferentiated abyss of non-being and Being, the primordial realm of origination. It is the no-thing that is also everything, potentiality without form. Boehme also called it Wonne, or bliss. But at a deeper level the *Ungrund* is not or cannot be characterized at all, except as the "ewiges Kontrarium."

Why is there Being rather than nothing?  In Boehme's terms there is no reason for this other than freedom or will. This will to create expresses separateness, individuality, and selfhood. The occurrence of Being and the threat of evil are necessary for the appearance of all creation. So for Boehme neither creation, nor non-being, nor God, nor man nor nature are evil as such. But evil represents a moment in the theogonic process when freedom takes on the form of necessity. Creation implies the drama of destruction and construction.

At the depth of God is the *Ungrund*, groundlessness, the eternal silence. The *Ungrund* is anterior to God and is eternally a mystery to him, because it is what he was before he became conscious of himself. In *De Signatura Rerum*, Boehme describes the *Ungrund* as "the abyssal eye that sees in the nothing for it is the abyss."[28]  The *Ungrund* is the absolute in-itself (en-soi), it is in Boehme's terms the all and the nothing.[29]  The *Ungrund* is the eternal silence because, though it contains within itself all the antinomies, all the contradictions are still in harmony, for they are only potential, not yet differentiated. Though the *Ungrund* is the ground of being it is not Being itself: it is the abyss from which Being is born. So freedom, as pure potentiality, is anterior to Being and lies in the eye, the core, of God and creation.[30]  The *Ungrund* is not the personal creator God but the absolute in-itself, a moment at the commencement of the divine life and process of self--creation and revelation of Being and the Divine.[31]

---

[27]Boehme, *Mystérium*, vol. I p. 50.  Koyré, p. 313.

[28]Jacob Boehme, *The Signature of All Things*, Emmet Rhys, ed. (London: Everyman, 1912), 3:2.

[29]Koyré, p. 304, 322.

[30]Boehme, *Signature*, 3:1, 16:16.  Koyré, p. 214.

[31]Boehme, *Mystérium*, 1:1.

## Desire and Will

Boehme writes that at the depths God is the nothing, sheer will, but this will will not will to be nothing.[32]   The nothing of the *Ungrund* is the craving for something. This striving, that is groundless, causeless, and simply "is," differentiates itself in the *Ungrund* and becomes the One, Deity.[33] But Deity is not to be confused with God: it is also only a moment in the self-creation and self-revelation of God. It is the idea of God, but this God-idea must reveal itself to God's self. The craving for something from the nothingness of the *Ungrund* creates the two movements of God--will and desire. Will is the aspiration to reveal itself, and desire, the destructive longing for the object of self-revelation. In this motion are created the two centers of God, light and darkness. It is here that Boehme begins to give a clear statement that God and creation are bi-polar in nature, that all things have polar opposites.

> This liberty (which is called God) is the cause of the light; and
> the impression of the desire is the cause of the darkness and painful
> source;   Now herein understand two eternal beginnings, viz., two
> principles, one of liberty in the light, the other in the impression in the
> pain, a source of the darkness, each dwelling in itself.[34]

It is only through the existence of light and darkness that anything exists at all; the light could not exist without the darkness and the darkness could not exist without the light.

> Hence arises the first enmity and opposition; for the two forms,
> which yet are but one, make themselves their own enemies; and yet
> if this were not, there would not be any essence, neither body nor
> spirit, also no manifestations of the eternity of the abyss.[35]

The opposition of these two principles, light and darkness, forms the ground of the *Ungrund*; what Koyré  calls the emptiness which knows itself.[36] Boehme uses the metaphor of a mirror: through a circular process of reflection, God begins

---

[32]Boehme, *Signature*, 14: 23.

[33]Boehme, *Signature*, 2:8.

[34]Boehme, *Signature*, 14:27.

[35]Boehme, *Signature*, 14:19.

[36]Koyré, p. 337.

128

to come to know himself. This is the birth of the spirit.[37] In this movement, the light center, the will, manifests itself in the trinity: the indeterminate will (father), the will possessing an identity (the son), and the self-revealing will (spirit).[38] But the differentiation that exists at this point is still an act of the spirit, the imagination; the trinity does not yet exist concretely. For God to realize himself concretely he must have an object.[39] Until the creation of a world which is the other of God, the One now manifested in trinity was only an idea of God's potential concrete form. It is through the relation with the Other, the world, that God accomplishes his own self-revelation.

### The Two Centers and the Seven Qualities

The first center of the will toward Being is positive, the second or negative center of desire is the Abgrund, non-being. Boehme uses the terms "yes" for will and Being, and the "no" for desire and non-being. Non-being for Boehme is not simply the absence of Being, it is the contrary of Being; the negation and destruction of Being. Although the Abgrund in itself represents death and negation, through its interaction with the will it is the source of life and continual creation.[40] The Abgrund, or "Centrum Naturae," also evolves and later in its development it receives a triadic structure. God's essence is defined by the interaction and interpenetration of the two centers. These two centers and the mediation between them is what Boehme describes as the seven qualities of God.

The fourth of these seven qualities, the mediating quality, is of particular importance to this discussion. It represents the triumph of the will of God over the dark center. God, through the mediating quality, transforms his potential destruction, the Centrum Naturae, into the source of life. The Centrum Naturae becomes the center of God's concrete nature, his body. God lives through the opposition of the forces of desire and will, chaos and order.[41] Boehme believes that all things spring from the divine desire, so life must be viewed much in the same fashion as the harmony of Heraclitus' bow, an eternal struggle between

---

[37]Boehme, *Mystérium*, I:3.

[38]Boehme, *Mystérium*, I:3.

[39]Boehme, *Mystérium.*, II: 8-9.

[40]Boehme, *Signature*, 16:I, 6:1-3. Koyré , p. 30, 369.

[41]Boehme, *Mystérium*, LXXXI: 19. Koyré , p. 374, 487.

destruction and creation. If destruction would end, so would creation.[42] Life becomes the great tie between the contradictions whereby God's inner nature is revealed to himself. Life is the illumination of the primal darkness, the *Ungrund*.[43] With the differentiation of the two centers and the concretion of the seven qualities, God moves toward having a natural essence, a Body. In fact, Boehme maintains that God must have a physical nature to be capable of creating.[44] Unlike others of the great mystics, Boehme does not think the visible and the finite are unreal or less real. The world is a divine revelation and a positive reality.[45]

### Creation, Fall, and Evil

Boehme maintains the world or a world is necessary to God.[46] The world is the reflection of God and was made from his own nature.[47] The world is created in a process much like that in which God himself is created. The world was spiritually created in the mind of God before it received its physical creation. But, as with God, the spiritual creation by the will is insufficient because it is only imagined and not realized. The Divine idea is less rich than reality; the world is richer after its history than at the beginning.[48]

Boehme thus gives a description of the fall and the existence of evil in the world that is far different from traditional theology. Since the essence of the world and man were determined by God's own being, the world and man are made up of the same two centers and seven qualities that formed God's essence. And since God is free, his creatures, though limited by their finitude, are also free.[49] The harmony of Heraclitus's bow is analogous to the in which Boehme sees the condition of the universe before the fall; it was a harmony of opposites. The light

---

[42]Koyré, p. 389.

[43]Koyré, p. 360.

[44]Boehme, *Mystérium*, V:10. Koyré, p. 449.

[45]Jones, p. 155.

[46]Koyré, p. 392. Boehme, *Mystérium*, LXXI: 20.

[47]Boehme, *Mystérium*, II:9. Koyré, pp. 348-349.

[48]Boehme, *Mystérium*, I:3.

[49]Boehme, *Signature*, 16: 15-16.

center in God is continuously victorious over the dark center. Evil begins with Lucifer's free choice of death and darkness over the light. This choice separated him from God, and represents the destruction of harmony. The willful distortion of reality was an act of complete separation of Lucifer from the totality. Lucifer refusing to return to the harmony of the whole completely denied the light within him and chose the darkness.[50] Because of freedom, the rest of creation also fell out of harmony. The potentiality for evil is in the negative character of freedom that Boehme centers in the passionate nature. But the passionate nature is of positive value because in projecting its nature one realizes individuality.

Evil is real. But it is not an ontological reality; it is related to the negative character of freedom. For Boehme, evil is not privation, it is not a negative form of the ontological order, it is rather the reverse of the ontological order. Boehme's description of evil prefigures Kant but it also prefigures Schelling's, Sartre's, and Berdyaev's discussion of a negative desire to be God. The categorical imperative grants a person the choice to choose the world in the way of the moral law or to deny it as such. The denial of the law is not its evasion but the reversal of the moral order. It is to will that chaos become universal. This is the core of Boehme's explanation of Lucifer. Lucifer wills the destruction of order and harmony through the creation of a false image of the universe of which he is the center. This reverse of the moral/ontological order occurs, according to Boehme, via Lucifer's desire to become God himself.[51] Hubris is the culmination of egoism, but it would be a misunderstanding to assume for this reason that Boehme regards individuality as the source of evil. Quite the contrary, it is through individuality that God reveals and comes to know himself and creation. It is through the bad usage of individuality, as the desire for individuality becomes the exaltation of the self, that evil comes to be. Differentiation and individuality provide both the possibility of revelation, of creation, and of evil.

Egoism represents the effort of the individual to turn into itself, turning away from the Other, thereby halting the creative advance. This is an ontological regression. Instead of existing and progressing with others, the egoist regresses and turns in upon himself, within his imaginary private universe. He takes a position against the rest of creation and condemns himself to isolation. Only the soul that gives itself to God and others receives divine intelligence or knowledge of the whole. For Boehme, the individual who does not exalt his own interest over those of the Other is a more rich individual than he was before. This is so because in his own will he only comprehends the particular, whereas in the abandonment of his will he comprehends the whole.[52]

---

[50]Boehme, *Signature*, 16:7.

[51]Boehme, *Three Principles*, 14:85.

[52]Boehme, *Mystérium*, 67:13.

But this abandonment does not signify the dissolution of personal existence; quite to the contrary, this is the fulfillment and creation of the person. Anticipating Kantian morality, the development of the person is based on freely controlling desire in the light of responsibility to the moral law which is really responsibility for the Other. Personal existence is only lost through egoism which is either the unthinking, or demonically willful surrender to desire and because it denies the reality of the Other is also a denial of reality. In egoism the individual wishes to see himself as the only source of his Being. He sees himself as God in the Sartrean sense of the desire to be God. Selfishness covets the independence of the Other and requires it for its own self-affirmation, so the egoist is perhaps more reliant on the Other than ever before, though he denies the import of the other.[53] He requires that the Other affirm his superiority but the Other, as a free being, can refuse this, or, as in the Heglian analysis of master-slave it can give up its freedom and in doing this the Other ceases to be a real Other. Either way for the Demonic egoist the Other represents a constant source of frustration, it constantly frustrates his attempts to live out its fantasy.

The Devil's power is limited by the Boehmian idea of fantasy which is to say that Lucifer's power rests on a lie, an illusion. The idea shows how Boehme can be true to the scriptural statements about the devil's powers and principalities and yet still maintain that he is powerless. There is a parallel between good and evil in that evil is a false image or a bad imagination of the order of being; an infernal counterpart or copy of reality. But none of the images created by evil can sustain itself in being because it turns into itself, it desires permanence but all its efforts at permanence are in vain for it denies the reality of the interdependence of beings. What fantasy represents is not simply the absence of the truth, but a feverish opposition to it. As with Kant's categorical imperative, in Boehme's conception of fantasy, Lucifer's act, if universalized, would return all of creation to the centerless chaos of non-being through the creation of millions of pseudo-centers. The demonic hope is self-destructive--it cannot be realized. The demonic attitude refuses to accept the existence of the Other as another equal and sees itself as the unique center of its world. Whether it is God or man, or devil or angel, the Other is the source of continual pain to the demonic because the demonic imagines the Other as the source of its misery, as the limitation of the possibility of realizing his vision of a private universe. There is a great similarity between Boehme's conception of the demonic and Sartre's description of the project of the desire to be God where hell is other people because they represent the destruction of "my" project. The Other eliminates the possibility of fulfilling in fantasy my desire to be God. Boehme describes hell as that darkness where each of the damned blaims the others there for her despair.

---

[53]Boehme, *De Signatura Rerum*, 15:12.

, In the Darkness there is in the essence only a perpetual stinging and breaking, each form being enemy to the other--a contrarious essence. Each form is a liar to itself, and one says to the other, that it is evil and adverse to it, that it is a cause of its restlessness and fierceness. Each thinks in itself: If only the other form were not, thou wouldst have rest; and yet each of them is evil and false. Hence it is, that all that is born of the dark property of wrath is lying, and is always lying against the other forms, saying they are evil; and yet it is itself a cause thereof, it makest them evil by its poisonous infection.[54]

This is the culmination of evil. Evil projects its negativity onto the Other and tells the truth about itself in the form of a lie. Even here one knows oneself through relation to the Other but, as a juggler, must immediately deny it.

For Boehme liberty is activity and the possibility of evil is within the possibility of Being itself. Freedom cannot be passive indifference, it is activity and has a tendency to manifest itself. From freedom is born Being, nature, and all reality. This aspiration for creation contains within itself all of the contraries and thus explains the possibility of evil, though not its actuality. Thus it is possible that evil could be destroyed because evil is only a potential reality that exists as an actual but not a necessary part of reality.

Thus Boehme emphasizes in a rudimentary fashion something quite new in the history of Western thought and provides the seeds for an explanation of human freedom that is quite different from Sartre's ontological dualism. For Boehme negativity and positivity, Being and nothingness, freedom and potentiality precede any form of positive Being.

## A Brief Sketch of Berdyaev's Appropriation of the *Ungrund* Myth

In *Dream and Reality* Berdyaev acknowledges his debt to Boehme. Like many Russians, Berdyaev discovered the German mystic quite early in his philosophical career.[55] Berdyaev maintained that Boehme's myth of the *Ungrund*

---

[54]Jacob Boehme, *Six Theosophical Points and Other Writings*, trans. John Rolleston Earle (Ann Arbor: University of Michigan Press, 1958), 9:2, p. 89.

[55]In his article "The Influence of Jacob Boehme on Russian Religious Thought" Zvednek V. David emphasizes that the influence of Western mysticism, and particularly of Boehme, on Russian religious thought has largely been neglected. Boehmeian theosophy was present in Russia from the late 17th century and exerted an important influence on a wide range of religious thinkers like Tikon of Zadonsk

was the only conception of freedom that he found to be nearly adequate for the type of philosophy he wished to create. Boehme's myth, describing will and freedom, is present in all of Berdyaev's mature philosophy. He did not claim to

---

and even governmental, officials including Prokopovitch. Hand-written manuscripts in Church Slavonic and old Russian were circulated in the towns and among the peasants, especially in the Ukraine. The "Russian Socrates," Gregory Skovoroda, employed Boehmist concepts and symbols in talking about the soul's relation to God and the "divinization of man." He is also presumed to have authored several manuscript translations of Boehme which he distributed during his wanderings. But the main point of entry for Boehme's theosophy, that laid the basis for its later influence on Russian religious thought in general, came through the Free-Masons. Here the imprint of Boehme is obvious and his theosophy was the most important single intellectual influence on Russian masonry. An understanding of Boehme was required of those initiates who would attain the highest degree in the lodges. Through the Masons, Boehmian theosophy became widely read among the educated classes. Boehme was also read outside of esoteric groups. In 1815 the poet Dimitiev complained that booksellers no longer imported any literature but "Boehme and the like." However, in 1824 the government suppressed the reading of Boehme. Berdyaev in his autobiography *Dream and Reality* writes of the suppression of Boehme's works: "But Boehme's memory was kept alive among the people where he was regarded as a saint." Despite the suppression, Boehme was read throughout the 19th century and not only by "the people." The influence of Schelling on the Russian romantic circles and the Slavophiles leads back to Boehme. The Russians' enthusiastic reception of Schelling was probably facilitated by the influence Boehme had in Schelling's later philosophy. Throughout the century Boehme was read by diverse groups of Russian thinkers both Westernizers and Slavophiles, including Peter Chaadaev, Ivan Kireevsky, Alexander Herzen. In the renaissance of Russian religious thought Boehme was read by Vladimir Soloviev, whose notion of Sophia was profoundly influenced by Boehme. Boehme's influence is also found in the writings of S. L. Frank and Serge Bulgakov.

Berdyaev said he came to his interest in Boehme through his contacts in "the Pit," a people's basement tavern on the outskirts of Moscow. The Pit was frequented by many whom Berdyaev labeled as "seekers after God." There were common people of a variety of religious groups: Baptists, Tolstoians, Old Believers, etc.. Berdyaev indicates that these common people spoke like Boehme and that because of his conversations in the Pit he began to reread Boehme, Tauler and Silesius. In 1911 with the publication of *The Philosophy of Freedom*, Berdyaev said that his thought had been inspired by reading Boehme. The influence of Boehme is reflected in almost all Berdyaev's work after this early publication to his death in 1948.

be true to Boehme in every respect and used Boehme's conception of the *Ungrund* in his own ways. He identified *Ungrund* with primordial freedom, which precedes all ontological determination.[56]

Berdyaev interprets Boehme to mean that the Absolute is not the creator God. The absolute cannot be a person. It cannot relate to other persons, but is only the undeveloped potentiality of freedom. The *Ungrund*, existence, freedom, is the Absolute, the primary basis of the existence of God, but freedom is also at the depths of all that is. He sees this as the great advance of German mysticism over Greek philosophy and Neo-Platonic mysticism. (Neo-Platonism certainly was a major direct influence on Eckhart and the Rhineland mystics but not Boehme.) In the following passage Berdyaev relates Eckhart's Gottheit and Boehme's *Ungrund* and explains that the *Ungrund*, will or freedom, is the basis of both God and creation. In it he distinguishes between cataphatic or positive theology and apophatic or negative theology. Cataphatic theology is dependent on the law of non-contradiction and only see opposites as distinct. Apophatic theology sees beyond the distinctions imposed by language to the unity of opposites, the identity and difference of all things. The absolute is the *Ungrund* that precedes creation, like the eternal Dao that is the eternal ground of Yin and Yang it cannot be spoken. This is not to say that Berdyaev is a monist. He is a dynamic thinker who see the absolute as only the ground and beginning of the process of creation and not its end.

The conclusions of German mysticism are that neither the Divine Nothing nor the Absolute can be the Creator. The Gottheit is not creative; It escapes all worldly analogies, affinities, dynamism. The notion of a correlative Creator and creature is a category deriving from cataphatic theology. God-the-Creator comes and goes with the creature. I should state this as follows: God is not Absolute, for the notion of God-the-Creator, God-the-Person, God in relation to the world and man lacks the complete abstraction which is necessary for a definitive concept of the Absolute. The concrete, revealed God is correlative to the world and man. He is the biblical God, the revealed God. But the Absolute is a definitive mystery. In consequence two acts are affirmed: Firstly, from the Divine Nothing, from the Gottheit, from the *Ungrund*, a God is realized in eternity, a triune God; and secondly, God, the triune God, is the Author of the world. It appears, therefore, that there is in eternity a theogonic process, a Divine genesis. And that is the inner, esoteric life of the Deity. The act of Creation, the relationship between God and man, is the revelation of the Divine drama, of which time and history are an inner content.

---

[56]Berdyaev, *Dream and Reality*, p. 103.

This conception, which can hardly be called pantheistic, is best of all expressed in Boehme.[57]

As Berdyaev points out this can hardly be called pantheism in the traditional sense. The absolute is not a perfection that underlies the whole of existence. Berdyaev's reading of Boehme influenced his interpretation of Kant and it is possible to get an idea of what he is attempting to say in this passage if we relate this passage to a possible interpretation of the Kantian noumenal realm. The noumenal can be understood as freedom, it is prior to and thus beyond the categories of objectification. But unlike Kant and more like Schelling's 1809 essay *Of Human Freedom* Berdyaev speaks of both an explicit experience of freedom and the Other and its symbolic and mythic representation. He does not shy away from the representation of the mystic experience. Creation implies the effort to express truth in language, music, art, etc.. And like Hegel in *The Phenomenology* he describes the development of freedom from its ground. Berdyaev argues the development of personality is superior to the absolute in-itself. But Berdyaev understood Hegel's idea of freedom to assert the priority of the universal over the individual moment. He rejects this and asserts that the primary value is the creation and development and relationship of God and individual persons. The absolute in-itself is valueless but this fecund ground provides for the possibility of the creation of persons and value.

Berdyaev expands Boehme's image of the genesis of God from the absolute to include not only the development of God but of humanity and the cosmos as well. But Berdyaev maintains that the descriptions of these processes can only be symbols representing the existential mystery. The dialogical relation between God and the world cannot be expressed in terms of ontology because it is an immediate relation outside the realm of being and necessity, it exists in the realm of freedom. The basis of the relation is freedom which is both being and nothingness. The *Ungrund* functions of the symbol of the inexpressible. "It is impossible to formulate a conception of the Ungrund; it is a myth and a symbol, the limit of any rationalization."[58] "Boehme's teaching about the *Ungrund*. . . was a vision rather than a rational doctrine."[59] "An initial, irrational, and mysterious void lies at the heart of the whole life of the universe, but it is a mystery beyond the reach of logic."[60] These passages are interesting in several respects. They reflect both the

---

[57]Nicholas Berdyaev, *Spirit and Reality*, trans. George Reavey (London: Geoffry Bles, 1939), p. 141.

[58]Berdyaev, *Spirit and Reality*, p. 115.

[59]Berdyaev, *The Beginning and the End*, 105.

[60]Berdyaev, *Freedom and the Spirit*, p. 165.

Boehmian and Kantian influences in Berdyaev's thought. When Berdyaev speaks of Boehme's image of the *Ungrund* as not being a rational construction, as a vision rather than a rational doctrine, he can be understood in Kantian terms. He means that the *Ungrund* cannot be grasped as an objective constitution of the categories of the understanding, but, like the postulates of practical reason, beyond proof. Freedom and its meaning have their own type of intelligibility that cannot be reduced to the categories of the understanding. In common with the mystic Boehme, Berdyaev believes that a mystical experience of the whole, of God, and of freedom is possible. In *Freedom and the Spirit* Berdyaev gives his interpretation of the meaning and importance of the great German mystics, Eckhart, Tauler, and especially Boehme, to philosophy.

The great German mystics made a distinction between God (Gott) and Divinity or (Gottheit). Such, for instance, was the teaching of Eckhart. Boehme maintained the doctrine of the *Ungrund* which was at a deeper level than God Himself. The meaning of the distinction between God and Divinity is not expressible in metaphysics or ontology. This truth can only express itself in terms of spiritual life and experience and not in the categories of a rigid ontology.. . . As rigid ontology this truth would degenerate into heresy. Eckhart describes the relationships between God and man which are revealed in mystical experience. God exists if man exists. When man disappears, God will also disappear; "before the creature existed God was not God." God becomes God only in relation to creation. In the primal void of the divine Nothingness, God and creation, God and man disappear and even the very antithesis between them vanishes. "Non-existent being is beyond God and beyond differentiation." The distinction between the Creator and creation is not the deepest that exists, for it is eliminated altogether in the divine Nothingness which is no longer God. Negative mystical theology penetrates beyond the Creator in His relationship to creation and beyond God in His intercourse with man. The Creator is manifested at the same time as creation, God and man appear simultaneously. It is a theogonic process of the divine Unfathomable which is the counterpart of the anthropogonic process.[61]

Berdyaev thinks that all the great German mystics recognized the mutual dependence of opposites. They all teach that God is, in a significant way, dependent on the existence of the creature. In this respect the inexpressible cataphatic theology forms the possibility for positive apaphatic theology. But the

---

[61]Berdyaev, *Freedom and the Spirit*, p. 194.

positive theology that develops from this insight is far different from the predominant theological position of the West. It recognizes the absolute importance of mutual dependence in the relation between individuals and God. This position is emphasized in the later Schelling's interpretation of the categorical imperative as the basis of a metaphysics of freedom. Each owes his personhood to the Other. Berdyaev argues that the relation between God and man makes the existence of both possible. Both exist only as individual entities in the relation between them. Freedom precedes this relation at a deeper level and makes it possible but in-itself is nothing. The *Ungrund* precedes both God and Nature and they arise from it. This is the mythic characterization of the priority of indeterminate possibility over Being.[62] It is a negative characterization because all literal characterizations are predicates of objects or beings, and free possibility is the absence of all such determinations. Boehme characterizes the *Ungrund* not simply as nothingness but as will. Berdyaev follows this characterization but cautiously asserts that it is a symbolic characterization. In Boehme's metaphor the *Ungrund*

---

[62]It is important here to point out what seems unclear in Berdyaev's thought. The exact relation of God and the *Ungrund*. Boehme's image of the *Ungrund* maintains that the *Ungrund* is at "the depths" of God. It is the primal will, pure potentiality, freedom that is prior to all determination and thus precedes creation and remains at its depth. Berdyaev claims that he differs from Boehme in that he locates the *Ungrund* outside of God.

I do not claim to be true to Boehme in every respect, but I regarded his teaching concerning the *Ungrund* as susceptible of my own interpretation, and I identified *Ungrund* with primordial freedom, which precedes all ontological determination. According to Boehme this freedom is in God, it is the inmost mysterious principle of divine life; whereas I conceive it to be outside God, preferring as I do, not to speak of the unspeakable and ineffable apophatic mystery of God's life. Berdyaev, *Dream and Reality*, p. 103.

But I don't think it is clear how even symbolically this can be. The *Ungrund* as pre-existential freedom provides a common link between both God and creation. It precedes them both and they are both grounded in it. To place the *Ungrund* outside the divine life thus makes little sense if we accept what Berdyaev has said elsewhere about the priority of freedom. The only possible explanation of this seems to be either: (a) a concession to traditional theology, or, (b) an effort to clear God of any possible responsibility for evil. If (b) were the case, then God seems to become simply a regulative idea in that He exists simply as the intelligible ideal pole in relation to the indetermination of freedom.

138

is blind will toward creation--that which cannot remain nothing.[63] That is to say, creation is the most fundamental feature of reality, it represents the genesis of entities from the merely potential, the emergence of novel forms which are more than what is contained immanently in antecedent efficient causes. This creation of the new is the only sense of creation ex nihilo that Berdyaev accepts. The new is different and not reducible to that which preceded it. The *Ungrund* is that which is not a being, rather than non-being, in the traditional Augustinian sense.

In relation to the *Ungrund* myth, Berdyaev works out his conception of *meonic* freedom on which he bases his anti-ontology. Freedom is prior to Being but, unlike other Western voluntarists, will is not reduced simply to the will of God. God's creation of the world is preceded by the theogonic process through which God himself emerges from the *Ungrund*. And the creation of the world is a part of the theogonic process as well. By the theogonic process, God is made distinct from the *Ungrund* which he did not create. Then from the *meonic* freedom of the *Ungrund*, God creates the world. Berdyaev still uses the term creation from nothing to describe the creation of the world from the abyssal freedom which he calls meon, meaning non-being. To understand *meonic* freedom as non-being in the traditional sense would be to misunderstand Berdyaev. He returns to the Greek ways of saying non-being which can be expressed in two ways as *ouk on* and *me on* and have quite different meanings. "There is nothing more sad and barren than that which the Greeks expressed by the phrase *ouk on*, which is real nothingness. The words *me on* conceal a potentiality, and this therefore is only half being or being which is not realized."[64] *Meonic* freedom is not something; and it is not

---

[63]In Berdyaev's metaphysical explanation of eschatology he gives what is about as good a definition of the *Ungrund* and *meonic* freedom as can be offered. From the explanation below it is apparent that freedom is necessary to creativity in Berdyaev's thought.

The *Ungrund*, then, is nothingness, the groundless eye of eternity; and at the same time it is will, not grounded upon anything, bottomless, indeterminate will. But this is a nothingness which is '*Ein Hunger zum Etwas*'. At the same time the *Ungrund* is freedom. In the darkness of the *Ungrund* a fire flames up and this is freedom, *meonic*, potential freedom. According to Boehme freedom is opposed to nature, but nature emanated from freedom. Freedom is like nothingness, but from it something emanates. The hunger of freedom, of the baseless will for something, must be satisfied.

Berdyaev, *The Beginning and the End*, p. 106-107.

[64]Berdyaev, *The Beginning and the End*, p. 97.

nothing. It is not a thing. In this sense it is closer to the Upanishadic expression of non-being as *netti netti*, than to Greek and Western uses of non-being.[65] *"Meonic,"* then, is not to be understood in the sense of non-being, as opposed to Being, but as the undetermined, the no-thing, the pure potentiality of the *Ungrund*. So God's creative activity is the creation of meaning and order in the chaos of potentiality and Being from non-being. This meaning stands under the constant threat of blind irrationality, of the collapse back into chaos.

The *Ungrund* is dynamic tension. It is beyond any possible characterization because it has no precise character. It cannot be described as a privation because it is the fullness of everything existing in potentiality. Non-being and being, finite and infinite, time and eternity, nature and spirit, are all present within the *Ungrund* as unmanifested potentialities. Berdyaev claims that this is not pantheism because the potentialities do not stand in a relation of identity. The *Ungrund* contains all

---

[65]James Gail Sheldon in his 1956 Dissertation on Berdyaev's relation to some of his principle intellectual influences offers some valuable historical analogies to Berdyaev's idea of *meonic* freedom. *Meonic* freedom is Berdyaev's creation. The term is constructed from the greek words *me on*, "not being." It expresses conditional negation very much like the Sanskritic term, *netti netti*, "not this, not this." This is found many places in the Upanishads. *Brihad-Aranyaka Upanishad* 2.3.6; 3.9.26; 4.2.4; 4.4.22; 4.5.15. On non-being as primal ground, see *Chandogya Upanishad* 3.19; 6.2; *Taittiriya Upanishad* 2.7; *Mundaka Upanishad* 2.2.1; *Prasna Upanishad* 2.5; 4.5. See Robert Ernest Hume, *The Thirteen Principal Upanishads translated from the Sanskrit, with an Outline of the Philosophy of the Upanishads and an Annotated Bibliography*, 2nd ed. (London: Oxford University Press. 1931).

Sheldon notes that *"eis to me on"* as early as the writings of St. Gregory of Nyssa, whose works Berdyaev knew very well. But St. Gregory's use employs the phrase for the place phantasms and hallucinations go when not present to a mind. This no where near Berdyaev's use of *"meonic"* as conditional negation. Sheldon points out that Berdyaev indicated the difference between his use of *"meonic"* and the usual Greek sense (*Spirit and Reality* p. 145.). On St. Gregory's use, see Jerome Gaith, *La conception de la liberté chez Gregorie de Nyssé, Études de philosophie médievale*, ed E. Gilson, no, 43 (Paris: J. Vrin, 1953), p. 140. In Greek, *me* is distinguished from *ou (ouk, oukh)* which expresses complete and absolute negation, total non-existence or non-being. Liddell and Scott, *Greek-English Lexicon*, 7th ed., s.v. *"ou"*: *"ou* is the negative of Fact, Statement, as *me* of the will, and thought; *ou* denies, *me* rejects; *ou* is absolute, *me* relative; *ou* objective, *me* subjective.
James Gail Sheldon, "Berdyaev's Relation to Jacob Boehme, Frederich Nietzsche, Henrik Ibsen and Feodor Dostoevsky." Dissertation, Indiana University Department of Comparative Literature, l956.

antitheses, but is itself beyond antithesis--there is nothing anterior to it.[66] The idea of potentiality, of an historical process in the depths of the divine life, in the inmost nature of God, is what Berdyaev takes to be the great discovery of what he calls apophatic or negative theology.[67]

> According to this point of view virtuality is regarded as the deepest element in being, as its inner mysterious origin in fact; it is presumed that it is always richer than its actual manifestation. This conception admits potentiality in God; He is not wholly in action.. . . It is only with such a conception of potentiality, as it is manifested by the infinite unfathomability of being, that the oppressive limitation of the finite can be transcended.[68]

The ultimate metaphysical ground is infinite potentiality in freedom. Boehme often referred to the *Ungrund* as Quelle or source. And for Berdyaev the *Ungrund* is the ultimate source of every manifestation. As with Sartre, for Berdyaev, freedom is the original nature of an existent and cannot be taken from it by an external force. In fact, Berdyaev defines evil as a phantasm in which freedom is denied in two senses: either the self regards itself in bad faith as determined, thus objectifying itself, or the self attempts to assert its will over that of the Other, and thus objectifies the Other.[69] Freedom connects the existent to the groundless "ground" of being in the pre-existential abyss. Since God is not the creator of human freedom, freedom is not a gift given by God. God cannot direct or revoke human freedom. The *Ungrund* is the "primal source and fount of being" from which being is constantly created.[70] The *Ungrund* is the source of every kind of actualization of being which is in potential in ". . . the unfathomable irrationality of freedom, in pure possibility, in the forces concealed within that dark void which precedes all positive determination of being."[71]

---

[66]Nicholas Berdyaev, *The End of Our Time*, trans. Donald Atwater (New York: Sheed and Ward, 1933), pp. 71-75.

[67]Berdyaev, *The Meaning of History*, p. 47.

[68]Berdyaev, *Freedom and the Spirit*, pp. 332-333.

[69]Berdyaev, *The Destiny of Man*, trans. Natalie Duddington (New York: Harper and Row, 1960), pp. 180-184.

[70]Berdyaev, *The Meaning of History*, p. 55.

[71]Berdyaev, *Freedom and the Spirit*, p. 165.

With the realization of the potentialities and the contraries that were present in bliss in the pre-existential abyss of the *Ungrund* come the strife and tragedy of existence. Tragedy is an inevitable part of the ordering of creation. Charles Hartshorne points out that tragedy is the exclusion and actualization of possibilities.[72]

## Ungrund and Antinomies

Berdyaev, like Boehme, attempts to explain the beginning of the theogonic process as the ungrounded craving, as the will to become something. The *Ungrund* is seen at this point not as the pure potentiality but as infinite craving "a craving for something, "the nothingness longs to be something."[73] The instant that this blind will asserts itself the balance of the *Ungrund* of bliss is shattered. The opposition of God and freedom is secondary from the point of view of eternity. In the *Ungrund*, the possibility of God and *meonic* freedom exist as the opposition between order and meaning, and chaos and absurdity. As was the case for Boehme, the antinomic character of the *Ungrund* is preserved in *meonic* freedom and in all products of the source. In God these antinomies are held in balance in creation: the dialectic of contradiction is the very nature of freedom. Like Boehme, Berdyaev distinguishes between Deity and God. Within the interior life of Deity there is an eternal birth of God, an "Auto-enfantment" or Auto-engenditure.[74] Thus Berdyaev maintains the notion of the continual birth of God and Being from the *Ungrund*. In the creation the irrational will of the *Ungrund*, the passionate desire of the no-thing to become something, bends itself to the ordering will of God in free response to his call.

That the contraries cannot simply be resolved but exist because of the nature of possibility is part of the tragic character of existence. Berdyaev maintains that to talk about the antinomies in this way is not to accept a dualist interpretation of the cosmos in a Manichean sense. Rather, it asserts the ultimate irrationality and irreducibility of the dynamic character of freedom. The tragic nature of the antinomies of existence is presented in the problem of good and evil.

The interpretation of the mystery of evil through that of freedom is a supra-rational interpretation and presents reason with an antimony.

---

[72]Hartshorne, "Whitehead and Berdyaev: Is There Tragedy in God," pp. 183-199.

[73]Berdyaev, *Spirit and Reality*, p. 145.

[74]*Berdyaev, Essai de métaphysique eschatologique*, p. 122.

The source of evil is not in God, nor in a being existing positively side by side with Him. . .. Thus evil has no basis in anything; it is determined by no possible being and had no ontological origin.. . . The void (the *Ungrund* of Boehme) is not evil. . .. It conceals within itself the possibility of both good and evil.[75]

God is not the creator of the antinomies. These issue from the fact of freedom.[76] The dualism that exists in Berdyaev's thought is an existential dualism between good and evil, not an ontological one. Thus evil is real, existentially real. But it is not ultimately or ontologically real; and so it is not an essential element of existence. And thus the logical possibility of its eventual elimination exists.

**The Significance of the *Ungrund* for Berdyaev's Conception of Freedom and the Rejection of Ontology**

Charles Hartshorne sees the image of the *Ungrund* that Berdyaev employs to illustrate process, freedom, and creation as similar to Whitehead's metaphysical principle of creativity. For Whitehead the abstract principle of all reality is creativity. Creativity is not identical with God, neither is it a rival reality, nor is it superior to God. "It is a mere universal or an ultimate abstraction." As an unviversal it is real only as it appears in individuals including the one essential individual, God. So God is not identical with creativity because all creatures including you and I are also creative. Hartshorne notes that Berdyaev and Whitehead held similar positions on this point.

And Berdyaev tells us that this freedom is a principle uncreated by God and not identical with him and that the process of creation involves God, the uncreated principle of freedom, and the creative and partly self-creative action of the creatures. God's "call to man" is not answered by God himself or by man using solely elements which God has created in him but by man creating new realities, new qualities of experience.[77]

---

[75]Berdyaev, *Freedom and the Spirit*, pp. 164-165.

[76]From this it follows that the myth of hell and Satan cannot be ontologically real but is rather what Boehme terms fantasy. In *The Destiny of Man* Berdyaev refers to it as a Phantasm. *The Destiny of Man*, pp. 180-184, *Freedom and the Spirit*, p. 165.

[77]Hartshorne, "Berdyaev and Whitehead: is there Tragedy in God," p. 185.

Berdyaev argues that freedom is prior to being, but again it seems strange that one could argue that freedom can be prior to Being. With Kant, Berdyaev holds that freedom cannot be derived from the observation of phenomena. Berdyaev argues that if we deny the realm of the spirit and assert that the objectified world is all there is to reality, we must also deny the existence of human freedom because freedom "cannot be derived from being, for it would then be determined."[78]   But opposed to Kant, Berdyaev insists there is an inner experience of freedom.  For Berdyaev, metaphysics is possible (though on a radically different basis from traditional metaphysics), because freedom is experienced inwardly and is not just a moral postulate. Freedom and the noumenal can be known through experience but that experience is spiritual in nature.  The apparatus of our objective knowledge is limited to the world of experience.  An integral experience is volitional and emotional as well as intellectual and is possible because of the rootedness of the individual in the *Ungrund*, in freedom.  For Berdyaev, the individual is a microcosm of the whole and as such has the possibility of participation in the whole being.[79]

It is important to qualify the definition of "Being" that we have been using thus far. Berdyaev uses the term "Being" in several senses and until now we have only discussed it in its negative sense signifying ontology and objectification. Berdyaev, because he most often uses the term in this way, is easily misunderstood. But Berdyaev also uses "Being" in the sense of the symbolic and created nature of the natural world.  Most importantly however, he sometimes uses "Being" to signify meaning and order or intelligibility--this is the being which is created by God, and in the creation of which huamn beings also participate. Indeed, God is taken to be meaning and order and the principle of being.  For example, in his explanation of theodicy, in *The Destiny of Man*, Berdyaev acquits God of responsibility for evil by saying that the world is made of Being (meaning) and *meonic* freedom.  God is responsible for the Being of the world but not for freedom, which is also the source of His Being which He shares with the creation and man.  There can be no causal explanation of freedom and only a symbolic explanation of the existence of Being.  Freedom is a source and condition of existence but there is no direct causal link between freedom and existence. Nothingness does not exist but it has existential significance.[80]  For Berdyaev, freedom or will is prior even to existence.  This is in sharp contrast with Sartre's famous definition of existentialism.  Instead of "existence precedes essence" for Berdyaev, freedom or will precedes existence, which precedes essence, which is

---

[78]Berdyaev, *Toward a New Epoch* p. 98.

[79]The possibilities of human knowledge receive a fuller treatment below in the discussion of Berdyaev's idea of the concrete universal.

[80]Berdyaev, *The Beginning and the End*, p. 143.

144

constantly changing. The freedom of the *Ungrund* is the deepest reality in both man and God. The *Ungrund* is neither good nor evil, it conceals within itself the possibility of good and evil. t is the source of every actualization of being. It is: "an initial, irrational, a mysterious void lies at the heart of the whole life of the universe, but it is a mystery beyond the reach of logic."[81]

As we have seen, Berdyaev objects to Sartre's adoption of the name existentialist for his philosophy precisely because Sartre's existentialism is based in an ontology. Berdyaev's rejection of ontology has its roots not only in the voluntaristic mysticism of Berdyaev's interpretation of Jacob Boehme but also in Berdyaev's reading of Kant.[82] This appreciation of Kant is also the key to Berdyaev's preoccupation with objectification. He fully accepts Kant's contention that the categories by which we interpret the phenomenal world do not have any access to the things themselves. The science of ontology fails to describe reality because it is tied to the rationalist's faith that reality must conform to the categories of his rational system or conform solely to a rational order in being which are inventions of the intellect. Berdyaev believes that Kant demonstrated through the antinomies "an end of metaphysics of the naturalistic type."[83] Kant shows that no account of the rationalistic type can be made that adequately describes reality. That the human intellect has demonstrable limits shows that reality cannot be enclosed in concepts. In particular, there is no adequate account of how the actual comes out of the possible.

The rationalist objectifies living realities that exist outside of the limitations of his categories. "Abstraction and the hypostatizing of abstraction created both spiritual and materialistic metaphysical systems."[84] For Berdyaev, the objective world with all its causal connections is a projection of human consciousness. The categories of the mind deal with the phenomenal world and are practical tools that function in their sphere. But it is a mistake to suppose that they describe reality in-itself.

From the explanation offered above it seems that one could hold God responsible for objectification in that he has created a world and not simply a

---

[81]Berdyaev, *Freedom and the Spirit*, p. 165.

[82]Berdyaev, *Dream and Reality*, p. 93.

[83]Berdyaev, *The Beginning and the End*, p. 9.

[84]Berdyaev, *Freedom and the Spirit*, p. 1. Berdyaev was, early in his career, influenced by marxism. But he soon broke with the marxists. And in his autobiography he mentions a conversation with Plekhanov, the father of Russian marxism, to the effect that rationalism, and especially materialistic rationalism, are based "on the dogmatic presupposition concerning the rational nature of Being in general, and of material being in particular."

spiritual entity. Nature as being is not evil. Berdyaev is not a Manichean, neither is he a Neo-Platonist because he does not think that the body is less perfect than the spirit or mind.[85] When Berdyaev opposes spirit and nature, he is not opposing the soul to the body. But he opposes ideas of matter, substance, and necessity which are products of the categories of understanding. Spirit is not an objective reality. But neither is it simply subjective, because to conceive of it as such would be, once again, to perform a subtle form of objectification through labeling it as a sort of substance, as subjectivity opposed to objectivity. The problem of objectification arises when we look at the Other as merely an object and not as another freedom.[86] The key to reading Berdyaev is to see that he, like Schelling,

---

[85]In *Slavery and Freedom*, Berdyaev discusses the relation of the body and the soul and the importance of what he calls the form of the body, to personality. Personality is the ordering of the potentiality of nature by spirit. The body belongs to the personality. It is both a receptacle of creative action and the opposition that makes creative action possible.

> The problem of personality is a problem of an entirely different order from the ordinary problem of the relation of soul and body. Personality is certainly not the soul as distinct from the body, which links man with the life of nature. Personality is the entire image of man in which the spiritual principle has the mastery over all the powers of man's soul and body. The unity of personality is created by the spirit. But the Body belongs to the image of man. . . .The form of the body belongs to the spirit-soul. Here is personality in its entirety. . .. This presupposes a modification of Christian consciousness and the overcoming of abstract spirituality, which places spirit and body in opposition and sees in the body a principle which is hostile to the spirit. The spirit includes the body also in itself, it spiritualizes the body, and communicates another quality to it. They are ceasing to consider the body as a material physical phenomenon.

Berdyaev, *Slavery and Freedom*, trans. R.M. French (New York: Scribners, 1944), pp. 31-32. (See also p. 54 for Berdyaev's discussion of immortality and the body.)

[86]Berdyaev's discussion of the face of the Other as the portal of the spiritual world of the freedom of the Other indicates the creative action of spirit in the natural world.

> The form of the human body is already a victory of the spirit over natural chaos.. . . The form of the body is certainly not matter, it is certainly not a phenomenon of the physical world. The form of the body is not only of the soul, it is spiritual. The face of man is the summit of the cosmic process, the greatest of its offspring, but it

regards the phenomenal world as real, but symbolically so. Objectification is to see the symbol not as a symbol but as the ultimate reality, reifying the symbol. The phenomenal world is a symbol of a spiritual reality that is deeper than object-ification. The problem comes when human beings see the phenomenal world as the only reality. In Kantian terms we could say that Berdyaev would insist that pure reason, though more precise in its realm, is not concerned with primary reality and must be subordinated to pure practical reason which is concerned with this reality.

In this way Berdyaev can say that both the Other and God are outside of the categories of human reason. It is only our idea of the Other that is an object, never the Other herself who exists as a center of freedom. God exemplifies what is ultimately true for all other subjects. For Berdyaev, God cannot be referred to in naturalistic terms. He cannot be the first principle of a metaphysical system or the ground of Being. God is an independent locus of Being. Berdyaev maintains that the only possible approach to God or to the Other is through an immediate experience that transcends the antithesis between subject and object and the substantialist conception of them.[87] But in this experience there is no loss of the human subject; the subject still subsists in his independence as a freedom.[88] Berdyaev maintains the monadic and pluralistic structure of individuals, though he ultimately wishes to transcend this position as well.[89]

---

cannot be the offspring of cosmic forces only, it presupposes the action of a spiritual force, which raises it above the sphere of the forces of nature. The face of man is the most amazing thing in the life of the world: another world shines through it. It is the entrance of personality into the world process, with its uniqueness, its singleness, its unrepeatability. Through the face we apprehend, not the bodily life of a man, but the life of his soul. And we know the life of his soul better than his bodily life. The form of the body belongs to the spirit-soul. Here is personality in its entirety.
Berdyaev, *Slavery and Freedom*, p. 31.

[87]Berdyaev, *Freedom and the Spirit*, p. 55.

[88]Berdyaev, *Spirit and Reality*, p. 133, 136-137, 149.

[89]Some of Berdyaev's statements in his autobiographical essay *Dream and Reality* would seem to indicate that he regards consciousness as no less monadic and ultimately separated and trapped in its solitude, isolated from the Other, than does Sartre. This would be true if we were to ignore the importance of both eschatology and objectification for Berdyaev. Berdyaev regarded the objective world of physical objects as not ultimately real and thought that each human being is a microcosm of reality. Ultimately he thought that through creative action it

At this point Berdyaev radically breaks with Kant and moves to what is ultimately a non-rational position because he asserts that in mystical experience the distinction between subject and object is suspended and yet the independence of the two beings is maintained. This kind of a description of the experience is dependent on the notion that freedom as a non-rational will precedes Being and thus also precedes the capacities of rational language to describe it. The mystical experience that Berdyaev describes does give its subject knowledge. But it is a pure experience that can be expressed only in the form of symbols. "Knowledge of the divine is a dynamic process which finds no completion within the fixed and static

---

would be possible to break through the separations caused by the objectification of the world. Berdyaev is here as elsewhere unabashedly Christian and sees the creation of unity only coming about through the joint action of both God and man united in the symbol of the God-man, Christ.

> I have minimized rather than exaggerated the gulf which divides me from the things around me, and which yawns at me whenever I turn; the commonplace, and the common man, the "we," the "all of us", the collective mind, and so on and so forth. And yet I continued throughout life to hover between solitude and independence vis-a-vis the world, on the one hand, and an intense desire for communion with my fellow-men and for the establishment of just and free social relations, on the other.
>
> I have never tried, willingly or unwillingly, to shut myself in a private world of my own; rather, I desired to find a way out into the open, to be present in the world and to make the world present within me, but to be present dangerously and freely. Man is created as a microcosm and his vocation is to re-create the cosmos within himself. . .. The whole universe dwells within, and is personified by, man, and nothing should be regarded as external to him. But the phenomenal, empirical world, as in fact it represents itself to me, is not my own; on the contrary, it impinges on me from without and is intent on destroying me, and I am not the microcosm I ought to be. Man's actual condition is such as to make the intensity of his self-awareness a measure of his enslavement to an alien world, nature and society which stand over against me; what is mine is exceedingly slender and intangible in comparison with them, so slender indeed as to elude entirely the claims of nature, society and the world at large. I can only agree to submit to, and be merged with, that nature or that society which is capable of entering into me and of being my own.

Berdyaev, *Dream and Reality*, pp. 64-65.

categories of ontology."[90]   What we might be able to say about the experience
is that the self and the Other are united in an intuitive and empathetic way. This
is possible because they share the same source, *meonic* freedom. What happens in
Berdyaev's I-Thou experience is a free creation of a bond between two beings, the
self and the Other, based on their common experience of freedom. Berdyaev
claims that such conceptions as substance and cause are inapplicable to individual
freedom because freedom is prior to being. In the relation of the self and the Other
the causal nexus disappears because it is a part of the objectified world. The
experience of the Other is immediate and prior to all the categories.

Berdyaev's appropriation of Boehme also stems from the kind of philosophy
that Berdyaev is seeking to create. From his reading of Kant, Berdyaev took a
strong sense of the antinomic character of reality and of the radically unobject-
ifiable character of freedom. Berdyaev then asserts that all human objective
knowledge is necessarily anthropocentric, and thus excessively subjective, because
it must proceed from the categories of the understanding. This is why metaphysics
and ontology have failed in their attempt to characterize reality: they have imposed
on reality metaphysical categories of being and substance, but they are posterior to
that reality and have their origin in human reason. In his characterization of reason
Berdyaev resembles Nietzsche. Berdyaev claims that philosophers forget that
rational categories are human creations and endow them with real and not simply
symbolic status. Boehme, however, broke with the tradition of placing Being over
will and maintained that will is prior to Being.[91]

---

[90]Berdyaev, *Freedom and the Spirit*, p. 65.

[91]Like Nietzsche, Berdyaev argues that it is through reason that man orients
himself to the world of objects but he thinks this has more to do with pragmatic
living in the world than it does with ultimate truth which is beyond objective
categories. But against Nietzsche, Berdyaev would argue that the basis of moral
reason is not arrived at pragmatically, but is rooted in freedom. Berdyaev, *The
Beginning and the End*, pp. 45-51.

In *The Will to Power*, Nietzsche discusses the relation of reason to the
pragmatic orientation to the world.

> Logic is bound to the condition: assume there are identical cases.
> In fact, to make possible logical thinking and inferences, this condition
> must be treated fictitiously as fulfilled. That is: the will to logical
> truth can be carried through only after a fundamental *falsification* of
> all events is assumed, from which it follows that a drive rules here
> that is capable of employing both means, firstly falsification, then the
> implementation of a point of view: logic does not spring from the
> will to truth.

Boehme stands out as the first voluntarist in European thought. In the dark void, anterior to being, freedom is kindled. Boehme's vision discloses being and dynamic depths of being, much vaster probably, than being itself.[92]

Berdayev's assertion that Boehme is the first voluntarist in European thought needs to be understood in the sense that Berdyaev understands it. Certainly it could be objected that William of Ockham, John Calvin, and others are voluntarists. But in these thinkers the freedom of creation is only given to God. Berdyaev thinks in Boehme's mysticism is found the implicit assertion that freedom is the primal datum of reality. Berdyaev sees in Boehme's voluntaristic metaphysics the possibility of avoiding some of the problems associated with traditional metaphysics. A good deal of Sartre's criticism of traditional metaphysics relies on the metaphysician's inconsistent attempts to bridge the gap between the self and the Other, change and permanence, and the one and the many which results in an impure and magical blending of both sides of each dichotomy. Berdyaev thinks the voluntaristic metaphysics avoids these problems. Berdyaev explains that the world in which we exist is pluralistic but fallen from an original unity. In this he is not much different from Sartre or Plotinus. But Berdyaev's version of the original unity is far different from either Sartre or Plotinus. In Berdyaev's metaphysics the original unity is not pure positive Being. The original unity rather incorporates pure potentiality, pure possibility. The fall from this original unity represents the realization of possibility--its breaking out from simple potentiality. But this original unity now is shattered in plurality, in what Berdyaev calls the

---

A morality, a mode of living tried and proved by long experience and testing, at length enters consciousness as a law, as dominating--And there with the entire group of related values and states enter into it:  it becomes venerable, unassailable, holy, true; it is a part of its development that its origin should be forgotten--That is a sign it has become master--

Exactly the same thing could have happened with the categories of reason: they could have prevailed, after much groping and fumbling, through their relative utility--There came a point when one collected them together, raised them to consciousness as a whole--and when one commanded them, i.e., when they had the effect of a command--From then on, they counted as a priori, as beyond experience, as irrefutable. And yet perhaps they represent nothing more than the expediency of a certain race and species--their utility alone is their "truth"--

Friedrich Nietzsche, *The Will to Power*, trans. and ed. Walter Kaufmann and R.J. Hollingdale (New York:  Vintage Books, 1967), pp. 277-278.

[92]Berdyaev, *Spirit and Reality*, p. 145.

inevitable tragedy involving existence and creation. It inevitably involves the actualization of some possibilities to the exclusion of others.

In *Freedom and the Spirit* Berdyaev discusses the dichotomy that develops in actualization between freedom and spirit, which he also designates as nothingness and being or pure potentiality and intelligibility. The nothingness that opposes being in actualization is different from the original nothingness of the *Ungrund* which held all the potentialities in the state of potentiality that Boehme called "Bliss." The being and nothingness that come about through the fall from the original unity are what Berdyaev calls spirit and freedom but the nothingness that is freedom is a good deal different from Sartre's conceptions of consciousness, for to say that freedom is nothing or non-being is not simply to say that it is negation. For Berdyaev freedom is possibility, the possibility of the affirmation and creation of, or the denial of, the order of being.

> In the beginning was the Logos, the Word, the Meaning and the Light. But this eternal truth of religious revelation only meant that the kingdom of light and of meaning has been realized initially in being and that the Logos triumphed from the beginning over darkness of every kind. Divine life is a tragedy. Even at the beginning, before the formation of the world, there was the irrational void of freedom which had to be illuminated by the Logos. This freedom is not a form of being which existed side by side with the Divine Being, the Logos, or mind. It is rather that principle without which being could have no meaning for God, and which alone justifies the divine plan of the world. God created the world out of nothing, but it would be equally true to say that He created it out of freedom. Creation must be grounded upon that limitless freedom which existed in the void before the world appeared. Without freedom creation has no value for God.[93]

What all this discussion of potentialities, antinomies, and their actualization amounts to is that, like Whitehead's, Berdyaev's metaphysics is based on the first principle of creativity. Freedom and meaning are the elements that bring about the actualization of potentiality. In *The Meaning of History* Berdyaev writes that the significance of the world process is the illumination of the *Ungrund* or the bringing into actualization the possibilities of potentiality. This is the illumination of the possibilities latent in freedom. "The whole significance and essence of the world process consists in the illumination of this dark irrational principle in cosmogony and theogony."[94]

Berdyaev is often accused of being a dualist who splits reality into two competing elements of freedom and being, chaos and meaning, or *Ungrund* and

[93]Berdyaev, *Freedom and the Spirit*, p. 165

[94]Berdyaev, *The Meaning of History*. p. 56.

God. This is how Berdyaev's student and commentator, church historian Matthew Spinka has interpreted him.[95] But Berdyaev always claimed that there was no Manichean dualism in his philosophy.[96] Dualism implies an ontological dualism and Berdyaev maintains that freedom precedes Being and actually contains the potentiality of being within itself. The *Ungrund* is not Being or a being so there can be no dualism involved here. He is not talking about two spheres of being. It is only in the objectified world that an ontological dualism can take place. In fact, Berdyaev argues that traditional metaphysical/theological dualism and monism have gone hand in hand, with reality only residing in Being or God and not at all in the creature. This is the result of objectification that creates the dualism between creator and creature akin to Buber's I-it relation in *I and Thou*. The I-it relation is always in the past and objectified--like the monist version that bases the creature's reality in the Being of God.

Moreover, naturalist theology makes exactly the same mistake. The extreme dualism of Creator and creation, and of supernatural and natural, is allied here to an extreme monism with regard to both reality and being. The supernatural is on the same ascending scale as the natural, for it, too, is natural, though at a higher level. The antinomy existing between spirit and nature does not provide us with a dualistic metaphysics of being, but it introduces a distinction in the comprehension of reality itself. It is above all things the antithesis between life and thing, between liberty and necessity, between creative movement and passive submission to exterior impulses.[97]

The idiom of traditional kataphatic or positive theology and metaphysics is incapable of explaining ultimate reality. Only an apophatic knowledge which is symbolic and mythic in nature can point to the reality that is beyond the limits of the categories of reason. The *Ungrund*, God, and freedom, are symbols that convey truths about our existence that cannot be conveyed in conceptual frameworks. Contingency and creativity are real features about the world and they are found in every human personality. But the attempt to explain them fully only results in explaining them away, because to see them in such a way as to be able to explain them is to see them as conceptually and ontically subordinate to Being. The "ontological totalitarianism" of modern philosophy is the subordination of concrete experience to a reified abstraction. This makes the most important aspects of our lives appear as illusions. Berdyaev's metaphysics seeks to replace the concepts of Being and pure act with *meonic* freedom.

---

[95]Matthew Spinka, *Nicholas Berdyaev: Captive of Freedom* (Philadelphia: The Westminster Press, 1949), pp. 118-121.

[96]Berdyaev, *Dream and Reality*, p. 102.

[97]Berdyaev, *Freedom and the Spirit*, p. 7.

The next step in Berdyaev's explanation of freedom is his discussion of Godmanhood which is Berdyaev's version of the Sartrean problem of the creation of meaning in relation to freedom and the desire to be God.

# VI. BERDYAEV'S IMAGE OF GODMANHOOD AND THE DESIRE TO BE GOD

## Freedom and Intelligibility

Schopenhauer once declared that the major preoccupation of metaphysics, indeed the reason that metaphysics had come to exist, was the question of evil. For almost two thousand years, Western metaphysics has mainly seen the problem in only two ways: dualism or privation. But in either case evil has always been associated with the appearance of the negative. For Christianity and Judaism the arguments centered around privation, rejecting dualism which posits a principle that is independent of God. Kant's noumenal self marks a radical break with this tradition. The conception of the noumenal self sees evil not as a privation in an ontological sense, but in the practical sense of a basic choice. This is also the heart of Boehme's conception of a dialectical voluntarism in which evil is a positive principle; its possibility is a part of the character of freedom. There is nothing dualistic or Manichean about this. Evil is not a necessarily existing being. But the possibility of evil is always present as one of the possibilities of freedom. Evil is the denial of the possibility of relation. Freedom is not created by God; it is not a being and has no essence. God is not responsible for evil; evil, as well as good, is a possibility of free choice--one of the possibilities that may be realized in creation. Freedom is not created by God but is rooted in the *Ungrund*. Neither is it completely determined by God it is part of the nothing our of which the world is created. Freedom gives rise to evil and God cannot be held responsible for freedom.

> Man is the child of God and the child of freedom--of Nothing, of non-being, *to meon*. *Meonic* freedom consented to God's act of creation; non-being freely accepted being . . .. He creates out of nothing the world and man and expects from them an answer to his call--an answer from the depths of freedom. At first the answer was rebellion and hostility toward God, a return to original non-being.[1]

---

[1] Berdyaev, *The Destiny of Man*, pp. 25-26.

This last statement that God "expects from them an answer to His call"--an answer from the depths of freedom--indicates the next major component of Berdyaev's philosophy: the dialectic of the Divine and the human. Human beings are creators of meaning in relation to God. What was implicit and potential in the *Ungrund* is made explicit in creation and the meanings to be forged are meanings that are created in the dialectical relation between God and man. This dialectical and dialogical relationship, though framed in the image of Boehme's theory of the *Ungrund*, goes beyond anything found in Boehme's thought. The cosmogonic and anthropogonic processes are parts of Berdyaev's existentialism, and not so much parts of his relation to mysticism. But the dialectic of the Divine and the human, which implies the dialogical relationship of reciprocal love, is implied in Berdyaev's reading of Boehme. Boehme's conception of desire, of the presence of desire and movement in God, implies relation to another. As Berdyaev puts it,

> God longs for His "other," His friend; He wants him to answer the call to enter the fullness of the divine life and participate in God's creative work of conquering non-being. God does not answer His own call: the answer is from freedom which is independent of him.[2]

Because God cannot guarantee how freedom will respond to his "call," there is a tragic threat to all divine creativity. God "cannot avert the possibility of evil contained in *meonic* freedom.. . . The myth of the Fall tells of the powerlessness of the Creator to avert the evil resulting from freedom which He has not created."[3] And "It appears that liberty is bound up with imperfection, with a right to imperfection."[4] Tragedy and suffering are the inevitable consequences of the creative character of reality. They are not accidents or consequences of gratuitous evil but a consequence of the infinite possibilities and conflicts of freedom. The possible contains an infinity of mutually exclusive ends. Intentions, even divine intentions, can never completely determine results because whatever is created has within its being the essential freedom out of which it was created. Thus, even for God, and hence for all others, creation conceals an element of ineradicable surprise and disappointment. Chaos is an irreducible part of reality.

This explanation of creation and reality could have a particularly nihilistic character in that the movement toward order is constantly changing and seems to have no ultimate aim except perhaps greater diversity and creativity. There seems to be no particular reason to favor creativity over the bliss of the pure potency of

---

[2]Berdyaev, *The Destiny of Man*, p. 25.

[3]Berdyaev, *The Destiny of Man*, p. 25.

[4]Nicholas Berdyaev, *The End of Our Time*, trans. Donald Attwater (London: Sheed and Ward, 1933), p. 188.

the *Ungrund.* Berdyaev argues that nihilism can only be avoided by taking an eschatological perspective. The doctrine of redemption is the overcoming of the tragedy inherent in freedom by using that very freedom to attain supratemporal values such as love, truth, and beauty. This is the heart of the idea of a creative advance. Creation comes to mean the creation of permanent relationships between independent beings.[5]

There is a moral imperative that gives impetus to this creative advance. The moral law that gives a limited form to that creative advance is based on the Kantian notion of the infinite worth of persons and the Boehmian myth of the ultimate unity of reality. The moral imperative is based on the basic likeness of all monads of freedom, all of whom participate in freedom. This basic likeness insures a basic equality that is not unlike the second formulation of the categorical imperative that all persons should be treated as ends and never as means. The individual person shares with all others the responsibility to recognize the others for what they are: not things but, at least potentially, independent centers of free, creative activity. This moral law is given through both Berdyaev's epistemology and his metaphysics. The epistemology supplies a framework for creative activity that implies a permanent value structure in relation to the absolute worth of persons that Sartrean existentialism does not allow. This value is founded on the basic reality of the freedom of the individual and Berdyaev's metaphysical claim of the priority of freedom. The moral imperative thus given provides a minimum of meaning and structure to the infinite possibilities of freedom.

Berdyaev maintains that the atheist does not really reject God because of the existence of evil in the world, for the talk about evil presupposes a standard of good, of meaning, that is God. Meaning is synonymous with God for Berdyaev. Any belief in meaning is an implicit belief in the lasting character of that meaning and thus an implicit belief in God. This is why Berdyaev, in reference to Sartre's attempts to create meaning in a meaningless universe, says that a thorough-going atheism is almost impossible. Evil presupposes freedom and a standard of worth with respect to which it is evil. Thus there is a link between God and man as facets of the "real myth about man."[6] Man cannot be without some notion of meaning.[7]

Berdyaev insists that we have no guarantee of the world's meaningfulness, for belief in meaning involves commitment and faith. Meaning is related to freedom and freedom requires a choice on our part. That we have no guarantee of the world's meaningfulness does not signify that there is no possible meaning to

---

[5]Berdyaev, *The Destiny of Man*, pp. 284-297.

[6]Berdyaev *The Beginning and the End*, pp. 41, 148-157.

[7]Berdyaev, *The Divine and the Human*, trans. R.M. French (London: Geoffrey Bles, 1949), p. 183.

the universe, only that meaning cannot be ontologically guaranteed. Commitment to any form of meaningful activity involves faith, belief in some sort of permanence or intelligibility in the cosmos. Berdyaev is unabashedly Christian in his explanation of what this permanent structure of intelligibility is. It is the Godman, Christ, who provides a link between the two principles of Berdyaev's metaphysics: the need for meaning, and *meonic* freedom. Together they form the basis of creativity. The Godman is the existential concrete union of poles of reality: meaning (the divine, infinite, eternal, etc.) and freedom (the human, finite, temporal). One of Berdyaev's main objections to Sartre's existentialism concerns the idea that meaning might be created without hope or commitment to the ultimacy of that meaningfulness. For Berdyaev, meanings that are solely isolated and particular and have no characteristic of permanence are not meanings at all but only partial statements that add to the objectification of reality. In *The Meaning of History*, he sets forth his vision of human possibility and the creation of relation with the Other that is radically different from Sartre's.

> In the destiny of mankind, I must recognize my own destiny, and in the latter that of history. This is the only way we can commune with the mystery of the historical and discover the great spiritual destinies of mankind. And inversely, this is the only way we can . . . unite our own individual destiny with that of universal history instead of merely discovering the void of our isolation in opposition to all the riches of universal historical life. Thus the real goal of the philosophy of history is to establish a bond between man and history, between man's destiny and the metaphysics of history.[8]

For Berdyaev, the philosophy of history is a moral undertaking. It is the search for shared meaning, an effort to discover a commonality that can be shared by all human beings. The radical freedom and pure possibility of the *Ungrund* cannot provide for the possibility of the creation of order and meaning in human history. But a metaphysics of the Will or freedom by itself is not adequate. A voluntary metaphysics could easily degenerate into mere arbitrariness in which everything is radically de-centered or in the tyranny that Berdyaev see in traditional ideas of God in which there is only one arbitrary being in the universe surrounded by slaves who unlike the Hegelian variety are always the innessential consciousnesses. Freedom must be accompanied by spirit.[9]

Berdyaev desires to create a complete metaphysics that is concerned with a freedom that has acquired value and meaning and not one that is simply chaotic as is the freedom of the primal will. The *Ungrund* or the primal groundlessness is the

---

[8]Berdyaev, *The Meaning of History*, p. 17

[9]Berdyaev, *The Realm of Spirit and the Realm of Caesar*, p. 102.

condition of movement in the Divine life. It is the condition of any notion of freedom. The process of the development of the divine life is secondary when compared with this primal groundlessness. The whole purpose of the world is the illumination of freedom, the realization of the potentialities of the *Ungrund* insofar as that is possible--that is the tragic destiny of God and man. "Will, that is, freedom, is the beginning of everything.. . . The *Ungrund*, . . . the abyss, the free nothingness.. . . The divine *Ungrund*, before its emergence, is in the eternity of the Divine Trinity."[10] History is the illumination of the *Ungrund*, it is the realization of the possibilities of freedom.

If Freedom is prior to God's intelligibility, then Berdyaev seems to contradict himself when he says that both freedom and Christ, the Godman, are the metaphysical bases of history. In *Dream and Reality*, Berdyaev writes that he considers himself to be in a tradition that stems from Heraclitus that maintains that the world is antinomic in character. And the ultimate antinomy seems to be the one between meaningfulness and *meonic* freedom. In the silence and bliss of the primal abyss the antinomy that exists between freedom and intelligibility is never posed. It is only in existence that the antinomy is posited. Berdyaev seeks to reconcile the paradox of the Divine Logos and Freedom. For Berdyaev, there must be a tie between the theogonic, cosmogonic, and anthropogonic processes because in his mind all share the same spiritual meaning.[11]

In the creative act something new breaks through in the form of an illuminated freedom. Berdyaev intends that the coming of Christ does not eliminate the chaotic element of freedom but gives it a goal toward which it can strive. Christ represents the divine-human dialectic. He is the concrete universal, he represents the synthesis of divine intelligibility with human freedom.[12] Berdyaev introduces the historical process into the profoundest reality, the Absolute. By doing so, Berdyaev is able to posit a voluntarism in which Will is supreme, and yet Logos, intelligibility, is supreme too, because it aims at the complete illumination of Will at the end of history.

Berdyaev discusses three types of freedom. The first is the original *meonic* freedom of the *Ungrund* which precedes and contains the others. The latter two freedoms pre-exist in the bliss of the unrealized *Ungrund*. In existence they possess a meaning and delineation as the negative freedom of chaos and the

---

[10]Berdyaev, *The Beginning and the End*, p. 107.

[11]Berdyaev, *The Meaning of History*, p. 61.

[12]The notion of the divine-human dialectic presented here is much like Whitehead's conception of the absolute and consequent nature of God in which the absolute meaning affects and is affected by finite meanings. At the basis of Whitehead's metaphysics is a conception of creativity as the primary metaphysical datum of the universe.

freedom of creativity that is directed toward a meaning. Both are, of course, related but the second has submitted itself to a purpose. The original freedom of the *Ungrund* is ungrounded and causeless, an irreducible mystery. Existence reveals this freedom in two aspects or forms. The first is wholly irrational, chaotic and destructive. It is the freedom of denial. In Boehme's imagery, this freedom is represented in the image of the dark center, the destroyer of all forms and is necessary to the light, affirming, creative center. The second type of freedom is freedom that accepts form, this is the origin of Being and God. As in Boehme, it is the balance of the two centers that makes the creative advance possible.

Berdyaev claims the first freedom by itself is a wholly negative freedom, nihilistic in character. The exercise of this freedom may turn to mere negation, self-assertion, and egoism. It may locate the center of the universe in the self and refuse relation with the Other, because it refuses to grant the Other equal reality with the self, because it merely negates the world outside of it. Thus, freedom may lead back to chaos, the creation of an atomistic society and the end of the possibility of human community. It can manifest itself in the desire to return to the chaos of the *Ungrund*, it is the denial of meaning and is in that sense demonic. But even egoism's desire to return to the chaos of the *Ungrund* is a denial of reality, for the egoist denies the unity of the pre-existential abyss and desires above all to maintain his own independent existence.

Berdyaev's two types of freedom are in some respects similar to the two types of freedom that Sartre envisages in his essay on "Cartesian Freedom." Sartre rejects God's freedom to create as magical and though he doesn't consider the possibility of balance between the two he would consider this also a magical desire. What Sartre calls "Cartesian Freedom," which he considers the only real form of freedom, relates to the first type of freedom. It is wholly negative, the capacity of the individual to refuse being, to refuse God. Berdyaev calls it a merely "formal freedom." In this sense Sartre's "Cartesian freedom" is not much more than a version of the traditional arguments for the "freedom of the will" that involved the negation of being--the product of the ontological conception of non-being that dates back to Augustine and to Neo-Platonism. Indeed, in Sartre's reasoning, Descartes shows that in the theological structure human freedom was only freedom for the negative, freedom for evil. Despite all protests to the contrary Sartre's discussion of freedom reveals the closeness of Sartre's ontology to the theological tradition he so adamantly attacks.

Berdyaev's second type of freedom requires the first, negative freedom. It combines the wholly irrational undetermined freedom with the possibility of meaning. In this sense it resembles the Kantian moral postulate that affords the possibility of choosing the moral law. It also resembles the creative freedom of the divine and Berdyaev calls it the freedom of the spirit. It is the freedom to create and thus is closer to the second type of freedom that Sartre considers magical because it depends on the possibility of permanent meaning which Descartes reserves for God. For Berdyaev it is the freedom of the Godman, freedom in relation to meaning. The freedom of the Godman is the most perfect freedom because, according to Berdyaev, it entails not only the creation of community in relation to a common ideal, but also the creation of the ideal itself, at least in respect to its manner of realization. But this type of freedom may degenerate into the worship of form and structure and thus the denial of freedom. The second type of freedom implies the possibility of the creation of new forms of thought, and the creation of new social forms. But if it denies the reality of the negative it also becomes distorted; it may lead to the creation of a society in which freedom is not tolerated, in which created meanings become idols.[13] This occurs when the nature of created forms is forgotten and the forms themselves are seen as eternal, permanent, unchanging attributes of Being that are independent of either human or divine will.[14]

This discussion of two types of freedom indicates the di-polar character of Berdyaev's metaphysics. Seen by itself, the first type of freedom, irrational freedom, tends to degenerate into isolated particularity, egoism and chaos. The

---

[13]Berdyaev, *Freedom and the Spirit*, pp. 133-136.

[14]Berdyaev expands this idea of the two kinds of freedom and the tragedy that is involved in their realization in *Freedom and the Spirit*.

> The existence of two kinds of freedom has been revealed to us and each possesses its fatal dialectic through which it degenerates into its opposite, that is, into slavery and necessity. Indeed the kind of freedom, which is in itself irrational and unfathomable, by no means alone guarantees that man will follow the right path, that, he will come to God, that truth will dominate in his life and that freedom will in the long run be supreme in the world. Unlimited force makes possible the most varied and opposite manifestations.
>
> The first kind of liberty does not necessarily mean an adherence to the life in truth and in God. It may mean the choice of the path of discord and hatred, of the affirmation of one part as against another, the way of disunion in the spiritual world, that is to say, of the way of evil. Initial freedom has not been sanctified in love, it has not been illuminated by the inner light of truth.
>
> When freedom precipitates man into the world of division and egotistical self-affirmation, he necessarily falls under the domination of the laws of natural necessity and becomes a slave of the lower elements. . ..
>
> The second kind of freedom can lead to necessity and authoritarianism, forced to submit to perceived truth and goodness. . ..

Berdyaev, *Freedom and the Spirit*, pp. 131-132.

second type of freedom, freedom that accepts form, can degenerate into mere form in which structures become idols and freedom and creativity are lost. This tension is indicative of the polar tension between individuality and unity, the one and the many in Berdyaev's thought. Berdyaev seeks to preserve the possibility of unity and meaning without sacrificing the independence of individual personality to mere oneness.

## God, Meaning, and Objectification

For Sartre the problem of the objectification of the for-itself was endemic to the whole program of metaphysics. For Berdyaev objectification represents an individual's failure to break out of the solitude of subjectivity.

> Man desires to go out from the closed circle of subjectivity and movement always takes place in two different and even opposite directions. Emergence from subjectivity proceeds by way of object-ification. This way leads out into society with its forms of universal obligation, it is the way of science with its laws of universal obliga-tion. On this path there takes place the alienation of human nature, its ejection into the object world: personality does not find itself. The other path is emergence from subjectivity through the process of transcendence. This is a passing over into the trans-subjective and not to the objective. This path lies in the deeps of existence, on this path there takes place the existential meeting with God, with other people, with the interior existence of the world. It is the path not of objective communication but of existential communion. Personality reaches full realization of itself only on this path.[15]

In this passage Berdyaev discusses the two ways in which the individual endeavors to break out of the solitude of his subjectivity. The first, objectification, is a failed attempt at breaking out of the self because it never gets beyond subjectivism, i.e., the subjectivism of living in the world of the created social forms that have become idols and barriers to freedom and communion with others. In objectificaition knowledge is limited to the categories of the understanding, so extreme objectivity is a form of excessive subjectivism. The second, the path of transcendence, represents the goal of intersubjectivity and the creation of existential communion in *Sobornost*. It represents the possibility of actual communion with the Other.

---

[15]Berdyaev, *Slavery and Freedom*, p. 29.

Objectification deals with all forms of creation of objects and not simply empirical knowledge. Like Nietzsche, Berdyaev thinks that even logical rules are ultimately parts of metaphysical systems. They are pragmatic in nature and have more to do with social convention and norms of communication than with ultimate truth.[16] Objectification is part of the tragedy of existence: in the creation of values from the pure potentialities of freedom, only some possibilities can be realized. The problem of objectification arises when interpretations of reality acquire a necessary character that eclipses the creativity and freedom they were meant to illuminate. He uses the traditional representation of God in Western theology as an example of this kind of objectification. In Berdyaev's characterization, the God of the Western theological tradition resembles the ideal Sartrean God, the in-itself-for-itself, a magical entity. He is that being who is both changing and unchanging, to whom the world is related but is not related to the world. He is the God to whom human beings are related but who is not related to them. The objectified notion of God is that of a despot.

This idea of God has been deeply impressed upon the Christian world and continues to exercise an influence even today. Man is the slave of God, the subject of an autocratic potentate, who must carry out his Master's will whatever it may be. The Fall is a formal transgression of the will of the Lord, an act of disobedience to the law of the Master of life.. . . God, personified as an autocrat and a despot with limitless power, demands from man, not the performance of a truth and a righteousness which have a meaning for him and some correspondence with his spiritual nature, but the carrying out of His formal will and of His orders, even if they are devoid of meaning and completely transcendent so far as human nature is concerned. Man, so it is held, must carry out the will of God without even asking in what this will consists and what it means. But the fulfilling of the will of God does not enlighten us as to its nature, and in this case the question is still put in a juridical fashion. If God is infinite love one consents to do His will, however difficult it may be; but if God is hate, one would refuse to do His will, even were it easier. In one's picture of God one cannot separate the idea of God from Intelligence, Love, Truth, Righteousness, and Beauty. Such a separation means slavery for the spirit, and God becomes simply an Asiatic despot.[17]

Like Kant, Berdyaev argues that God is not found in the natural world order. The only knowledge we have of God is afforded to us by our intuitions of

---

[16]Berdyaev, *The Beginning and the End*, pp. 74-75.

[17]Berdyaev, *Freedom and the Spirit*, p. 148.

transcendent values. God cannot be separated from ideas of "Intelligence, Love, Truth, Righteousness, and Beauty." If we do, we deprive the idea of God of any meaning. God is a concrete universal; transcendent values like love and truth have no independent existence of their own but are realized in the relations between individual entities. God is the ideal person, the embodiment of transcendent values. Berdyaev's personalism is close on this point to American Personalist Idealism. Just as Hegel in in *The Phenomenology of Mind* Berdyaev argues for a polar tension between ideal and concrete individual. The two are mutually dependent. The complete refusal of the ideal means the end of the individual, for it would lapse back into the chaos of *meonic* freedom. On the other hand the ideal does not exist independently of the individuals who seek to bring the ideal into actuality. The ideals such as Love, Truth, and Righteousness, like the Kantian categorical imperative, only exist in relation to concrete individuals, they arise from the relation between them. It is impossible for God to will the meaningless. This is not because He/She is limited by a standard of truth, goodness and beauty that exists independent of God as a Platonic ideal. But because God is truth, goodness, and beauty. Belief in freedom requires free action on the part of all members of the divine-human relation.

> God cannot will that which has no meaning because He is Meaning, and Meaning is the immanence of His idea. The Wisdom inherent in God cannot will bondage because that is an evil. God can only will freedom because it is His idea and his plan for the world. He cannot desire that man should carry out his will in a formal spirit of blind submission, because his will cannot be separated from the idea of God, of Meaning, of Truth, of Righteousness, and of Freedom, without which there is neither meaning nor Righteousness. Above all God expects freedom from man.[18]

Like Buber's I-thou relation, the relation of the divine and the human is beyond objectification, but unlike Buber, Berdyaev argues that we must give at least a symbolic metaphysical explanation to the characterization of the divine and the human and that this symbolic characterization represents an actual reality that lies below the ontological pluralism of existence. Because of the unity of our participation in freedom, each individual monad is potentially a mirror of the Other. In this respect it is not like Buber's I-Thou encounter but an interiorization and empathy with the Other. This is what Berdyaev attempts to do with his development of Boehme's *Ungrund* myth and the discussion of the dialectic of the divine

---

[18]Berdyaev, *Freedom and the Spirit*, p. 148.

and the human. But it must be recognized that the divine-human relationship is seen symbolically through the inescapable anthropocentrism of human reality.[19]

Berdyaev believes with Kant that all arguments that purport to prove the existence of God are unsuccessful. Thinking of God as a being is itself a confusion of an abstract mental object with a real existent. But he goes further than this to assert, like Sartre and Feuerbach, that even our concept of such a being is merely a subjective projection onto an imaginary supernatural plane of properties belonging to ourselves and society.[20] He further claims that this is unavoidable. We have a need to ask questions about the divine and to make images of the divine. When we attempt to bestow ultimate reality on our symbols we objectify the existential realities that we wish to understand.

Objectification arises from the consciousness' desire to break out of the closed circle of subjectivity, but acquiesces in the temptation to reduce reality to either immanence or transcendence and thus lose sight of reality's di-polar nature. There is a bond between the divine and the human. The infinite and the finite objectification affirms one of these principles in the abstract. This has occurred in much of traditional thinking about the infinite and the finite, the transcendent and the immanent, the impassive and passive. Theologians and metaphysicians have favored the infinite, transcendent, impassible, etc. over the finite, immanent and passible. But this can only be done in the abstract. Real life is the constant reminder of the inter-relation between the one and the other.[21] Thinkers like Sartre have moved to the other extreme, and though they point out the impossibility of thinking about the absolute and solely infinite, impassible and totally transcendent, they submit to a similar impossibility in committing to the finite opposite pole of the relation.

Berdyaev recalls a Platonic theme that implies the meaninglessness of the finite envisaged in-itself. When only the human is affirmed as real, the divine, authentic life comes to an end and its dramatic character exists no longer. Life

---

[19]Berdyaev, *The Divine and the Human*, p. 185.

[20]Berdyaev, *The Beginning and the End*, p. 10.

[21]In *The Divine and the Human* Berdyaev uses the example of immanence and transcendence to illustrate the interdependence of opposites.

> The transcendent becomes immanent and without its immanence it is abstract and lifeless. It is merely objectification at its limit. And equally the immanent postulates a process of transcendence. Pure immanentism which denies the transcendent is continuance in a circle which has no outlet.

Berdyaev, *The Divine and the Human*, p. 184.

implies tension between the immanent and the transcendent. When the transcendent is thought of exclusively as immanent and there is no transcendent mystery and remoteness, the immanent is deprived of life and content. In order for the immanent to have meaning there must be some conception of permanence, something that transcends the finite situation. But in order for the eternal, transcendent values to be they must appear in concrete finite existence.

The preservation of the tension between immanence and transcendence aims at the creation of an image of God that is free of the idea of the perfection of power and self-sufficiency that Sartre describes as the human desire to be god and Berdyaev calls sociomorphism. To Berdyaev the notion that God is sufficient unto himself, a potentate who wields unlimited "magical" power (in Sartre's sense), with all others dependent on Him and He dependent on no other, is idolatry. It represents a type of objectification of the divine that removes it from the realm of freedom and meaning and places it in the realm of necessity and power--asserting that the latter realm is prior to the former. It is only the conception of the suffering God, yearning for his Other, that preserves the dialectic between immanence and transcendence.

The similarity and difference between Sartre and Berdyaev is reflected in the discussion of God and meaning. Sartre writes that God is felt in our hearts in the same way that Descartes, in the *Third Meditation*, argued that God must exist. We have the notion of perfection in our minds though we ourselves are not perfect beings. The Cogito proves, for Descartes, the existence of God because I doubt, I hesitate between assertion and certainty, and this split in my knowledge implies imperfection. But I have within me at least an implicit understanding of perfection of that which I lack that would create the lost totality of being. According to Descartes, this idea of perfection cannot come from myself, since I am an imperfect being, but must have come to me from without, from perfection, from God. But, says Sartre, this is exactly the reason that God cannot exist. Consciousness is imperfect in relation to the brute perfection of the in-itelf. It is even less perfect before its projection of the magical being that could be both in-and-for-itself, both consciousness and substance. The perfect cannot be conscious. Sartre maintains that although human beings have something very like an a priori conception of God, this is actually the acute awareness of the lack of the negative character of freedom before the absolute being of the in-itself. The magical entity that human beings call God is the projection of consciousness' own would-be totality. But this totality is not possible because, by definition, consciousness is a lack; a conscious totality is impossible. Still the fundamental lack of totality in us intends some final unity and Sartre takes this unity to be the brute existence of being-in-itself. The lacked totality of consciousness announces God in our hearts as the fundamental human project; we try to imitate God. For Sartre, to be human is the attempt to be God. Man is fundamentally the desire to be the magical entity we call God.

It is Sartre's adoption of the Cartesian cogito, and the autonomous nature of consciousness that it implies, that dooms the program of any conception of totality.

The way he interprets the cogito through the ontological split of the in-itself and for-itself leads directly to his philosophical anthropology. Sartre sees human freedom attempting to break out of its individual negativity toward a positive creation of totality. But this desire to be God is ruled out by the ontological natures of the in-itself and the for-itself.

Both Sartre and Berdyaev agree that the desire for totality is the basic desire of human beings. But Berdyaev's understanding of the divine is fundamentally different from Sartre's. The lack of totality is the source, not only of human suffering, but of Divine suffering. The Divine is essentially related to the Other. God suffers along with human beings, sharing in their destiny.[22] The heart of suffering is the seeming impossibility of ever overcoming the gulf that separates human beings from totality. "In the depth of human suffering is the experience of insurmountability, inevitability, and irrevocability."[23]

It is apparent that for Berdyaev God cannot be the Absolute. What is Absolute is the restless, infinitely fertile *Ungrund*, but the Absolute then is nothing. God is the directive principle. The complexity and order of experience can only be explained through the existence of God: "freedom must be linked to a cosmic aim."[24] The doctrine of the *Ungrund* is a myth, figurative rather than literal, because freedom can never be described as an existent. Freedom is not an existent but is prior to and in all existents. "Free will in God is the *Ungrund* in God, the nothingness in Him."[25] At this level the *Ungrund* is really identical with God but it is also identical with all that is, in other words, with all beings.

God is the ultimate locus of creative action, and creative action is primordial freedom informed by purposefulness. The mythical assertion that the world is the creation of God means that the world is a process within the life of God, perpetual movement from potential to realized values. For Berdyaev God is not the single-handed constructor of values and creation, God is the creator of creators. The world order is derivative, arising from the creation of free existences. Creation is an ongoing process brought about through the agency of all "creatures," not an

---

[22]Berdyaev's metaphysics shows a basic similarity with Whitehead's process metaphysics on this point: "God is the fellow-sufferer who understands." Boehme says that suffering is the source of creation. Suffering is important in the divine as well as the human. "Here everything turns upon the union of the suffering of the human with the suffering of the divine, for in that the disruption and alienation between the human and the divine is overcome." Hartshorne, "Whitehead and Berdyaev: Is there Tragedy in God," p. 199.

[23]Berdyaev, *The Divine and the Human*, p. 70.

[24]Berdyaev, *Truth and Revelation*, p. 69.

[25]Berdyaev, *The Beginning and the End*, p. 108-109.

occurrence in the remote past. The divine aim is embodied only through the cooperation of independent beings. The meaning of reality is a combination of the anthropogonic and theogonic processes. Both God and man participate in the ever-changing creation of meaning. This meaning affects God as well as man. They are two complementary aspects of the essential creativity of reality.

God exists, in Berdyaev's account, as meaning, truth, righteousness, and creative freedom. God is the intelligible nature of the universe. But since Berdyaev's philosophy is anthropocentric in character, this intelligible meaning of the universe must also be personal.[26] Berdyaev asserts that the very idea of man can only be constructed because there is an idea of God. The divine image in man provides human existence with meaning and an end toward which all experience organizes itself. If the divine image in human beings is effaced, then the human cannot long endure. Human beings need meaning in order to be human; without any transcendent value meaning is not possible. Humanity returns to the chaos of freedom and loses the ability to create cosmos from chaos, being from freedom.[27]

Like Kant, Berdyaev affirms a relationship between freedom, meaning and the possibility of ethics. Both freedom and the basic categorical imperative that recognizes others as independent centers of freedom precede any empirical experience of the world. Evil results from the objectification of the Other, seeing the Other as a means toward the affirmation of the self and not an end in herself. This is why egoism constitutes the original source of sin and evil and leads to the annihilation of the being of the individual. It represents a turning away from the possibility of meaning which, by its nature, implies a shared meaning toward the creation of community. In egoism, the ego not only remains in individuality but implicitly denies the otherness of the Other and sees herself as the unique center of the universe. This is Sartre's "desire to be God." But this position cannot be maintained. If meaning is denied the individual cannot maintain his place in being. "The natural man cannot preserve his qualitative originality, his unique place in the hierarchy of being, when he finally denies the spiritual man and loses the basis of support which he possesses in the other world."[28]

But this possibility of meaning and the essential respect for the Other is not simply the product of practical reason, as in Kant. Berdyaev thinks that the noumenal reality of the Other can be known through experience. The experience is spiritual in nature and tied to the emotional and volitional sides of our

---

[26] The world has fallen away from the principal of the integral man. The key to Berdyaev's cosmology is the inner identity of spirit and nature. Objectification of the cosmos is a fallen idea of it. It is fallen as it was for Boehme's conception through bad imagination. See Berdyaev, *Freedom and the Spirit*, p. 162.

[27] Berdyaev, *Freedom and the Spirit*, p. 217.

[28] Berdyaev, *Freedom and the Spirit*, p. 217.

humanness, not only to reason. The possibility of metaphysics arises from this intuitive awareness of the Other that Berdyaev explains mythically through the image of the original unity of all existents in the pre-existential abyss of the *Ungrund*.[29]

Berdyaev thinks that Kant, better than any other philosopher, has shown the priority of freedom. But Kant denies the possibility of any experience of the Other. And so, Berdyaev turns to Boehme to explain what he thinks is the noumenal experience of the Other, of the thing-in-itself that is the foundation of metaphysics. Berdyaev follows Kant in claiming the categories of pure theoretical reason can only deal with phenomena but thinks that the reality of the other's freedom is more than a postulate of practical reason. It is knowledge grounded in an empathetic experience of the Other.

---

[29]This is Berdyaev's most important disagreement with Kant and it reflects the mystical element of Berdyaev's thought. Unlike Kant, Berdyaev thinks that the noumenal world can be known through experience, but that experience is spiritual in nature.

Kant recognized that there is a metaphysical need implanted in our nature; it is deeply inherent in reason. But he repudiates spiritual experience as a basis of a possible metaphysics. Or rather, more accurately, he reduces spirituality to practical ethical postulates which open up another world to view. But Kant would not acknowledge outright that non-conceptual, spiritual, existential apprehension of a noumenon is a possibility. He was right only in a negative sense: the whole apparatus of our knowledge by concepts is applicable only to the world of appearances. . ..

The criticism, however, of purely intellectual contemplation seems to me to be true. If intuitive knowledge is possible it cannot be purely intellectual, it can only be integral, concrete, that is to say it must also be emotional and volitional. Thinking and knowing are always emotional, and the emotional is the deciding element. Judgement presupposes freedom and a choice of the will. Judgments of value are emotional and volitional. It was a fundamental mistake of Kant that he recognized sensuous experience, in which appearances are the data, but he did not recognize spiritual experience, of which the data are noumenal. Man remains, as it were, corked up in the world of phenomena; he is unable to break out of it, or able to break out only by way of practical postulates. Kant regarded man as, from man's point of view, an appearance; man was not revealed to himself as a noumenon.

Berdyaev, *The Beginning and the End*, pp. 14-15.

### The Microcosm and Knowledge of the Other

Berdyaev adopts another Boehmeian myth to explain personality, the myth of the microcosm. According to Boehme the microcosm is the perfect mirroring of the universe within the self, perfect openness to the whole of reality, the Other, and God. The truly personal represents what could be called, in Hegelian terms, a concrete universal. The success of the project of personality depends on how well the individual is able to integrate the world within herself. There is no sense of a Sartrean being-in-itself here because there is no ontological separation of being and personality.

All egos resemble each other in that each is unique and distinct. Each Ego is an entity, a world in itself, postulating the existence of other Egos without seeking to identify itself with them. The Ego I have in mind is the extra-social and non-objective Ego. The Ego's existence precedes its materialization in this world, and yet it is inseparable from the existence of the other Self and of other Egos.[30]

The uniqueness and distinctness of every Ego is a condition of human freedom, so Berdyaev insists that each ego is a world in itself, a microcosm. The ego is separate, its discreteness precedes its materialization and yet it is inseparable from the existence of the Other Self and of other Egos. Berdyaev wants to show that the ego is completely free, a microcosm. It is self-determined; yet it cannot be in solitude and isolation from others. The Ego postulates the existence of other Egos. In knowing them it knows, and thus illuminates, the irrational basis of freedom which it shares with the Others. As its openness to the Other increases, so does its self-knowledge.

Self-consciousness implies consciousness of others; it is social in the depths of its metaphysical nature. Man's life, insofar as it is the expression of the Ego's, presupposes the existence of other men, of the world, and of God. The Ego's absolute isolation, its refusal to communicate with anything outside it, with the Thou, would be suicidal. The Ego's existence is threatened whenever it denies the potential existence within itself of another Ego, or of the Thou.[31]

But in postulating the existence of other the ego Berdyaev does not prove the existence of the Other. The preceding explanation seems to jump to the conclusion

---

[30]Nicholas Berdyaev, *Solitude and Society*, Trans. Geaorge Reavey (London: Geofrey Bles, 1938), p. 90.

[31]Berdyaev, *Solitude and Society*, p. 90

that the Other is known to the ego. I think at this point Berdyaev's mysticism and existentialism are apparent. As a proof, Berdyaev's description of the microcosm as the basis of knowledge of the other fails abominably. It doesn't even work very well as phenomenological description. But I think this is to misunderstand what he is attempting. Here, as elsewhere Berdyaev, once again, shows his debt to Kant and Boehme. From the point of view of Berdyaev's Kantianism the Other is a postulate of practical reason. One cannot conceive of practical action otherwise. The experience of the microcosm, however, is based in Boehme's mysticism. It is founded on the experience of communion with the Other. And this experience of the free relation to the Other is outside of the objective realm. In order to accept Berdyaev's "vision" on this point, as on many others, we have to share his desire for communion. Berdayev would argue that as the highest form of knowledge, this belief cannot be coerced but can only be chosen freely. As with other parts of Berdyaev's system no adequate proof does or could exist. Berdyaev only tries to show the possibility is there and that it is a possibility that can be chosen.

Knowledge of the microcosm, self-knowledge, is the highest form of knowledge, but true self-knowledge is also knowledge of the whole, because the self is really the microcosm or mirror of the whole. Truth is in the depths of the subject. As for Sartre, the ego, the self, is a creation. There is no "moi profond," but only will, a will that desires to express itself. So just as God is creativity, the expression of to will to be the individual ego is a microcosm and microtheos. It arises from freedom into being. Since the roots of the subject are in the noumenal or spiritual, they belong to the relation of freedom and meaning. The ego is potentially personal and potentially relational; it contains within itself the unrealized knowledge of the whole. "But it [self-knowledge] is within me in a drowsy state and the awakening of it within me is an awakening of truth."[32] This sounds somewhat like Socratic self-knowledge and the Platonic doctrine of recollection but there are important differences. There is no world of ideal rational forms in Berdyaev's conception of self-knowledge. Rather, I contain within myself, at the deepest level, the shared source of all Being, noumenal freedom. What I have to do is to realize it in actuality.

Knowing the self is the basis of knowledge. But Berdyaev does not make self-analysis the method for the arrival at knowledge of the self, rather knowledge is a communal activity. It is only arrived at in communion with the Other. "The We is a qualitative content immanent in the Ego, for every Ego is invariably related not only to the Thou but also to the multiple mankind."[33] Through common grounding in the freedom of the *Ungrund*, the We is in an unrealized sense already present in the Ego. For Berdyaev the Other, as rooted in freedom, is already

---

[32]Berdyaev, *The Beginning and the End*, p. 47.

[33]Berdyaev, *Solitude and Society*, p. 107.

immanent within the self, for both have their source in the pure potentiality of the *Ungrund* and their goal in the Godman, though the way and the extent to which they realize this goal may be different for each individual. One knows his own personality through that of the Other. The personality cannot be understood except through communion. This is the basic importance of the overcoming of solitude.[34]

As we have seen, Berdyaev contrasts this trans-subjective way of communion with the way of objectification. In trans-subjective awareness he finds within himself a reflection of the inner spiritual life of each concrete existent in the cosmos as it arises from the *Ungrund*. This trans-subjective awareness is a type of empathy possible through the common experience of noumenal freedom in which all beings have their source. Not only people, but also animals, plants, minerals, stars, forests and seas each have an "inner existence," an "inner life" of their own.[35] Berdyaev already includes all these, as a microcosm, within himself. Instead of trying to know something objectively, he "ought to be that something," consciously mirroring within himself its noumenal or spiritual reality.[36] The more this happens, the more consciously universal he himself becomes and the more he is in communion with all that is Other. In contrast with Sartre, Berdyaev thus not only claims that communion is possible, but that it involves the highest form of knowledge.

Berdyaev does not reject objective knowledge, however. He regards it as a pragmatic method for approaching the object world. The problem is that in the objective stance we fail to see the object world as symbolic. Like Sartre in his account of knowledge and possession, Berdyaev sees objective knowledge as an effort to create the object and possess it. In this sense it is a transcendence of subjectivity that is bound to fail for the same reason that it failed in the Sartrean interpretation, because of the existence of the Other. In *Solitude and Society*, Berdyaev cites Freud's explanation of narcissism as one pattern of objective knowledge. The Ego splits and projects itself so that it becomes its own object. In the objectification of the world everything is reduced to an object to be encountered and possessed, but the Ego only possesses its own fantasy projection. Real escape from subjectivity fails.[37] But knowledge does not end with the failure of objective knowledge. Objective knowledge points to something beyond the objectified world and subjectivity. The light of the Logos is reflected even in the

---

[34]Berdyaev, *Solitude and Society*, p. 110.

[35]Berdyaev, *Slavery and Freedom*, p. 94. *Solitude and Society*, p. 112.

[36]Berdyaev, *Dream and Reality*, p, 287.

[37]Berdyaev, *Solitude and Society* p. 113.

general principles of objective knowledge because all systems are inherently the creations of human Egos.[38]

The nature of knowledge is conjugal. It can be either simply erotic or it can approach Christian love. On this point, the discussion of love and knowledge, Sartre and Berdyaev approach each other. (Although Sartre would certainly not accept the title Christian love he might accept Berdyaev's understanding of Christian love as the free relation between persons.) Through knowledge, the individual aims at breaking out of the circle of closed subjectivity toward the Other. In his description of the desire to be God, Sartre reduces sexual desire and knowledge to the desire to possess. Sexual desire and objective knowledge reflect the effort to create a link between the inner I and the outside object. They wish to consume the object and yet leave it there in its entirety. Berdyaev, like Sartre, sees sexuality as the effort to overcome dividedness. The difficulty with simple erotic love is it sees the other as an object of possession and thus dividedness can never be overcome. The Other is always a brute object that cannot be consumed by me and still retain its independence. Both Sartre and Berdyaev would agree that objective knowledge and erotic love fail to overcome the gulf that separates the self and the other. Sartre, in the radical conversion passages points to community beyond the desire to be God in free relation to the Other. Berdyaev argues that communion with the Other, the Thou, is possible because the We is already potentially within us. Like Sartre, Berdyaev admires Hegel's discussion of the Master-Slave dialectic. But Berdyaev is truer to Hegel's idea of development (though he is opposed to Hegel's ideal of Absolute spirit). Berdyaev accepts the idea that one comes to know the self in the Other. "The essential quality of love . . . consists in the discovery of another's unique personality, in the fact that the personality expands only in relation to another personality."[39] Personality is created in relation to the Other. It is only through love that one breaks out of solitude into communion because in Christian love one approaches the Other as a person, a completely unique Thou.

> The personality and love are intimately related, for love transforms the Ego into a personality. Only love can effect that complete fusion with another being which transcends solitude. The pursuit of knowledge cannot achieve this unless it be inspired by love.[40]

In love the self emerges from its subjectivity in quest of the Other Ego as opposed to another impersonal or collective Self. "But the Ego is only an embryonic

---

[38]Berdyaev, *Solitude and Society*, p 117.

[39]Berdyaev, *Solitude and Society*, p. 195.

[40]Berdyaev, *Solitude and Society*, p. 120.

personality; to become one it must commune with the Thou and the We."[41] The communion that Berdyaev seeks is akin to mystical ecstasy and is not found in human friendship alone but also exists in the communion with nature. What is necessary is that being able to get past the objective and possessive status of the object world to an empathetic relation with the Other. The key to this is in the idea of the We, the fundamental connection of all beings in the pre-existential abyss. Communion requires the free openness of each individual to the Other. In the mythical terms that Berdyaev used in describing the relation between God and man it is the free response to God's call.

> *Communion implies reciprocity:* it can never be one sided; there can be no communion in unrequited love. In a state of communion both the Ego and the Thou are active, whereas there can be no reciprocity in the symbolism of objective communication. In order to achieve communion on an existential plane, it is necessary for the Ego to commune with another Ego, which must also be a Thou, an active Thou. The Ego remains isolated as long as it can only communicate with the object; its solitude can only be vanquished by the communion of personalities, of the Ego and the Thou, in the innermost depths of the We. [Berdyaev's emphasis].[42]

The movement from solitude to communion is dangerous and entails the constant possibility of objectification and, because the Other is free, of rejection. The ego's solitude keeps it safe from the world and objects, from the constant danger of objectifying the Other, of turning the Other into my object or of reading the Other through the eyes of society. Still this solitude can and must be transcended. Solitude is only overcome when the Ego identifies itself with the Other in love and friendship. But like Berdyaev's interpretation of the myth of the Fall, there is no way of avoiding the tragedy that is associated with freedom and existence. Conflict with Others is unavoidable.

> But there is no way of avoiding such ruptures, however painful they may be, once man has embarked upon the path of spiritual progress; for solitude can only be transcended on the spiritual plane, only in mystic experience, wherein all things participate in the Ego and the Ego participates in all things.[43]

---

[41]Berdyaev, *Solitude and Society*, p. 114.

[42]Berdyaev, *Solitude and Society*, p. 111.

[43]Berdyaev, *Solitude and Society*, p. 124

The experience of love is, for Berdyaev, ultimately a mystical and intuitive one. Because it is an experience of the noumenal reality, it is by its nature beyond the categories of pure theoretical reason. The Other is approached immediately but our description of the encounter is always in the language of myth and symbol. It is the same in speaking about God. The Other can only be known in communion. God can be known, but his being known is inexhaustible in this sense--he is both knowable and unknowable. This is true of others who are free and in the image of God. "The process of knowing God is a movement of the spirit which has no end."[44]


**Godmanhood**

Freedom and intelligibility, immanence and transcendence are embodied in what Berdyaev calls the "real myth about man," Godmanhood.[45] The Russian philosophical doctrine of Godmanhood is the basis of Berdyaev's personalism. Godmanhood entails the relation of the divine and the human in the person of Christ. The idea originates in the nineteenth century Russian philosopher Vladimir Solovyev's *Lectures on Godmanhood*. Solovyev argued that humanity can assume Divinity only in the absolute totality of the Godman, Christ. For Solovyev, the Godman is necessarily collective and universal.[46] Because of its emphasis on cosmic unity, Berdyaev found Solovyev's version of Godmanhood too collectivist and verging on pantheism. Instead, Berdyaev sought a form of relation of the divine and the human which would preserve the integrity of the participants in the relation while still being universal in character. He called it the theandric process. Theandric--taken from the Greek theos, god, and aner, man--refers to the union of the divine and the human. The idea hinges on the notion that the universal must also be concrete and individual and encompass both the finite and infinite, immanent and transcendent, passive and impassive poles of experience. It is also based on a conception of a concrete universal. The universal must be truly universal and also concrete and particular; this union is found in the Godman, Christ. "In the eternal ideal of him, man is rooted in God-manhood and linked with the God-man.. . . Humanity exists in eternity and ought to be realized in

---

[44]Berdyaev, *Solitude and Society*, p. 124.

[45]Berdyaev, *Slavery and Freedom*, p. 50.

[46]Vladimir Solovyev *The Lectures on Godmanhood*, trans. R.M. French (London: Dobson, 1948), p. 61.

174

time."[47] The birth of man in God is a part of the theogonic process, something that occurs within the divine life. Eternal man is the eternal idea of man, the eidos, the ideal of man, Christ or Godmanhood. Humanity exists in eternity in Christ.[48] As Christ is the eidos or eternal man, man "ought" to realize this image in time. ". . . The Son is not only God but man in the absolute and spiritual sense of the world, that is, the Eternal Man."[49] Christ is thus the source of intelligibility, the ideal of the human and is the meaning of history. Godmanhood is an eternal ideal; in it the ideal of personality is expressed. This ideal is dialectically related to the world and must be realized in different fashions according to the historical epoch. In it freedom is not suppressed by the existence of ideal meaning, but given a creative character. Through the dialectical relation of the ideal and freedom, the possibilities of freedom come to realization. The development of this ideal in the world process is the meaning of history.[50]

---

[47]Berdyaev, *The Divine and the Human*, p. 111-112.

[48]Berdyaev, *The Divine and the Human*, p. 182.

[49] Berdyaev, *Freedom and the Spirit*, p. 137.

[50]In *Slavery and Freedom*, Berdyaev describes the relation of the divine and the human with reference to the creation of personality which he considers to be the ultimate value. Personality is created as the individual moves from the egoism of his particular desire to relation with the Other.

The mystery of Christ does not lend itself to rationalization; it is the mystery of the paradoxical union of the one and the many. Christ represents the whole of humanity. He is the universal Man and at the same time a concrete individual Man, in space and time. The mystery of Christ throws a light upon the mystery of human personality. The individual is only particularized; he belongs to the world of the many. Personality on the other hand is connected with the One, with the image of the One, but in an individually particularized form. Precisely for this reason personality is not a part of the world of the many in which everything is particularized.. . .
The hypostatization of man, the endowment of him with the qualities of personality is the real myth about man and it also requires imagination. In accord with this myth man is not a part, he is not particularized, because he is the image of the One and is a universe. This is the God-likeness of man; but the other side of this God-likeness is the man-likeness of God. This is true anthropomorphism, not false. For this reason alone a meeting of man and God is possible, a relation between man and God. Man is personality because God is

**The Ego and Personality**

Like Kant, Berdyaev locates freedom in the individual. If the freedom of the *Ungrund* is the starting point of Berdyaev's metaphysics and philosophy of history, then the individual ego is the starting point of Berdyaev's epistemology. Berdyaev maintains that our knowledge of reality is fundamentally anthropocentric.[51] The ego represents no more for Berdyaev than original existence, the existence of the individual in relation to the world. Viewed against the background of his use of the *Ungrund* image and his contention that freedom is both prior to and the basic datum of existence, Berdyaev's conception of the ego becomes clear. It is the primitive starting point of possibility. As in Sartre's view, in order for there to be choice there must be limitation, negation, and individuality. The finite individual confronts his situation. Also as with Sartre's view, this starting point is ever changing rather than permanent and unchanging. But it is nevertheless monadic in that it is existentially independent of other individuals. So like Sartre's Berdyaev's thought is monadic in character. And, somewhat like Kant's view, reality consists of separate centers of freedom which constitute appearances between them. The ego is the starting place for Berdyaev's epistemology. In itself it is not personality or community, but only a center of free action.

> The Ego is primitive; it can neither be deduced from nor reduced to anything. . ... It is not true to say, "I think therefore I am;" but rather "I am surrounded on all sides by impenetrable infinity, and therefore I think." I am, in the first place. The ego belongs to the sphere of existence. The Ego is primarily existential. . . it is synonymous with freedom.[52]

When Berdyaev says that the ego belongs to the sphere of existence and is primarily existential he is alluding in Kantian fashion to the conception of the primary reality of existence/primal freedom as the thing-in-itself. Like Hegel and

---

personality and **vice versa**. But personality presupposes the existence of its other. It has a relation not only to the One but also to the many. How can this be in the case of the personality of God? Personality is an existential center and in it is a capacity to feel sorrow and joy. There is no such thing as personality if there is no capacity for suffering.

Berdyaev, *Slavery and Freedom*, p. 50.

[51]Berdyaev, *The Beginning and the End*, pp. 8-13.

[52]Berdyaev, *Solitude and Society*, p. 87.

Schelling, Berdyaev develops a conception of the ego based in an irrational and willful principle that is illuminated in the course of history. In both seeing the will as the basis of the ego and in treating the metaphysical principles of freedom and existence in relation to a doctrine of the ego, Berdyaev's thought resembles Fichte. But Berdyaev criticizes Fichte's conception of the ego for two reasons: first, because it is universal and not individual; and second, because it does not recognize a concrete Other but sees the Other only as the non-ego.[53] Berdyaev claims that the German idealists lost the impetus given to them by Kant because they objectify and universalize the subject.[54] Berdyaev's notion of the ego presupposes the existence of others.

For Berdyaev, the fundamental problem of existential philosophy is the development of personality from the primitive point of view which is the ego. One is an ego before she becomes a personality. "The Ego is primary and undifferentiated; it does not postulate a doctrine of the personality. The Ego is postulated ab initio; the personality is propounded." The ideal meaning of the ego is to realize personality: this involves a struggle and is by no means a necessary development in the life of the individual. "Many rather renounce their personality than endure the suffering which its realization involves."[55]

There is, says Berdyaev, a double ego in man, the deep ego which is creative and potentially personal and the false ego that is created by the passions and the imagination which denies the reality of the Other and God. In Berdyaev's conception, similar to Sartre's discussion of the magical character of the ego in *Transcendence of the Ego*, the false ego is created in order to secure some sort of changeless character for the individual. By granting the false ego primary existence, the imagination denies the fundamental reality of change and freedom and attempts to provide its present state with a necessary character. This created fantasy (projected as uncreated and necessary) is an example of the desire to be God. But Berdyaev's position once again diverges from Sartre's because of the possibility of meaning and value that is inherent from the starting point of Berdyaev's metaphysics. Like Sartre, there is for Berdyaev a free, creative, willful, changing, monadic point of view. Sartre calls this point of view consciousness and Berdyaev, the deep ego. But unlike Sartre, Berdyaev maintains there is also the possibility of a real but created being that recognizes the free and changing character of reality but attempts, through the willful creation of value, to create unity over time. This Berdyaev calls personality. Personality is created and represents a struggle against the multitude of false egos created by the imagination. "Chaos stirs within man; he is connected with the chaos which is hidden

---

[53]Berdyaev, *Solitude and Society*, p. 67.

[54]Berdyaev, *The Divine and the Human*, p. 26.

[55]Berdyaev, *Solitude and Society*, p. 159.

behind the cosmos."[56] Out of the possibilities of chaos are born false, illusory egos. Every passion that man possesses can be reified into an object ego. The creation of personality is a creative act that involves the unification of being. It is the creation of the unity of the person with the cosmos. "Man is in greater need of psycho-synthesis than of psycho-analysis."[57]

Berdyaev resembles Sartre in as much as he asserts that both egos, the false and the personal, are the creation of the human imagination in its aim at totality. But because Berdyaev's anti-ontology is fundamentally different from Sartre's ontology, they come to opposite conclusions. Sartre denies the possibility of an authentic ego. Berdyaev maintains that a distinction can be made between a false and a true ego. Both are created by the monadic center of freedom that is the deep ego. The created false ego represents an attempt to assert the self as the ultimate unchangeable individual which is a denial of reality. The created personal ego aims at the creation of unity of the personality with itself and other persons across the flow of change and represents a possible fulfillment of the desire for totality in an authentic fashion. The possibility of an authentic ego only exists if freedom is not simply non-being, the radical negation of being, but the *Ungrund*, the no-thing or limitless potentialities of being and nothingness. It is possible to imagine the creation of unity that pre-exists in the mind of God as an ideal and in freedom as a possibility. The creative advance is the movement toward cosmos. In fact there can only be an advance because of the pre-existing possibility of the goal.

Personality is created by the individual in relation with meaning. The spiritual principle alone constitutes personality and gives it a permanent center. Personality is created by the logos. "The personality postulates further the existence of a dark, violent and irrational principle. . .." which is the destructive nature of negative freedom that allows for the possibility of creative change in relation to being.[58] But without the logos, without the spiritual principle, personality disintegrates.[59] The Ego as the independent principle of freedom returns to the nothingness of the original abyss, if it is not directed toward intelligibility. Berdyaev calls the spiritual principle the logos, because it ultimately refers to the perfect prototype of meaning, the Godman. Personality relies on a transcendent truth. It is the triumph of meaning over chaos. It represents the illumination and exploration of the possibilities of freedom. The personality is the symbol of the

---

[56]Berdyaev, *The Divine and the Human*, p. 110.

[57]Berdyaev, *The Divine and the Human*, p. 134.

[58]Berdyaev, *Solitude and Society*, p. 161.

[59]Berdyaev, *The Destiny of Man*, p. 189.

creation of value, it is spirit, and in itself valuable. In fact the recognition of the value of the Other, of personality, is the foundation of all value.

> The personality . . . also postulates the soul's ultimate and everlasting triumph over this irrational principle. But although it is rooted in the unconsciousness, the personality implies an acute self-consciousness of its unity in the midst of change. It is sensitive to all the currents of social and cosmic life and open to a variety of experience, but it takes care not to lose its identity in society or the cosmos.[60]

Personality represents the creation of the realm of the spirit. "Spirit is the realm in which the divine and the human are united."[61] Spirit emanates from God but is not just a divine creation; it is rather an effusion of meaning in reality. In this sense Spirit is the creative force itself. It is the dialectical relation of the divine and the human. Meaning is offered to the freedom of the individual ego but Spirit is the creation of new forms in the interaction between intelligibility and freedom. Spirit is related both to Deity and to the primal existential freedom of the *Ungrund*. This is the fundamental paradox of spirit. ". . . it is a Divine emanation, and at the same time it can reply to the Deity in terms not dictated by it.. . . it is freedom in God and from God.[62]"

## Evil and Objectification: The Denial of the Divine and the Human

The denial of the possibility of shared meaning with the Other is the denial of meaning. According to Berdyaev, it amounts to the total objectification of reality. The Judeo-Christian myth of the Fall represents both a fall up and down, a descent from unity into plurality but also an ascent to self-consciousness and the possibility of conscious totality. In the Fall man asserts his individual nature.[63] But, as in Boehme's description of egoism, he attempts to become a center in him and denies the Other as another. He objectifies the world and the Other, turns them from spirit into things. It is only now that the nothing which is not evil

---

[60]Berdyaev, *Solitude and Society*, p. 161.

[61]Berdyaev, *Freedom and the Spirit*, p. 47.

[62]Berdyaev, *Spirit and Reality*, p. 34.

[63]Berdyaev, *The Meaning of History*, p. 78.

becomes evil. Rebellion against God is a return to non being which assumes, for the rebel, the form of illusary being. He places reality in objectification.[64]

Evil is the isolation of the self from the Other, God and meaning. Evil is the desire for life apart from God and hence from all meaning and reality. It seeks to invest non-being, chaos, with the character of being and meaning. Basically it asserts that all meaning is completely determined by the individual ego. It originates in freedom and the individual asserts himself, his ego, as the center of being. But this self-assertion means the end of the freedom of the spirit and the establishment of the tyranny of necessity. Objectification implies slavery to the myths created by the ego in its attempt to center itself in the world. Human beings create myths to please their egocentricity. They create myths about nature, being, their family, country, their class, church, or themselves in order to improve their position. In essence all of these myths imply a natural necessity in being that enslaves and isolates the individual or the group from the rest of being. The only form of unity that now exists is unity of the group in opposition to the others. Evil implies the loss of unity and disintegration of being, followed by violent conflict between the separated elements. "The world breaks up into isolated individual units unknown to one another and therefore hostile." Real unity of choice becomes impossible and the disparate elements can only be united by compulsion. Apart from meaning everything falls into chaos.

> Apart from God everything is alien and remote and is held together simply by force. Satan by dint of his superior spiritual powers has succeeded in leading men astray by suggesting to them that they will become as gods. But by the pursuit of evil and by the substitution of himself for God, man, so far from becoming the God-like being of his dreams, becomes the slave of his lower nature, and, at the same time, by losing his higher nature becomes subject to natural necessity and ceases to be spiritually determined from within.[65]

The preceding strongly resembles Sartre's negative description of the desire to be God. Man seeks to be the God-like being of his dreams. He aims at Feuerbachian projection of himself as the center of all meaning. Like Sartre, Berdyaev sees this as the "natural" attitude of human beings. Also, as was the case for Sartre, he thinks that the desire to be God represents the loss of freedom in the slavery of necessity. Love is not natural for human beings. It is natural for human beings to hate and kill one another. It is a mistake to say that equality and freedom are the primitive states of mankind. They do not belong to the natural or

---

[64]Berdyaev, *The Destiny of Man*, pp. 25-26.

[65]Berdyaev, *Freedom and the Spirit*, p. 169.

phenomenal world but the noumenal world of the spirit. In the natural phenomenal state human beings are fragmented. But Berdyaev believes that the ideal of God as the goal and as the initial creative and ordering agent of freedom is necessary if any kind of value or community between individuals is possible. "Real union among human beings is evidence of the divine-human link. People can be united only in Godmanhood, not in the human; a unity of the human does exist but it is a spiritual unity, a unity of destiny."[66]

The other side of the denial of meaning is the denial of the human in the affirmation of the transcendent. This is the mistake made in much of the metaphysical and theological tradition. The denial of the divine human link is thus also a denial of both humanity and God. Berdyaev maintains that when there is no dialogue between God and man there is also no link between them. Man no longer worships God, he worships the first principle of metaphysics which is no longer God but an impersonal image. The concrete living creature is a higher value than the abstract idea of the good or any metaphysical principle, any principle of well being and the like. The denial of the human is as much a denial of Godmanhood as is the denial of the divine.

Thus the denial of the divine and the human occurs in two fashions: in the dissolution of man before God in which man is a mere nothing, and, in the audacity of man where he denies the human and becomes the superman, God. Both are examples of the desire to be God. The first is a projection of the human

---

[66]Berdyaev has insisted that all our knowledge is fundamentally anthropocentric. But this does not mean that the myths created by human beings have to be egocentric. Humanity centered on itself alone is the denial of any kind of transcendent meaning and ceases to be human.

> There is a true and a false criticism of humanism (humanitarianism). Its fundamental falsity lies in the idea of the self-sufficiency of man, of the self-deification of man, that is to say in the denial of Godmanhood. The aspiration of man and his attainment of the heights presuppose the existence of something higher than man. And when man is left with himself, shut up in his humanity, he makes himself idols without which he cannot rise. Upon this the true criticism of humanism is founded. The false criticism on the other hand denies the positive significance of humanistic experience and leads to the denial of the humanity of man. It may lead to the brutalizing of him when an inhuman god is worshipped. But an inhuman god is in no degree better and is indeed even worse than a godless man.

Berdyaev, *The Divine and the Human*, p. 115.

desire to control and eliminate freedom projected in the ideal of an ontological tyrant. The second isolates the individual from meaning or the rest of humanity. In either case the human is denied and destroyed. The theological traditon has destroyed the human in the first sense by subjecting humanity to the image of God as an imperial despot. Both Marx and Nietzsche destroy the human in the second fashion: Nietzsche in the creation of superhuman individuals that destroy the link between themselves and the rest of humanity; and Marx in the vision of a perfect humanity that is only achieved within a Utopia based on the suffering of the billions of the de-humanized who precede it.

### Personality as the Unity of History: The Microcosm or Concrete Universal

Personality is the affirmation of both the divine and the human, of the dipolar nature of reality. It is the effort at the creation of unity, of meaning, out of the chaos of freedom. Without such an affirmation of both meaning and freedom there is no unity or totality in the world, only the meaninglessness of unlimited possibility or absolute determinism. ". . . outside personality everything is partial, even the world itself is partial.. . . Such is the whole objectivized world."[67] The individual is an existential center. All of the universal categories of existence and of knowledge are only to be found in concrete individuals, they have no existence of their own. "The cosmos, mankind, nation, etc, are to be found in human personality as in an individualized universe or microcosm."[68] Objectification is the creation of myths that place ideal generalities into the world of external reality, granting them a kind of independent and hierarchical existence of their own. This is the meaning of the myth of the fall--the subordination of the human to impersonal, objectivized categories. The impersonal is fragmented, it creates the two worlds of the internal and the external, the subjective and objective. The impersonal is, therefore, always partial.

The personal aims at creating a unity of being. "There is no wholeness, no universality of any kind outside personality, it exists only within personality."[69] T        o understand why Berdyaev thinks that the personal aims at totality while the impersonal loses it, it is necessary to see what he means by personality. As we have seen, Berdyaev adopts another Boehmeian myth to explain personality, the myth of the microcosm. The microcosm for Boehme is something like a universe

---

[67]Berdyaev, *Slavery and Freedom*, pp. 41-42.

[68]Berdyaev, *Slavery and Freedom*, p. 42.

[69]Berdyaev, *Slavery and Freedom*, p. 41-42.

within a universe or, better, the perfect mirroring of the universe within the self, perfect openness to reality. Thus, the personal represents what could be called a concrete universal. The success of the project of personality depends on how well the individual is able to integrate the world within her. There is no sense of a Sartrean being-in-itself here because there is no ontological separation of Being and personality. The world is created in the free action between separate centers of freedom, consciousnesses, in a dialectical fashion.

The way that universals and particulars are united in reality is not the same way they are united in thought. The universal is always located in individuals. Spirit is activity by which the individual entity incorporates more of the universal into the unity of its experience. This movement is the ground for experience of meaning and value. God represents the highest possible incorporation of experience. Instead of being the most self-sufficient, God is the most relational. It is thus that God is the most universal of individuals. We realize the universal in the creative acts of love, morality, relation, cognition and artistic creation. Reality, thus, is a plurality of separate agencies each of which embodies supra-individual relations and values and moves toward the self-realization of a united meaning that transcends each individual.

Berdyaev's personalism is monadic in character. Each individual is radically free in incorporating and interpreting the world that presents itself before him. This world is the product of the interpretation of other conscious beings as well. Creative activity is the incorporation and interpretation of as much experience as possible.

> He who creates is a microcosm . . .. The world is my creative act.
> Another man is my creative act. God is my creative act. . .. Beauty
> in the world is a creative act not an objective reality. Creative
> transformation must therefore go on all the time.[70]

Spirit is not an epiphenomenon of the material. Rather, the material is the epiphenomenon of the spiritual. It is the creation of spiritual existence because looking at the outside world as material is to select a certain stance toward the world. The creative act is both immanent and transcendent. When Berdyaev says that the world, another man, or God is my creative act he means that as we create myths about the realities around us we aim at a higher and higher approximation of the realities which our interpretations symbolize. These symbols may become idols and barriers when we cease to see them as myths and symbols of our own creative attempts to disclose others or God and begin to see them as ontological realities. Ideally, though, it is through the subjective disclosure of the Other that

---

[70]Berdyaev, *Truth and Revelation*, pp. 75-76.

the self is also disclosed. Myths disclose the world of the meta-historical or meaning of history because they reflect upon the creation of concrete universals.[71]

In *The Beginning and the End: An Essay on Eschatological Metaphysics*, Berdyaev endeavors to illuminate the notion of microcosm and microtheos, explaining that they represent the penetration of the individual by the universal. He argues that the universal and the individual are only opposed in philosophical systems. In reality universals and individuals interpenetrate. God is the highest universal and at the same time the most concrete individual. God encompasses the whole of experience. He is the only personification of the universal that is true and accessible.[72] The God-likeness of persons is that they are the finite beings who are potentially open to the infinite.[73] It is a mistake to create a realm of pure essences separate from individuals; the essence cannot be separated from the individual. This blurring of the distinctions between individuals and universals, man and God, existence and essence, points toward philosophical monism and pantheism and Berdyaev seeks to avoid this through a pluralism of monadic centers of freedom. But Berdyaev is equally wary of a simple pluralism because of its atomistic and partial character. He endeavors to create a synthesis between the one and the many through the idea of Godmanhood, the concrete universal in which each incorporates the others into himself. Berdyaev attempts to maintain the tension between the poles of monism and pluralism. His thought is existentially pluralistic but eschatologically aims at monism. But the unity that is aimed at eschatologically, aims also to preserve the existential pluralism because unity is only possible between individuals. The eschatological moment would be the illumination of the infinite possibilities of the *Ungrund*. This is a continual process.

Berdyaev maintains that the problem of interpreting reality is not a matter of a thing-in-itself as an object hidden behind appearances, but that reality is not objective. It does not exist as what philosophers call being or substance, or as a thing; but in their innermost essence all entities are free. They are not things but creative acts.[74] They are not determinate objects but active agents or subjects.

---

[71]Personality cannot be thought of as having been generated by the mechanism of nature. It is the child of meaning of transcendent values and the creativity of the individual in relation to God and the Other. "Personality is not the offspring of a generic process; it is the child of meaning, of truth. There is a concrete universalism in truth which not only is not opposed to personality but presupposes its existence." Berdyaev, *The Beginning and the End*, p. 44.

[72]*Berdiaeff, Essai de métaphysique eschatologique*, pp. 190-191.

[73]*Berdiaeff, Essai de métaphysique eschatologique*, p. 259.

[74]Berdyaev, *The Beginning and the End*, p. 104.

Real existence is synonymous with becoming. It is the original knowledge of action and creation that affords us some knowledge of the inner activities of other entities that are only accessible to us through the life of the spirit. Berdyaev's speculations are based on the idea that human personality is an instance of the kind of reality constituting the cosmos and not an idiosyncracy or an illusion.

> Outside personality there is no absolute unity and totality in the world, to which personality would be subordinate.. . . An existential center, and a suffering destiny are to be found in subjectivity, not in objectivity.. . . And everything which is existential in the objectivized ranks of the world, in mankind, in the cosmos, etc. belongs to the inward being of personality.[75]

Realization of totality is not guaranteed. Each agent freely creates his meaning in relation to the transcendent meaning. Thus some are more concretely universal or more fully personalities than others. The extent to which personality is realized is related to the degree of universality subjectively realized in an individual's creative experiences of meaning and value. All values arise from spiritual existence and thus could be measured in degrees of spirituality which involve relation to other agencies, ranging from those of the least personal entity up to the ideal values of divine personality. God, as the meaning of the world, is both the most universal and the most individual of realities, the epitome of personal existence.[76] But God is not the unique unity of the cosmos, because the unity of the cosmos as universal is contained in all individual spirits. Each person is potentially a microcosm. Berdyaev calls this the "interior concrete universalism of personality."

> Personality is a microcosm, a complete universe.. . . Personality is not a part and cannot be a part in relation to any kind of whole, not even to an immense whole, or to the entire world. This is the essential principle of personality and its mystery.. . . For personality . . . in its self-revelation is directed towards an infinite content. And at the same time personality presupposes form and limit.. . . It is the universal in an individually unrepeatable form.[77]

---

[75]Berdyaev, *Slavery and Freedom*, p. 41.

[76]Berdyaev, *The Beginning and the End*, pp. 119, 120, 129-130.

[77]Berdyaev, *Slavery and Freedom*, pp. 22-23.

**The Concrete Universal and the Existential Dialectic of the Divine and the Human**

The relation of the human and God, the universal and the individual, is possible because of the interpenetration of the individual by the universal. The individual becomes the universal as she opens herself to the Other, the world, and God. The earthly and heavenly destinies are intimately connected. The Divine and human are no longer viewed as the mutually exclusive attributes of God and man respectively, but as shared attributes that are in the process of creation in both God and man. In *The Meaning of History*, Berdyaev says that anthropomorphism is extremely important, for only such an interpretation, wrapped up in the human, gives a true picture of reality. Only this kind of mythology can approach the dynamic elements that pantheism cannot touch.[78] What has been wrong with anthropomorphism in the past is not that it ascribed to God human traits but that it ascribed to him the wrong human traits: inhumanity, cruelty, self-sufficiency, and love of power, instead of humanity and the need for responsive love.[79] Anthropomorphism mythically points to the reality of God because it ties the Divine and the human together and makes intelligible any notion of a relation between them. God and man both have roots in freedom, mythically described as the pre-existential abyss of the *Ungrund*, the dark nature of God.[80]

The significance and meaning of the world process is the illumination of the dark irrational principle, the calling into being of the non-being through the creative act.[81] Berdyaev makes the connection between the Divine and human destinies even more explicit. Freedom is the duty of man before God. In realizing himself man realizes the divine image. Humanhood is God-manhood. Humanity is necessary for the Divine life to be realized in its fullness. The relation of God and humanity is reciprocal and entails the humanization of God and the divinization of humanity; the birth of humanity is a part of the theogonic process.[82] Berdyaev believes this is the message of Christianity. This Christian conception of humanity is based on two ideas, that man is in the image and likeness of God, and that Christ is the God-man. Christianity is the religion of the God-man, the incarnation, the redemption and sacrifice; the appearance of the incarnate Christ is the moment of

---

[78]Berdyaev, *The Meaning of History*, p. 53.

[79]Berdyaev, *The Divine and the Human*, p. 3.

[80]Berdyaev, *The Meaning of History*, p. 56.

[81]Berdyaev, *The Meaning of History*, p. 57.

[82]Berdyaev, *The Divine and the Human*, pp. 110-111.

the humanization of the Divine.[83] But the incarnation also represents an important moment in the divinization of the human; it is the descent of God into the dark irrational element to enlighten it from within.

The humanization of the world is an ongoing process that entails the humanization of God and the divinization of humanity. Human beings work to return themselves and the world to God. Human beings are dual beings. Berdyaev calls humanity the child of God and *meonic* freedom, of both freedom and intelligibility. Appealing again to the myth of the Fall, Berdyaev says that because of its freedom, humanity was able to fall and now lives in a fallen world. But the Fall implies the break from the bliss of non-differentiation and unilluminated freedom or pure potentiality. This does not have to be a temporal decision but is an implication of the freedom of the individual ego. In the Fall humanity chose pain and tragedy in order to explore its destiny to its depths. God calls human beings to participate in the creation of meaning from out of the chaos of radical freedom. In part, human beings are creative because of freedom. But the possibility of creation also implies the creation of form and meaning. There is in humanity an element of primeval nothingness that is uncreated and can never be completely overcome. But this element can be given meaning because humanity is in the image and likeness of God. Human beings carry the Divine image, the potential for creation within them. But because they are by nature free, they may realize their divine destiny and return to being and God, or may destroy the image of God within them and return to non-being.[84] Personality is precisely the development of the divine idea in the individual--the attempt to incorporate in the person the reality of the Other and God. Thus personality is to be contrasted with individuality which is a naturalistic and biological conception. In order to truly understand himself the person must seek God. Seeking God is to seek the divine idea conerning herself and directing activity toward the realization of the idea.[85]

Personality is contrasted with individuality because personality is a concrete universal and not an isolated particularity. In personality the person seeks to encompass the Other in himself. In the creation of personality one seeks the divine ideal in oneself and then aims at its realization which is the realization of the universal. The universal is a moral concept. It entails that a human being is free to act morally or immorally, but more than this she is a creator of moral value. The capacity to create moral value does not mean however, that one is morally free to dominate another. As Kant's moral law proclaims no one should act so as to use another as only a means to his end. All Others are always ends in themselves. They are viewed as microcosms of the whole. Creative activity is aimed at the

---

[83]Berdyaev, *The Divine and the Human*, p. 53. *The Destiny of Man*, p. 28.

[84]Berdyaev, *The Divine and the Human*, p. 53.

[85]Berdyaev, *Freedom and the Spirit*, p. 213.

realization of the Kingdom of God which is the liberation of all human beings to the freedom of creative activity. Berdyaev's ethics of freedom and creativity is an ethics of compassion.

A good deal of what Berdyaev says "mythologically" in the explanation of personality as a microcosm of the universe can be understood in relation to the demand that universals must be concrete and individual as opposed to abstract and general. If individual centers of freedom are all that actually exist, then mythic language is the only kind of language that is appropriate in talking about universals. The universal is only found in concrete individuals or in the immediate relationships between them. The anti-ontology, which places freedom prior to being, demands an approach which denies a realist conception of universals.

> I want to emphasize in this connection that my whole philosophical approach is radically incompatible with a belief in the possibility of a rational ontology, that is to say, of a science of being in which the process of abstraction is pushed to the point where Being is regarded as devoid of all peculiarities and all concrete characteristics. I can only admit a phenomenology which describes metaphysical reality in symbolic terms. Any rationalization of the divine-human relationship, any attempt at expressing it in terms of a rational philosophy of being, makes nonsense both of that relationship and of that philosophy. It can only be spoken of in symbolic and mythological terms which leave the door open to mystery.[86]

Universality is created in the individual relationship between the person and the rest of existent being. This relation can only be approached in mythological or symbolic terms because it is concrete and individual. The project of creating an anti-ontology based on a metaphysics of freedom requires this kind of emphasis on individual freedom. But Berdyaev's commitment to the possibility of meaning requires some sort of universality. Rational ontology is based on an abstract conception of Being from which generalizations about reality follow. No such generalizations can be made about freedom itself. Freedom implies that there is and always will be an irreducible element of mystery involved in any description of reality. Tying freedom to the individual ego as Berdyaev does means that causation through freedom eliminates the possibility of abstract universals that could describe every case. The only means of talking about the radical plurality of individual egos is mythically. This is similar to the position of the later Schelling. When he was under the influence of Boehme, in *The Ages of the World*, Schelling came to the position that nothing universal exists. Only what is individual exists, and universal being exists only if the absolute being is both

---

[86]Berdyaev, *Dream and Reality*, p. 209.

188

individual and universal.[87] The universal being is only present in the individual. The key to the concrete universal is that it is opposed both to the isolated particularity and abstract universality; it is the individual being integrated in history.[88]

---

[87]F.W.J. Schelling, *The Ages of the World*, trans., Frederick de Wolf, Jr. (New York: AMS Press, 1967), p. 48.

[88]Even in Hegel there is a sharp contrast between the abstract universal and the concrete universal. In addition to Hegel and Schelling, discussion of the ideal of a concrete universal can be attributed to Whitehead's metaphysics. In fact, as Charles Hartshorne has pointed out in his article on Whitehead and Berdyaev, the points of similarity between their philosophies are astounding, especially since there is no mutual influence and the two seem so radically different in style. But both posit a universal character of freedom or creativity as the ultimate principle of all reality. Even though Whitehead considered creativity as an abstract principle of all reality, the universal of universals, it is only present in an individual.

> For Whitehead, there is an ultimate, though abstract principle of all reality, a universal of universals, which he calls "creativity." This he says is not identical with God, nor is it an individual, coordinate with or superior to God. It is a mere universal or an ultimate abstraction, the ultimate abstraction. Like all universals, it is real only in individuals, including the one essential individual, God. God is not identical with creativity, because you and I are creative too, with our non-divine but real creative action.

A fruitful comparison can be made here between Berdyaev and Whitehead to show that Berdyaev's notion of freedom is similar to Whitehead's idea of creativity. Hartshorne continues:

> And Berdyaev tells us that this freedom is a principle uncreated by God and not identical with him and that the process of creation involves God, the uncreated principle of freedom, and the creative and partly self-creative action of the creatures. God's "call to man" is not answered by God himself but by man through new realities, new qualities of experience.

The creation of meaning in the Divine-human relationship never fully exhausts the possibilities of freedom. "In the multiple-freedom or multiple decision of actualization inheres an element of not wholly eradicable chaos." The significance of this statement is that the chaos of freedom or the indeterminacy of the *Ungrund* is never wholly eradicable in the creative process by which being and order are brought to be. But chaos, or freedom allows for possibility. Freedom is not created but resides within the Godhead. Possible alternatives are found within freedom but not to freedom. Freedom is the basic datum of existence. Hartshorne, "Berdyaev and Whitehead: is there Tragedy in God," pp. 185-186.

# VII. BERDYAEV'S FINAL RESPONSE TO THE PROBLEM OF THE OTHER AND THE DESIRE TO BE GOD: *SOBORNOST*

## Berdyaev and Sartre on Community

In *Being and Nothingness*, Sartre's ontology divides human consciousness into separate centers of freedom and experience that are indicative of his Cartesianism. The notion of the desire to be God, the basic human project which acts as the pattern for all other human projects, is the exemplification of Sartre's conception of Cartesian freedom. It is antithetical to the creation of community among human beings because community necessarily comes to be seen as an attempt at the objectification of consciousness to escape its facticity. The Other as Other constantly drags us back because it limits the infinitude of our subjective world. Its world is not and can never be ours. Berdyaev argues against this point of view. Though Berdyaev characterizes one type of desire to be God in much the same terms that Sartre does--as egoistic and atomistic--he argues that this version of the desire for being is always tied to objectification. He differs from Sartre because he believes that not all projects that desire totality and unity necessarily ' objectify reality. He ultimately points toward the possibility of a unity in which · identity and difference are preserved. As mentioned previously a possible reading of the radical conversion passages from *Being and Nothingness* can place Sartre also near this position. And I think this interpretation makes more sense in view of some of Sartre's later remarks about *Being and Nothingness* and his discussion of the possibility of community in his later thought. Viewed this way, Sartre envisages, beyond the ontology of *Being and Nothingness* human activity and ethics based on freedom and not on the objectifing desire to be God. But even bearing all this in mind, we have endeavored to show that the ontological characterization of freedom as presented by the dualism of the in-itself and for-itself seriously cripples this attempt before it can be started.

Berdyaev takes the Kantian distinction between freedom and nature and applies it cosmologically. Nature is the objectified form, the manifestation of the activity of another freedom. The similarities between this and Sartre's description of the encounter with the Other are striking. Objectification is almost an inevitable consequence of existence. The expression and realization of spiritual potentialities requires their expression but their expression is also their alienation from the original intention. Objectification is the congelation of a subjective act into a public fact. Objects result from the projection of creative activity into the social sphere. Free subjectivities become encased in their spatio-temporal, externally related, causally determined substance. Objects become the mediating relationship between subjectivities. If this is the case, then objects must be understood as a form of symbolizing of the real, rather than as the real itself.[1] But at this point the similarity ends; it is only in the negative characterization of objectification that Berdyaev's description of relation to the Other resembles Sartre's. Personality is not created in the relation of the Cartesian self and the non-self, but through the relation of the self and the Other. The eschatological creation of meaning requires the ethical relation with the Other.

In the objectified world it is the absence of wholeness and the absence of true relation with the Other that is the source of suffering. In a world of isolated particularities, relation with the Other is impossible. Berdyaev appropriates Kierkegaard's characterization of suffering as the separation of the infinite and the finite in human beings and the inability of human beings to posit the relation between the two sides of their nature. Human suffering is connected with the fact that one is lonely, seemingly unable to break out of finitude. Like Kierkegaard and Sartre, Berdyaev thinks that humanity is caught between the finite and the infinite-- man is the finite being that strains toward eternity. This is the source of human suffering: man wants infinity but is confined by his finitude. Suffering is the antithesis of the feeling of infinity. Suffering presupposes the absence of integrity. Man lives in an objectified world and only very rarely gets beyond it to a world of "subsistence," of meaning that integrates the fragmented character of objective experience. Even within the individual there is much that seems not integral to the self. "Within me myself there is much which is alien to me, which is not mine (the 'Es' of Freud) and this element in my very self which is alien to me is a source of suffering."[2] The temptation is to attempt to impose the power of the ego against

---

[1] Berdyaev, *Solitude and Society*, p. 63.

[2] Much of human suffering is the result of the inability of the ego to accept the equal reality of the Other. Egoism is the attempt to force the Other to recognize the independence of my freedom without accepting the equality of hers. I objectify her freedom and try to turn her into an object for my manipulation. In *Being and Nothingness*, Sartre says that this structure is an unavoidable aspect of human relationships. The similarity between Sartre and Berdyaev on this point stems from their common debt to Hegel's analysis of the Master-Slave dialectic.

It may be accepted as beyond doubt that a large amount of suffering and unhappiness is due to being engulfed by one's ego, to egoism. At

this alien, objectified world outside and within me. This is one of the ways the desire to be God attempts to realize itself. But such projects are doomed to failure because they deny the basic reality that the world transcends the individual.

Suffering is a part of the tragedy of existence that Berdyaev takes as a part of the eschatological path to communion. God suffers along with humanity. But suffering is also indicative of the erotic desire for wholeness, for love. The possibility of communion, the finding of community and neighborliness, is the opposite of suffering and is necessary to the existence of personality. When one experiences the cosmos as a neighbor, as divine, it is no longer seen as an alien world of objects. One looks to a world that is beyond this one, the world that is in harmony. Communion is the reverse of suffering. Death represents the greatest suffering because it is the moment we pass through absolute isolation. Harmony is the discovery of community and is the antithesis of suffering.[3]

### Personality, The Concrete Universal, and Openness to the Other

Berdyaev's description of human beings as free agents creates a picture of reality that in many ways sounds like the independence of Leibnizean monads but there are important differences. Most importantly, agents in Berdyaev's personalism are not windowless monads. Nor is there any pre-established harmony. But they resemble monads in that they are not finally determined by external influences. This very freedom, however, requires openness and harmonious interaction with the Other. Indeed, the more universal, the more realized a personality, the more it incorporates the Other in the communality. This is the way Berdyaev explains his conception of *Sobornost*, the togetherness or community of spirits. The more realized an individual entity is, the more it has become universal and opens itself to the others. There can be no pre-established harmony, only the possibility of harmony that is to be created by subjects. Thus, Berdyaev desires to walk the narrow ridge between unity and difference, monism and pluralism.

Once again, Berdyaev's philosophy is existentially pluralistic but eschatologically monistic. As in Sartre's philosophy, the subjective tries to lend unity to the chaos that both precedes it and surrounds it. But unlike Sartre's view there is

---

the extreme limit this leads to madness which is always a state of being engulfed by one's ego, of being incapable of getting outside of it. The capacity to issue from the ego, to escape engulfment by it, is a condition of the realization of personality.

Berdyaev, *The Divine and the Human*, p. 70.

[3]Berdyaev, *The Divine and the Human*, p. 71.

no pre-established objective unity that exists apart from consciousnesses as illustrated by Being-in-itself. The universal is an attempt on the part of the subject to create unity from the mystery of freedom that surrounds it. Personality is the microcosm of the whole and it creates order and meaning out of the chaos of the changing world of freedom through the intelligibility of the divine principle in which it participates. Though this resembles Platonism, because there are ideals that determine chaotic being it is not a Platonism, because the only governing ideal is derived from existence itself. That the existence of a conscious entity implies the existence of Others. The relation to the Other is the fundamental structure of existence.

God is the most complete because He is the most open to relation with the Other, and thus also the most universal.[4] Personality is the opposite of individuality which is an isolated particularity. Personality is universality, the encompassing openness to the being, freedom, and experience of the Other. Viewed objectively, personality may be numerically singular, but Berdyaev's concept of personality, like Hegel's concept of plenitude, implies openness to the Other and the possibility of encompassing the non-Ego in the mirroring of communion: ". . . the personality. . . can do what no mere part can aspire to do--it can realize itself in the process of making its content universal. It is a unity in the midst of plurality, and can thus comprehend the universe."[5]

The realization of personality as the microcosm of the universe depends on the assumption that the individual human being contains at the basis of her being the primal undifferentiated unity of freedom, the *Ungrund*, but this freedom is unilluminated; it must become intelligible. In Hegelian terminology, it must become both in and for itself. The endowment of the ego with the qualities of personality, what Berdyaev calls "the real myth about man," requires a creative act of the imagination. "In accord with this myth man is not a part, he is not particularized because he is the image of (God) and is a universe." Persons are conceived as monads but also as mirrors of the whole.[6] The personality is a subject and a whole that seeks communion with others.

> . . .the personality is never a part but always a whole.. . . It is not of this world: when confronted with the personality, I am in the presence

---

[4]This is also Whitehead's position. Also, as in Whitehead's discussion of actual entities and the absolute entity, God, consciousnesses seeks to synthesize the reality that confronts them at each occasion.

[5]Berdyaev, *Solitude and Society*, p. 173.

[6]Berdyaev, *Slavery and Freedom*, p. 50.

of a Thou. It is not an object.. . . Thus the triumph of the personality
will mean the annihilation of the objective world.[7]

One knows his own personality through that of the Other. The personality cannot
be understood except through communion. This is the basic importance of the
overcoming of solitude.[8]

That the Other and God can never be fully known but are also infinitely
knowable is a justification of symbolism as the only mode of talking about reality.
Divinity and humanity are eternally mysterious in the unfathomable depth of their
being, for at the depths is freedom and creativity. "Thus it is that the knowledge
of the divine is a dynamic process which finds no completion within the fixed and
static categories of ontology."[9]   But because Berdyaev's idea of this relation is
eschatological it must be that there can be advances as well as regressions in the
use of symbols.[10]

---

[7]Berdyaev, *Solitude and Society*, p. 197.

[8]Berdyaev, *Solitude and Society*, p. 165.

[9]Berdyaev, *Freedom and the Spirit*, p.65.

[10]Some ways of symbolizing the Divine are better than Others.  Berdyaev is
thoroughly Christian and, though he appreciates aspects of Hinduism, he clearly
thinks that Christian symbolism reveals the Divine more adequately than Hindu
symbolism, even though he admits that it also conceals some things that Hindu
symbolism reveals.  Beyond this, he prefers some mystics to most theologians and
he even greatly prefers Eckhart's mystical writings to his theological ones.  Clearly
Berdyaev does not mean that all symbols reveal the divine but only those that
emphasize the relation between the divine and the human, freedom and meaning
that allow for the meeting and interpenetration of the divine and the human.  For
example, in *The Divine and the Human*, Berdyaev characterizes his attitude to
Christianity, Hinduism and Western thought about the divine in speaking once
again about the secondary nature of being and the divine-human relation.

> Being is secondary, not primary; it comes to light after the division
> between subject and object; it is a product of thought, of rational-
> ization.  In this respect Indian religious philosophy attains greater
> heights and goes deeper that Western ontological philosophy which is
> too much subject to the categories of Aristotle.
>     The only true path is the path of intuitive description of spiritual
> experience, and along the path it becomes clear that in revelation both God
> and man are active, that revelation has a divine-human character.  The
> religious phenomenon has two sides; it is the disclosure of God in man and

Existential knowledge is synonymous with community. For Berdyaev a major contribution of existentialist philosophy is the radical insistence on the import of the individual in the community of others.[11] Although Berdyaev accepts the existential primacy of the particular individual and is existentially a pluralist, eschatologically he is a monist. Like Hegel he would grant equal reality both parts of the dichotomy, but unlike Hegel he thinks the synthesis of the two is beyond the capacity of language to grasp. Still, for all his talk against rationality and objectification, Berdyaev is not an irrationalist. He aims at what he calls the supra-rational. He does not reject rationality in favor of the irrational. The irrational turns from the intelligible, which is the goal of history, back to the simple irrationality of the will. To attempt to return to the irrationality of the *Ungrund* is to move toward a totally isolated particularity as much as some forms of objectification. This represents the fall into the chaos of pure relativism. This indicates that Berdyaev, like Kant, thinks that the source of value lies in the development of personality and the development of personality in the relationships between persons. Value, truth, and meaning are all dependent on an ethical relation but this relation is created between persons. It is not an abstract conception of an ethical principle, but a concrete existential relationship. Reminiscent of Boehme, at the heart of all Berdyaev's discussion of the development of persons, of creativity, of value, is the supreme value of relation between persons. This bestows Berdyaev's philosophy with a concrete rationality that resembles Kant's moral reason. In essence Berdyaev believes that if freedom really is and human beings are really free, then each person is a center of the universe more important than any cosmic truth. But human freedom is only, and develops only, in concrete relations between beings. Berdyaev, like Hegel, sees objectification as only a

---

of man in God. The yearning of man for God comes to light in it and the yearning of God for man from the fear of introducing affective passionate life into God  For the rational concept of perfection does not admit of yearning and need in the notion of completeness; it prefers the perfection of a stone. In that case the relations between God and man cease to be a drama of two which is capable of resolution in a third. Revelation is a creative act of the Spirit; it has both a theogonic and an anthropogonic character. It is only mysticism which found another language and Christian theosophy (Boehme) which have risen above the naively realistic interpretations of revelation, above the rational and naturalistic understanding of God.

Berdyaev, *The Divine and the Human*, p. 15.

[11]Berdyaev argued that his position is different from either Fichte or Stirner. For them the relation between the ego and the non-ego was not a relation between an individual I and a Thou, but a relation between a generalized I and the non-ego which is not personal.

moment in the dialectical development of spirit toward unity. He speaks of the unhappy consciousness that accepts the split between the self and the Other, the subject and object, but this is only a stage on the way toward unity.[12] In order to achieve the unity that still preserves the integrity of the opposites, of a plurality of persons and unity of community, intelligibility and mystery, the infinite and the finite, necessity and freedom, the one and the many, they must all be aufhaben in the new synthesis of the supra-rational that transcends the opposition of the rational and irrational. Knowing is not only an act of the intellect but an act of love and the will. It aims at a synthesis of the will and the intellect that is based on the maximum integration of experience. "Philosophy is therefore based upon the maximum experience of human existence. This integrates man's intellectual, affective and volitional life."[13]

Berdyaev outlines the development of the individual ego to personality and community in an eschatological vision. Originally, there was no differentiation between the Ego and the "totality." The revelation of the existence of the non-Ego shattered this original unity. The Ego developed through its alienation from the totality. Berdyaev, like the German Idealists, seeks a finale that overcomes alienation and preserves all of history in a transfigured form.

> The stages of its development are as follows: Firstly, the undifferentiated unity of the Ego with the universe; secondly the dualist opposition of the Ego and the non-Ego; thirdly and finally, the achievement of the concrete union of every Ego with the Thou, a union which preserves plurality in a transfigured form.[14]

Like Sartre's, Berdyaev's existentialism aims at creating a philosophical position based on the freedom of human beings who are free creators of values. They both maintain that the creation of meaning is the fundamental human project. Both see meaning as ideally aiming at a notion of totality with Others and the universe. Man is situated in the indefinite and he creates meaning from this ambiguity. But where Sartre thinks the indefinite and the ambiguous represent the only fundamental characteristics about being and the nature of consciousness, Berdyaev argues for the possible existence of transcendent meaning and unity. The radical nature of human freedom has its roots in the pure potentiality of the *Ungrund* and the myth of the *Ungrund* grants a picture of unilluminated totality which is prior to the fragmentation of Being. The divine provides the ideal meaning of the existent plurality and points toward the possibility of creating a new

---

[12]Berdyaev, *The Beginning and the End*, p. 81.

[13]Berdyaev, *Solitude and Society*, p. 17.

[14]Berdyaev, *Solitude and Society*, p. 88.

unity that is also conscious of itself as such. The creation of the concrete universal represents the creative effort of individuals to break out of the solitude of particularity. The creator is one who creates a relation to the Other. Whether this creation takes the form of openness to the I-Thou relation or artistic or moral creation, it is in its essence religious because it aims at the totality of *Sobornost* or communion with others and God.[15] All truly creative activity wills the end of fragmentation and objectification and the creation of the Kingdom of God. Love is the basis of this kind of creation. "A genuine act of love is eschatological, it makes an end of this world of hatred and enmity, and the beginning of the new world."[16]

In *Being and Nothingness*, Sartre's description of creation is individualistic in essence and involves the creation of a wholly individual meaning in an ambiguous universe. Berdyaev's basic disagreement with Sartre on the fundamental nature of freedom is that Sartre's existentialism calls into question the possibility of creating any sort of meaning and basic to this problem is the creation of the in-

---

[15]For Berdyaev, any doctrine of totality must also include the past and even the dead. Berdyaev aims at the appropriation of all time in the eternal or existential time. One of the primary themes of Russian religious thought since Nikolai Feodorov in the late nineteenth century was resurrection. Feodorov argued that the natural process creates the enmity of Fathers and Sons because of the scarcity of natural resources. The younger generation depends on the death of the older. Feodorov felt that justice demanded this enmity had to somehow be overcome. His influence shows up in Dostoevsky's *The Brothers Karamazov* where Ivan rejects any future utopia because it would in no way justify the sufferings of persons in the past. The theme of resurrection in the novel is a response to this position. For Berdyaev, there are Thous and Wes in the past, there must be a personal communion with history.

> This spiritual memory. . . reminds man of the fact that in the past there lived concrete beings, living personalities, with whom we ought in existential time to have a link no less than with those who are living now. Society is always a society, not only of the living but also of the dead.

Berdyaev, *Slavery and Freedom*, p. 111. See also Nicholas Feodorov, "The Question of Brotherhood or Relatedness, and of the Reasons for the Unbrotherly, Dis-Related, or Unpeaceful State of the World, and of the Means for the Restoration of Relatedness" in James Edie, James Scanlan, Mary-Barbara Zeldin, and George Kline, eds. *Russian Philosophy*: Vol. III (Knoxville: University of Tennessee Press, 1976), pp. 11-55.

[16]Berdyaev, *The Beginning and the End*, p. 184.

itself and the for-itself. The problem is that Sartre's existentialism falls into important difficulties in attempting to derive freedom from Being and in rejecting the primal character of negation as co-equal with Being. In making the for-itself dependent on the in-itself, Sartrean existentialism misunderstands the question of nothingness and human freedom. This misunderstanding is the basis for Sartre's rejection of what he admits is the main intention of consciousness and even seems to be the intention of the in-itself.[17] Sartre must maintain that the intentional movement of consciousness toward totality is aimed at an imposibility. This leads to the absurdity of the human condition.

### Personality and the "We": *Sobornost*

For Berdyaev, the very nature of personality is relation to Others. The nature of personality is not to be isolated. This is a creative relationship like the evolution of symbolism in relation to reality. It improves as the Ego more and more fully comprehends the reality of the Thou and the We.[18] The aim of the universe, the ideal meaning that Berdyaev seeks, is the creation of community or the Russian ideal of *Sobornost*. There is no adequate translation of the term in English, but one of Berdyaev's translators, R. M. French, offered an approximation in the translator's note to *Slavery and Freedom*. *Sobornost* is catholic consciousness, symphony, "altogetherness," the dynamic life of the collective body.[19]  N.O. Lossky in his discussion of the early Slavophile philosopher Alexi Khomiakov, in *A History of Russian Philosophy*, writes "*Sobornost*, means the combination of freedom and unity of many persons on the basis of their common love for the same absolute values."[20] But this love of the same value is also organic arising from

---

[17]Sartre would argue that intention is read into the in-itself by the for-itself. *EN*, p. 124, 717. *BN*, p. 99, 762.

[18]Berdyaev, *Solitude and Society*, p. 171-172.

[19]Berdyaev, *Slavery and Freedom*, p. 4.

[20]Lossky thinks that this is the major donation of Khomiakov to Russian philosophy. N. O. Lossky, *A History of Russian Philosophy* (New York: International Universities Press, 1951), p. 41. *Sobornost* is related etymologically to the verb *sobirot* which means "to gather," "to collect," to assemble," "to summon," "to converse," "to prepare or get ready," " to intend." *Sobor* (n) also means "cathederal," "council," "assembly or synod." *Soborovat* means "to give extreme unction, the last accounting." *Sobranie* is "collection," "gathering", "session," "assembly," "meeting." *Sobrat* (*brat* = brother) is a "colleague or fellow."  I am

the community itself. It is not coerced, but is freely and spontaneously given. Lossky's definition is the most helpful in determining the importance of *Sobornost* for Berdyaev's philosophy and its relation to his doctrine of Godmanhood. God is the absolute value. Through the common love for the absolute value the alienation between persons is to be overcome. *Sobornost* is the norm of Berdyaev's ethics. Berdyaev himself says of *Sobornost*, as he did of the concrete universal, that it is not objectively definable, though he would insist that it is intelligible. "That to which Khomiakov gave the name of *Sobornost* and which is difficult to define in rational terms, is not an "objective" collective reality, it is an interior quality . . . an existential subjectivity."[21] *Sobornost* is intelligible but it is not simply reducible to description in objective terms. There must be a common experience and interpenetration of love. Communal knowledge is affective and loving. It is based on intuition that is not only the perception of something; it is also a creative penetration into meaning.[22]

Berdyaev maintains that since general validity is external and only related objectively, it must be replaced by a real knowledge that is a ". . .sense of community, spiritual kinship, and reciprocal penetration of feeling."[23] But such knowledge is based on a free relation, and by nature cannot compel acceptance. In one of the most telling passages in Berdyaev's corpus, in some ways reminiscent of Aristotle's categorizing of the levels of knowledge in the *Metaphysics*, Berdyaev outlines the levels of knowledge in his existential metaphysics. The description is, of course, quite different from Aristotle with the highest level of knowledge having the least universally binding character and the lowest the most universally binding. Consistent with the metaphysics of freedom the highest forms of knowledge would have to be freely chosen.

> . . . the universally binding character of cognition is to be found in its
> highest degree in mathematics and the physical sciences.. . On the
> other hand, knowledge in the historical and social sciences and in the
> sciences of the spirit and of values, that is to say, in philosophy, has
> a lower degree of universally binding character just because it pre-
> supposes a greater spiritual community in which people share. Least

---

indebted for the preceding etymology to Professor Richard Marshall of the Department of Slavic Languages and Literatures of the University of Toronto.

[21]Berdyaev, *Truth and Revelation*, p. 39-46.

[22]Berdyaev, *The Beginning and the End*, p. 38.

[23]Berdyaev, *The Beginning and the End*, p. 77.

of all universally binding are the truths of a religious character because they pre-suppose the maximum of spiritual community.[24]

It is precisely because of the lack of a universally binding character that the sciences of values and the truths of religion are more important. They require a much greater degree of free consent. They demand a high degree of spiritual community that can be shared by human beings, a commitment to a common meaning or good. This is the creation of the WE, the communion of the Ego and the Thou. This is a personalist and not a cosmological doctrine. The idea of communion as a goal of human life is essentially religious. Communion requires a common goal and at least some common symbols that are intelligible to the members of the community. But above all, it requires the free encounter of the Ego with a Thou. "The interpenetration of the Ego and the Thou is consummated in God."[25] It is a personal community in which the person is not simply absorbed in the impersonal collective.

---

[24]Berdyaev, *Slavery and Freedom*, p. 215.

[25]Berdyaev, *Solitude and Society*, p. 188.

# CONCLUSION

In this study we have examined two major areas in the philosophies of radical freedom put forward by Berdyaev and Sartre. On the question of freedom, Sartre's explanation of radical freedom involves the negative image of the tradition he criticizes. Sartre's derivation of freedom from the notion of non-being inherits all of the problems that he sees in traditional metaphysics. Given Sartre's critique of the theological/metaphysical tradition, Sartre's own ontology should provide something different. But in adopting the Cartesian existentialist position and creating the ontological distinction between the in-itself and the for-itself, Sartre does exactly what he has accused the classical tradition of philosophy of doing, he assumes the exalted position of the philosopher. He gives a "metaphysical" explanation of freedom arising from a predetermined ground. All of Sartre's important ideological pronouncements are based on the ontological dichotomy of the in-itself and the for-itself. The description of the human condition as the impossible desire to be God, and the impossibility of ever realizing the aim of totality with the Other, stems from the ontological definition of Being and nothingness. To the extent that Sartre insists on the static structure of the for-itself and the in-itself he remains in the metaphysical tradition that he criticizes.

In traditional theological discussions about God, creatures are said to add nothing to God's perfect Being. But this has always been extremely difficult for theologians to explain, whether they have been traditional theists talking about God and creatures, or pan-theists talking about ground and manifestations. The existing contingent thing does seem to add something to the lone necessary Being. God and the world do seem to be more valuable than just God alone. Similarly, the for-itself is supposed to add nothing to the in-itself. But in talking about the ways that objects appear in the world through the interrelation of positive Being-in-itself and negative determinative being-for-itself, Sartre's thought is plagued by the same inconsistencies that he criticizes in the metaphysical-theological tradition. Sartre's discussion of the past is one example of his inconsistency. Here, the for-itself creates its past which serves as the in-itself for it. Thus it appears that the for-itself does affect the in-itself. "Metaphysical mistakes," due to the desire to be God, resurface in the relation of the for-itself and the in-itself. Sartre's discussion marks no serious progress on this question over theological tradition. Finally, as we have noted, Sartre's position is weaker than the theistic tradition he criticizes because he cannot appeal to the inscrutable mystery of the will of God.

On this point, Berdyaev's position is much stronger. If we are going to talk about the reality of freedom and do it in the radical fashion that Sartre and Berdyaev have attempted, then freedom cannot be posterior to Being and determined by it but must be either prior or co-equal to it. To this extent the tradition that includes Boehme, Hegel, Schelling, and Berdyaev, which maintains either the priority of freedom or what we have called an ingredience of negation in Being, are much more consistent in explaining the possibility of freedom and becoming than those who try to derive it from a changeless Being.

But there does still seem to be a problem for Berdyaev and the process philosophy he advocates. For where the main problem for Aristotle and traditional metaphysics was to explain motion and becoming in a universe where truth was based in a changeless Being, and God becomes necessary as the Unmoved Mover, for Berdyaev a similar problem is posed, the problem of order in a universe where becoming and freedom provide the basic description of reality. God might have to function in such a universe as the "Unstopped Stopper," the provider of order to chaos. This is exactly the way that Berdyaev has described God except that he has included all other creatures with God as creators of order out of chaos. But the problem for Berdyaev does not go away with this characterization of agents as the providers of order. If freedom is prior to God and Being, how does order ever emerge? And even if it does, why is it not at the mercy of chaos? For if it is, it would seem that we have a very different application for William James' famous line that the things that matter most should not be at the mercy of the things that matter least. I maintain that Berdyaev does avoid this problem when he retreats from the position that freedom is prior to Being to the use of the mythic and symbolic images of the *Ungrund*. The *Ungrund*, as Berdyaev admits, is actually prior to both freedom and Being. It contains the possibilities of them both. So the poles of meaning and chaos are mutually dependent, as they are in Boehme's image of the theogonic process. Thus, if one wants to look for a reason for God's or his creature's necessary willing of order in the universe, it can only be in the respect or reverence for the moral law. And the moral law is the respect for the ultimacy and autonomy of each person as microcosm or center of freedom. But beyond this, the reason for the respect for freedom in the Other is only to be located in the inscrutable depths of freedom. Order exists to some extent merely because agents will it to exist. Here Berdyaev must make a concession to traditional theology. Where the theistic tradition ultimately is always forced to end its enquiries in the inscrutable will of God, Berdyaev, the process existentialist, is forced to end his in the inscrutable depths of freedom, or the inscrutable wills of the Divine and the human.

The second major point, the possibility of meaning and community, is in the groundwork of both Sartre's and Berdyaev's philosophies. Both contain conceptions about the possibility of meaning (Sartre's desire to be God) and how it relates to the possibility of communion with the Other. As we have said, although Sartre calls any attempt at the creation of totality an effort at founding values and thus the impossible desire to be God, what is strange about Sartre's position is that being-for-itself and being-for-others both presuppose this totality which, according to Sartre, cannot be. "The multiplicity of consciousnesses appears to us as a synthesis and not as a collection, but is a synthesis whose totality is inconceivable." He insists there is no vantage point from which to observe totality, no third observer who stands outside, insuring the totality.[1] The relation to the Other is always surrounded with the halo of totality but this totality is only an idea; it is a part of the human predicament never to be able to attain it. But Sartre speaks about this as if from a totality. As we have seen, despite his rhetoric, Sartre assumes something near to the theological tradition in relation to a totality. In spite of his claims that his ontology is based on phenomenological analysis, it appears that its dualistic and ultimately monistic character is metaphysical and must be evaluated in metaphysical terms.

Within this realist ontology is the subjective starting point of the Cogito. Sartre's description of the relation with the Other maintains that no trans-subjective or empathetic experience grants me the subjectivity of the Other. Sartre maintains that it is the feeling of my own objectivity before the Other that grants me the Other as other. I suffer because of the Other's entrance into my world. He turns me, the subject of my world, into an object in his. But I still cannot say I have any trans-subjective awareness of him. It is not the experience of an alien Other that I suffer. It is in the interior experience of my own objectivity that the subjectivity of the Other is supposed to be revealed to me. If this is the case, the Sartrean theory of social ontology can, in the final analysis, only be an interpretation of the meaning of my own objectivity. This feeling of my own objectness is in reality the subjectivity of the Cartesian Cogito. Then Sartrean existentialism cannot break out of isolation any more than the theories of the Other that Sartre criticizes.

Berdyaev's position is not plagued by these problems. As Sartre admits, the in-itself and for-itself seem to imply a higher synthesis, albeit an inconceivable one. But the synthesis ceases to be inconceivable if we abandon the static structures of Sartre's ontology. Berdyaev has done this through the adoption of the *Ungrund* myth. Boehme speaks of the genesis of God from an original but imperfect plenitude and a theogonic process that culminates in a universe that is superior to that which precedes it by the very fact that God becomes conscious of the Other and brings the Other (His creation) back into unity with Himself. For Berdyaev, this movement toward unity is possible, though unity cannot be thought of as static and must be constantly recreated. This creation of totality, prefigured in the *Ungrund*, is what makes relation with the Other a possibility also. The *Ungrund* is the symbol of the coincidence of being and nothingness, unity and determinate-

[1]*EN*, p. 363. *BN*, p. 370.

ness, that precedes both existent being and nothingness. While the pre-existential unity of the *Ungrund* is not the metaphysical guarantee of unity the way that traditional pantheism is, against which all of the existentialist philosophers are in rebellion, it guarantees the possibility of unity through creative action. The *Ungrund* as the mysterious primal abyss does indicate that there is a primal unity that points the way, a vague pre-figuring of the human project, or, the Divine-human project. This is not to say that there is a prior necessity that determines the project, but that the meaning to be created is, in an imprecise way, pre-figured in the principle of creation that implies a relation between the self and the Other. That unity is prefigured in the primal unity of the *Ungrund*. When applied to human history, politics or ethics, this conception of human freedom and the possibilities of the creation of meaning and community answers many questions but creates many others.

Politically, Berdyaev was an anarchist, but an anarchist who realized that the tragic condition of the world made anarchism an ideal. Berdyaev's ideal of unity must be freely chosen. The universally binding character of the "hard" sciences relegated them to the lowest rung of the levels of knowledge in Berdyaev's metaphysics. The least universally binding truths of religious character that must be freely chosen occupy the highest level. They presuppose "the maximum of spiritual community." The unity of community is pre-figured in the *Ungrund*, made explicit in the moral law, but has no means of making human beings adhere to it.

The final question we must ask here is this. Is Berdyaev too much of an optimist? Although the logical possibility of *Sobornost* does exist, is there any reason to think that it could ever be made actual? Berdyaev seems to think it can and this is the basis of the commitment to an eschatological vision of human history. But it seems that there can be no guarantee that *Sobornost* will be achieved. If, as Berdyaev claimed, God has less power than a policeman, He cannot guarantee the creation of community which is the goal of personality. God could only guarantee that personality, the concrete universal, serves as the prime example of community for an individual person. But, there is, perhaps, a negative guarantee of community in the explicit doctrine that to turn away from it is to turn toward the disintegration and destruction of the personality. Here we once again return to the problem of order in Berdyaev's philosophy. If freedom is primary, why should order ever come to be? Ultimately it seems impossible to tell how it comes to be or why there should be beings rather than nothing. But in Berdyaev's defence, to explain this would explain away freedom which must ultimately remain a mystery to philosophical investigation.

# SELECTED BIBLIOGRAPHY

## Sartre

*Cahiers pour une morale*. Paris: Éditions Gallimard, 1983.

*Équisse d'une théorie des émotions*. Paris: Hermann, 1960. *The Emotions: Outline of a Theory*. Translated by Bernard Frechtman. New York: Philosophical Library, 1948.

*L'être et le néant: Essai d'ontologie phénoménologique*. Paris: Éditions Gallimard, 1943. *Being and Nothingness: An Essay on Phenomemological Ontology*. Translated by Hazel E. Barnes. New York: Philosophical Library, 1948.

*L'Existentialism est un humanisme*. Paris: Les Éditions Nagel, 1946. *Existentialism is a Humanism*. Translated by Bernard Frechtman. New York: Philosophical Library, 1947.

*L'Imaginaire: Psychologie phénoménologique de l'imagination*. Paris: Gallimard, 1940. *The Pyschology of Imagination*. Translation anonymous. New York: Philosophical Library, 1948.

*L'Imagination*. Paris: Presses Universitaires de France, 1963. *Imagination: A Psychological Critique*. Translated by Forrest Williams. Ann Arbor: University of Michigan Press, 1962.

"Kierkegaard: L'Universel singulier," *Kierkegaard Vivant* allocation de René Maheu. Paris: Gallimard, 1966. "Kierkegaard: the Singular Universal," in *Jean-Paul Sartre: Between Existentialism and Marxism*. Edited and translated by John Mathews. New York: New Left Books, 1974.

*Les Mots*. Paris: Gallimard, 1964. *The Words*. Translated by Bernard Frechtman. New York: George Braziller, 1964.

208

*La Nausée*. Paris: Gallimard, 1938. *Nausea*. Translated by Lloyd Alexander. Norfolk: New Directions, n.d.

*Saint Genet, comédian et martyr*. Paris: Gallimard, 1952. *Saint Genet, Actor and Martyr*. Translated by Bernard Frechtman. New York: George Braziller, 1963.

*Situations I*. Paris: Gallimard, 1947. Essays cited, together with pages: "Une Idée fondamentale de la phénoménologie de Husserl: L'Intentionalité," pp. 31-35.
"L'Homme et les choses," pp. 245-293.
"La Liberté cartesienne," pp. 314-335. "Cartesian Freedom." In *Sartre, Literary and Philosophical Essays*. Translated by Annette Michelson. New York: Collier Books 1962.

*Situations II*. Paris: Gallimard, 1948. "Qu'est-ce que la littérature?" *Literature and Existentialism*. Translated by Bernard Frechtman. New York: Citidel Press, 1962.

*La Transcendence de la ego: Equisse d'une phénoménologique*. Paris: Librarie Philosophique J. Vrin, 1965. *The Transcendence of the Ego*. Translated by Forrest Williams and Robert Kirkpatrick. New York: Noonday, 1957.


**Berdyaev**

*The Beginning and the End*. Translated by R. M. French. London: Geoffrey Bles, 1952.

"Deux études sur Jacob Boehme." in Boehme, Jacob. *L'Mystérium Magnum*. Translated by Nicholas Berdyaev. Paris: Aubier, 1948.

*The Destiny of Man*. Translated by Natalie Duddington. London: Geoffrey Bles, 1945.

*The Divine and the Human*. Translated by R. M. French. London: Geoffrey Bles, 1949

*Dostoevsky*. Translated by Donald Attwater. New York: Sheed and Ward, 1934.

*Dream and Reality*. Translated by Katherine Lampert. London: Geoffrey Bles, 1950.

*The End of Our Time.* Translated By Donald Attwater. London: Sheed and Ward, 1933.

*Freedom and the Spirit.* Translated by Oliver Fielding Clarke. New York: Scribner's, 1935.

*The Meaning of the Creative Act.* Translated by Donald A. Lowrie. New York: Harper and Bothers, 1955.

*The Meaning of History.* Translated by George Reavey. London: Geoffrey Bles, 1936.

*The Realm of the Spirit and the Realm of Caesar.* Translated by Donald A. Lowrie. New York: Harper and Brothers, 1954.

*Slavery and Freedom.* Translated by R. M. French. New York: Charles Scribner's Sons, 1944.

*Spirit and Reality.* Translated by George Reavy. London: Geoffrey Bles, 1939.

*Solitude and Society.* Translated by George Reavey. London: Geoffrey Bles, 1938.

*Toward a New Epoch.* Translated by Oliver Fielding Clarke. London: Geoffrey Bles, 1949.

*Truth and Revelation.* Translated by R. M. French. London: Geoffrey Bles, 1953.


**Boehme**

*Le Mystérium Magnum.* Translated by Nicholas Berdyaev. Paris: Aubier, 1948.

*Six Theosophic Points and Other Writings.* Ann Arbor: University of Michigan Press, 1958.

*Personal Christianity.* Edited by Franz Hartmann. New York: Ungar, 1964.

*The Signature of All Things.* Translated by Emmett Rys. London: Everyman, 1912.

*The Way to Christ.* Translated by Peter Erb. New York: Paulist Press, 1978.

210

## Selected Secondary works on Sartre

Anderson, Thomas C. *The Foundation and Structure of Sartrean Ethics*. Lawrence: The Regents Press of Kansas, 1979.

Barnes, Hazel E. *An Existentialist Ethics*. Chicago: University of Chicago Press, 1967.

Bell, Linda. *Sartre's Ethics of Aunthenticity*. Tuscaloosa, Alabama: The University of Alabama Press: 1989.

Catalano, Joseph S. *A Commentary on Jean-Paul Sartre's Being and Nothingness*. Chicago: University of Chicago Press, 1974.

de Beauvoir, Simone. *The Ethics of Amibiguity*. New York: The Philosophical Library, 1948.

Detmer, David. *Freedom as a Value*. La Salle, Illinois: Open Court, 1988.

Desan, Wilfred. *The Tragic Finale*. New York: Harper Torchbooks, 1960.

Fell, Joseph P. *Emotion in the Thought of Sartre*. New York: Columbia University Press, 1965.

Fell, Joseph P. *Heidegger and Sartre: An Essay on Being and Place*. New York: Columbia University Press, 1979.

Greene, Marjorie. *Sartre*. New York: New Viewpoints, 1973.

Greene, Norman. *Jean-Paul Sartre: The Existentialism Ethic*. Ann Arbor: University of Michigan Press, 1963.

Hartmann, Klaus. *Satre's Ontology: A Study of Being and Nothingness in the Light of Hegel's Logic*. Evanston: Northwestern University Press, 1966.

Jeanson, Francis. *Le problème moral et la pensée de Sartre*. Paris: Éditions de Seuil, 1965. *Sartre and the Problem of Morality*. Transated by Robert V. Stone. Bloomington: Indiana University Press, 1980

King, Thomas, M. SJ. *Sartre and the Sacred*. Chicago: University of Chicago Press, 1974.

Marcel, Gabriel. "Existence and Human Freedom" in *The Philosophy of Existentialism*, Translated by Manya Harari. Toronto: Citadel Press, 1977.

Marcel Gabriel. *Homo Viator*. Paris: Aubier, 1944.

Salvan, Jaques L. *The Scandalous Ghost: Sartre's Existentialism as Related to Vitalism, Humanism, Mysticism, and Marxism*. Detroit: Wayne State Unversity Press, 1967.

Poster, Mark. *Existential Marxism in Postwar France*. Princeton: Princeton University Press, 1979.

Schillp, Paul Arthur ed. *The Philosophy of Jean-Paul Sartre*. La Salle: Open Court, 1981.

Schroeder, William Ralph. *Sartre and his Predecessors: The Self and the Other*. London: Routledge & Kegan Paul, 1984.

Silverman, Hugh J. and Elliston, Frederick A. eds. *Jean-Paul Sartre: Contemporary Approaches to His Philosophy*. Pittsburg: Duquesne University Press, 1980.

## Selected Secondary Works on Berdyaev

Chaddick, Lloyd. "Berdyaev's Theodicy and the Nature of God" in *King's Theological Review*, vol. 8, pp. 12-16, Spring, 1985.

Dietrich, Wolfgang. *Provokation der Person: Nikolai Berdjajew in den Impulsen seines Denkens Bd. 1-5*. Berlin: Burckhardthaus Verlag, 1975.

Dye, James Wayne, "Nicholas Berdyaev and His Ideas on the Fundamental Nature of All Entities," in *Ultimate Reality and Meaning*, vol. 2, no. 3: 109-135, 1981.

Friedrich, Hans Peter. "Ein Sohn der Freiheit: Nikolai Berdjajew" in *Ökumenische Rundschau* bds. 37&38, pp. 426-437, pp. 61-66, Oct. 1988, Jan 1989.

Idinopulos, Thomas A. "Berdyaev, Meland, and Dagenais on what it is to be Human" in *Encounter*, vol. 46, pp. 289-307, Autumn, 1985.

Ignatow, Assen. "The Dialectic of Freedom in nikolai Berdjaev" in *Studies in Soviet Thought*, Vol. 38(4), pp 273-289, Nov. 1989.

Hartshorne, Charles. "Whitehead and Berdyaev: Is there Tragedy in God" in *Whitehead's Philosophy*. Lincoln: University of Nebraska Press, 1972.

Hefner, Phillip J. "God and Chaos: The Demiurge vs. the Ungrund" in *Zygon*, 19, pp. 469-485, Dec. 1984.

Lampert, Evgueny. "Nicholas Berdyaev and the New Middle Ages." in *Modern Christian Revolutionaries*. Edited by Donald Attwater. New York: Devin Adair Co., 1947.

Markovic, Marko. *La Philosophie de la inégalité dans les idées politiques de Nicolas Berdiaev*. Paris: Nouvelles éditions latines, 1978.

Nucho, Fuad. *Berdyaev's Philosophy: The Existential Paradox of Freedom and Necessity*. Garden City N.Y.: Doubleday and Company, 1966.

Richardson, David Bonner. *Berdyaev's Philosophy of History*. The Hague: Martinus Nihoff, 1970.

Shestov, Lev. "Nikolai Berdyaev: Gnosis and Existential Philosophy" in *Speculation and Revelation*. Translated by Bernard Martin. Athens, Ohio: Ohio University Press, 1982.

Slaatte, Howard A. *Time, Existence and Destiny: Nicolas Berdyaev's Philosophy of Time*. New York: Peter Lang, 1988.

Slaate, Howard A. *Time and Its End*. Washington D.C.: University Press of America, 1980.

Spinka, Matthew. "Berdyaev and Origen" in *Church History* vol. 16, March 1947.

Spinka, Matthew. *Nicolas Berdyaev: Captive of Freedom*. Philadelphia: The Westeminster Press, 1950.

Wood, Douglas Kellogg. *Men Against Time: Nicolas Berdyaev, T. S. Eliot, Aldous Huxley, & C. G. Jung*. Lawrence: University of Kansas Press, 1982.

**Selected Secondary Works on Boehme**

Jones, Rufus. *Spiritual Reformers of the 16th and 17th Centuries*. Boston: Beacon, 1959.

Koyre, Alexandre. *La philosophie de Jacob Boehme.* New York: Burt Franklin, 1968.

Weeks, Andrew. *Boehme: An Intellectual Biography of the Seventeenth-Century Philosopher and Mystic.* Albany: SUNY Press, 1991.


**Selected List of Other Works Consulted**

Bergson, Henri. *Oeuvres.* Paris: Presses Universitaires de France, 1963.

Brown, Robert. *The Later Philosophy of Schelling: The Influence of Jacob Boehme on the Works of 1809-1815.* Lewisburg: Buchnell University Press, 1977.

Buber, Martin. *Between Man and Man.* Translated by Ronald Gregor-Smith. New York: Macmillian, 1965

Buber, Martin. *Eclipse of God: Studies in the Relation Between Religion and Philosophy.* Translator anonymous. New Jersey: Humanities Press, 1952.

Buber, Martin. *Good and Evil.* Translator anonymous. New York: Scribners. 1953.

Buber, Martin. *I and Thou.* Translated by Walter Kaufmann. New York: Schribners, 1970.

Edie, James, James Scanlan, Mary-Barbara Zeldin and Kline, George eds. *Russian Philosophy: Volumes I-III.* Knoxville: University of Tennessee Press, 1976.

Gallagher, Keneth. *The Philosophy of Gabriel Marcel.* New York: Fordam University Press, 1975.

Griffin, David Ray. *Evil Revisited: Reponses and Reconsiderations.* Albany: SUNY Press, 1991.

Griffin, David Ray. *God, Power, and Evil: A Process Theodicy.* Philadelphia: Westminster Press, 1976.

Hartshorne, Charles. *The Divine Relativity.* New Haven: Yale University Press, 1948.

214

Hartshorne, Charles and Reese, William eds. *Philosophers Speak of God.* Chicago: University of Chicago Press, 1960.

Hegel, G W F. *Hegel's Science of Logic.* Translated by A.V. Miller. New York: Humanities Press, 1969.

Hegel, G.W.F. *The Phenomenology of Spirit.* Translated by A. V. Miller. Oxford: Oxford University Press, 1977.

Heidegger, Martin. *Being and Time.* Translated by John Macquerrie and Edward Robinson. New York: Harper and Row, 1962.

Heidegger, Martin. "What is Metaphysics." in *Martin Heidegger Basic Writings.* Edited by David Krell. New York: Harper and Row, 1977.

Hyppolite, Jean. *Genesis and Structure of the Phenomenology of Spirit of Hegel.* Translated by Samuel Cherniak and John Heckman. Evanston: Northwestern University Press, 1974.

Kant, Immanuel. *The Critique of Judgement.* Translated by J. H. Bernard. New York: Hafner, 1951.

Kant, Immanuel. *The Critique of Practical Reason.* Translated by Lewis White Beck. New York: Macmillan, 1985.

Kant, Immanuel. *The Critique of Pure Reason.* Tranlated by Normon Kemp-Smith. New York: St. Martins, 1975.

Kant, Immanuel. *Religion within the Limits of Reason Alone.* Translated by Theodore M. Greene and Hoyt Hudson. New York: Harper and Row, 1960.

Kierkegaard, Soren. *Fear and Trembling and the Sickness unto Death.* Translated by Walter Lowrie. Princeton: Princeton University Press, 1954.

Kierkegaard, Soren. *The Concept of Anxiety.* Translated by Reidar Thomte. Princeton: Princeton University Press, 1980.

Kockelmans, Joseph J. ed. *Contemporary European Ethics.* Garden City, New York: Doubleday and Company, 1972.

Lossky, N.O. *A History of Russian Philosophy.* New York: International Universities Press, 1951.

Marcel, Gabriel. *Etre et avoir*. Paris: Aubier, 1968.

Marcel, Gabriel. *Journal métaphysique*. Paris: Gallimard, 1968.

Marcel, Gabriel. *Man Against Mass Society*. Translated by G. S. Frazer. Chicago: Henry Regnery, 1967.

Marcel, Gabriel. *The Mystery of Being*. Translated by G. S. Fraser. South Bend: Gateway, 1950.

Marx, Werner. *The Philosophy of F. W. J. Schelling: History, System and Freedom*. Translated by Thomas Nenon. Bloomington: Indiana University Press, 1984.

Nietzsche, Friedrich. *The Will to Power*. Translated by Walter Kaufmann and R. J. Hollingdale. New York: Vintage Books, 1967.

Schelling, F. W. J. *Of Human Freedom*. Translated by James Gutmann. La Salle: Open Court, 1936.

Shestov, Lev. *Athens and Jerusalem*. Translated by Bernard Martin. Athens, Ohio: Ohio University Press, 1966.

Whitehead, Alfred North *Process and Reality*. New York: Free Press, 1978.

Zenkovsky, V. V. *History of Russian Philosophy: Volumes I-II*. Translated by George L. Kline. New York: Columbia University Press, 1950.

## Studies in Phenomenological Theology

Recent years have witnessed a burgeoning interest in the application of phenomenological concepts and techniques to issues typical of the philosophy of religion: the existence and nature of the Divine, and the modes of relatedness whereby the Divine is manifest in human experience. Seeking the highest standards of scholarship and philosophical penetration, this series promotes original and critical work in philosophical theology undertaken from the standpoint and with the methodological techniques of phenomenology.

Phenomenology involves the application of certain strategies of *reflection* to the investigation of *phenomena*. Philosophers maintain remarkably divergent views regarding "mill" and "grist." This series offers a forum for the entire spectrum of phenomenological persuasions. The phenomenology of Husserl is, of course, exemplary. But approaches more kindred in spirit to the "first-generation" phenomenologists, Heidegger, Sartre and Merleau-Ponty are equally welcome, as are those, remaining strictly within the parameters of reflection and phenomenological concern, more at home in the "second-generation" thought of philosophers such as Ricoeur, Gadamer, Foucault, and Levinas.

Please send submissions or inquiries to:

Steven W. Laycock, General Editor
Studies in Phenomenological Theology
Department of Philosophy
University of Toledo
Toledo, OH 43606
(419) 537-4417